The Mind's Eye

The
MIND'S EYE

Image and Memory
in Writing about Trauma

Marian Mesrobian MacCurdy

UNIVERSITY OF MASSACHUSETTS PRESS
Amherst

LC 2006033406
ISBN 10: 1-55849-558-4 (paper); 557-6 (library cloth)
ISBN 13: 978-1-55849-558-6 (paper); 557-9 (library cloth)

Designed by Steve Dyer
Set in Minion
Printed and bound by The Maple-Vail Book Manufacturing Group

Library of Congress Cataloging-in-Publication Data

MacCurdy, Marian M.
    The mind's eye : image and memory in writing about trauma /
Marian Mesrobian MacCurdy.
        p. ; cm.
    Includes bibliographical references and index.
    ISBN-13: 978-1-55849-557-9 (cloth : alk. paper)
    ISBN-10: 1-55849-557-6 (cloth : alk. paper)
    ISBN-13: 978-1-55849-558-6 (pbk. : alk. paper)
    ISBN-10: 1-55849-558-4 (pbk. : alk. paper)
1. Creative writing—Therapeutic use.   2. Creative writing—Study and teaching.
3. Psychic trauma—Treatment.   I. Title.
[DNLM: 1. Writing.   2. Psychotherapy.   3. Sex Offenses—psychology.
4. Terrorism—psychology.   5. Wounds and Injuries—psychology.
WM 450.5.W9 M133m 2007]
RC489.W75M33 2007
616.89'165—dc22   2006033406

British Library Cataloguing in Publication data are available.

An earlier version of material in chapter 1 was first published in my essay
"From Trauma to Writing," in *Writing and Healing: Toward an Informed
Practice,* ed. Charles M. Anderson and Marian M. MacCurdy, 158–200
(Urbana, Ill.: National Council of Teachers of English, 2000); an earlier
version of chapter 5 was published in *Literature and Medicine* 19.1
(Spring 2000): 115–32. I thank the publishers for permission to reuse
that material here.

For Robbie and Meline,
my white doves,

Mark,
the basso continuo of my life,

and my mother, Arpena Sachaklian Mesrobian,
who taught me the power of the word

Contents

Preface

*So while our art cannot, as we wish it could, save us from wars,
privation, envy, greed, old age, or death, it can revitalize us
amidst it all . . . Writing is survival.*

RAY BRADBURY

IT IS LATE SEPTEMBER in Ithaca, New York, a glisteningly bright day
with that late summer shimmer, a product of the sinking of the sun in the
southern sky that presages winter. I am in my office grading papers when I
hear a faint knock on the door. I open it to face Cory, one of my students in
my personal essay class. He is tall, blond, handsome, and with a face more
frozen than any I have ever seen. Classes have been in session for close to three
weeks, but Cory has yet to write a single word. In class he is silent, stuck to his
seat, looking angry and disenfranchised, and my inquiries and invitations to
come to my office and talk have been met with silence—up to now.

He sat stiffly upright and told me that his brother had been murdered in
Boston two weeks before school started. He was angry, so very angry that he
could barely speak. I looked straight into his pale blue eyes. I saw no tears,
only that blankness Vietnam War veterans call the thousand-yard stare. I
know this face because it peered back at me the day of my husband's memorial service: a Byzantine widow, hollow sunken cheeks under sharp, high
cheekbones, flat black vacant eyes, staring at nothing, at the air, at herself with
such disbelief.

I broke my usual male student rule: I reached out and took his hand. I told
him I know a little of grief. My husband died suddenly a year ago; my two
young children are fatherless. We talked of grief, of anger, of death. We talked.

Cory's stiff face began to soften, and he could speak. His mind had been frozen along with his tears.

From then on he began to write. He wrote in his journal and offered a few tentative motions toward full papers. He still would not speak in class. Finally, toward the end of the semester, he read from his paper in which he described his brother's murder, his reaction to it, and his movement toward emotional health. His hands were shaking as he held the paper and read about going down to the Charles River where his brother was murdered, sitting on the bank, and struggling with how to live. He realized looking out at the water that his brother would not want him to be tortured forever, would not want him to discard his life. He decided to come back to school and engage as best he could. When he was finished, Cory looked up at the students, his eyes wet, but his hands no longer shaking.

The students were speechless. Then, one by one, they spoke: "Thank you for trusting us with this story. Thank you for your honesty." From then on Cory was a part of the class. As he said to me later, "I created a barrier that let no one in. This barrier was made of the thickest material: silence. When I looked into your eyes I saw what I have seen so many times before—hurt. It was not your hurt, but instead you were mirroring me. Because I knew you had been in my shoes, I felt touched by your words. Things became much clearer for me, and I could understand why I feel the way I do. I finally realized that I was not alone in my world. My whole perspective on life changed."

I had spent a year trying to decide how to *be* in the world. This young man had figured it out so quickly. It's not only murder that kills people; it is silence, interior and exterior. For two months after my husband died I was mute; I could write nothing, could barely speak, except in the classroom, when automatic pilot took over. I remember little of those days, although the nights are etched into my mind like dark tattoos. The first I could write was two and a half months after his death, after having dinner with a friend, a gentle soul who let me sit quietly in his space and remain mute. I needed peace, and for two hours, sitting in front of a wood stove, I felt warm and quiet. I drove home, and at one in the morning I started writing. From then on, my journal became a map, a guide I could refer to to chart my progress through the ocean of grief. And singing became my escape. I could barely speak, but I could sing, and I did. Bach, Mozart, Schubert—and my journal—became my allies in a war with myself. In the evenings I sang; at night I wrote. Grief is a process of separation from the loved one. And I had a lot to separate from, having been with this man since I was nineteen years old. The person that loved him wanted to stay attached; the person I had to become could not.

Picasso once said something about art sweeping away the dust of life. I decided to offer a Schubert song recital both because of the beauty of the music and the opportunity to find a voice to externalize my grief. "Shepherd on the Rock" was a challenge, as it is for most sopranos. It requires sweetness and strength, lightness and legato; it also calls for intensity born of grief and joy. I had the intensity, certainly the grief, but where to find lightness and joy in a sad soul?

A week before the concert I am rehearsing Schubert's "Shepherd on the Rock" in the greenroom at Barnes Auditorium at Cornell University. My musical partner, Trevor, a doctoral student of Malcolm Bilson in fortepiano performance, is playing the opening bars of the first movement while Malcolm stands, his arms folded, listening for every inflection, every nuance. I look out the windows down to the lake far below and begin to sing. Trevor and I move easily together, we communicate wordlessly, but something is missing.

Malcolm, the premier fortepianist in the world, stops us: "Yes, yes, it's almost right, but it's a waltz, you see, a waltz." And he begins to dance around the room in waltz time: *"Wenn auf dem hochsten Fels ich steh, in's tiefe Thal herneiderseh, und singe, und singe"*—When on the mountain top I stand, so far above the meadowland, and sing, and sing.

Trevor begins to play again and I sing and Malcolm dances, and suddenly the Shepherd is singing on the hill and the music dances, turns, lilts up and back on the air effortlessly.

We complete the first movement and begin the second: *"In tiefem Gram verzehr ich mich, mir ist die Freude hin"*—In deepest grief I am consumed, to me is joy gone from the earth. Malcolm leans over to me, stretches his arms out: "Pull this music out of you; stretch it as long as you can until you can't pull any longer. That high B must hang overhead as long as possible. This is one of the hardest movements to sing in all music." This I know. How will I sing these words without weeping?

Then we come to the last movement and I know how: *"Der Fruhling will kommen, der Fruhling, meine Freud . . . Je weiter meine Stimme dringt, je heller sie mir wiederklingt"*—Spring is coming, my joy . . . The further my voice carries, the brighter it resounds. And the allegretto music skips like running water over rocks.

When I perform "Shepherd on the Rock" one week later, I see Malcolm dancing and smiling in front of us, his genius so simple, so right, and that high B soars out of me and hangs in the air just long enough to show I am still alive.

I had frozen myself, just as Cory had, but memories embrace all that we are—joy and sadness, grief and wonder. Art saves us, connection saves us, memories save us. Art brings the white dove of hope.

My Armenian grandmother was one of those people who always believed in her version of reality and acted on it. She might accede to another's wishes or needs, but her view of the world still maintained inside her head. As a child I remember how that frustrated me. It's hard to grow up with a force of nature in your house. But I remember my husband saying to me when I insisted on trying to grow a peach tree in our cold climate, "Marian, you bend existence to your will," and I think of my grandmother.

We lived together for the first six years of my life and after that saw each other many times a week, grew strawberries together, knit, baked baklava, sang together. I heard her stories, all those stories, for all those years—stories of hiding on the roof from the Turks during the 1896 massacres of the Armenians, getting stung by a hive of bees, trying to sing as a young wife and finding that church was the only acceptable place. I heard these all like I felt the snow in winter, the rain in spring. They were the fabric of my life, my way to order the world. But I never knew that this is what makes a writer. Writers remember, and she had the best memory I have ever known. I sat next to her on her love seat, took her withered hand, and watched as her eyes focused back on a past more real than any present would ever again be. She smiled softly as she remembered her husband's proposal of marriage, laughed openly as she told of jilting an earlier beau who had hurt her, spoke with pride of loading rifles to defend themselves against the Turks attacking their village during the 1909 massacres.

As a child I thought her hands to be so powerful when she caught that baby bunny eating her lettuce and spanked it. I remember her hands mixing, kneading, and rolling dough for *banir bereg*. I watched her throw it around as if playing with a small child. I remember her hauling laundry in a wicker basket on one hip to hang it on the clothesline outside on warm spring days. I remember her sticking a peach pit in the ground and a few years later picking peaches off the tree that grew from it. I remember her comparing these peaches to the ones the size of navel oranges in her birth city of Aintab, her hands moving like small birds around her body as she recalled picking and eating them. I remember her trudging up the hill from our bus stop, her arms loaded down with groceries, and wondering what treats she brought home this time.

I remember her remembering. And now I know that she was the writer in our family. I always knew that singing had passed from her to me, but I never knew that those stories she told would thread their way through my genes until I, too, would "remember."

William Carlos Williams said to prospective doctors about the patients they were trying to heal: "Their story, yours, mine—it's what we all carry with us on this trip we take, and we owe it to each other to respect our stories and learn from them." Our stories make us who we are. Our art arises from them. And that is the purpose of this book: to help writers not to hide from memories but to embrace them, not to fear remembrances but to learn from them, not to run from the past but to celebrate it—to help writers remember.

The Mind's Eye

Introduction

Silence, Voice, and Pedagogy

It is, in the end, the saving of lives that we writers are about . . .
the life we save is our own.

ALICE WALKER

As I stepped out of the office in which I released a burden that weighed down my heart, a glint of hope flickered . . . that allowed me to sit with my housemate an hour later and describe who I really am and the traumatic events that have haunted me for over 15 years. It was the glint of hope that allowed me to go on later that night and do my daily routine rather than completely crumbling. As I lay in bed that night, my mind was swirled with happy, yet heavy thoughts. It was the oddest feeling; I was simultaneously empty of my burden, full of hope, raging with pain in my temples, exhausted by listening to the words of my own life. I fell asleep wondering how my disclosure of suffering will allow me to go on, how I can get past the illusory world I constructed as a safe haven for my own self. I feared integration, feared moving on from what I "know." Despite this fear, I knew that change was ahead, because I was about to elicit it.

THIS IS A JOURNAL ENTRY written by Sharon, a student in my senior capstone honors class. She had tentatively peered into my office that day to ask if I had a minute to speak with her about her responses to the class and to her own journal. She was finding herself thinking about long-forgotten memories, moments she knew—when being scrupulously honest—that she had tried to forget. The denial only resulted in compulsive overeating, anorexia, and depression. Was it O.K. to write about this in her journal for my class, she asked? After letting her know that it was her journal, her life, her choice, I asked her how *she* felt about this writing. I spent the next hour listening. Sharon erupted with years of unclaimed experience with the trauma, more a result of how it was handled than the original trauma itself. Once Sharon understood that she had found a safe venue—her journal, which I would read only if she chose—she realized that she had work to do to and began doing it. For her that work involved talking, writing, finding a therapist, and, especially, being utterly honest with herself. That meant locating the guilt and shame that childhood sexual abuse produced, investigating it, and integrating it into the person she would become. Writing was, for her, a method for this self-discovery.

Silence perpetuates trauma and the shame and guilt that often accompany it: Why didn't I run? Why didn't I say no? Why wasn't I strong enough to save him? Why was I so "bad" that my parents got divorced? The list of "whys" is as long as the list of traumas that can afflict us.

Current research shows that writing can have a therapeutic effect on painful life experiences in two ways. First, by unlocking these experiences from the parts of the brain that store iconic images and allowing us to put words to our difficult moments, it is not only cathartic but it also creates understanding. We can realize just how bad we felt, that we are not going crazy, that indeed these traumas were hard to endure. Our emotions are validated. Second, writing can join the cognitive and the emotional, resulting in a sense of control over that which we cannot control: the past. Writing produces a sense of agency that the trauma has threatened. We write our trauma; our trauma does not write us. The person who experienced the trauma and the person writing about it are not one and the same. Writing requires construction of a persona—and a point of view—that is different from that of the protagonist. In *Acts of Meaning* Jerome Bruner defined one of the characteristics of autobiography as "an account given by a narrator in the here and now about a protagonist bearing his name who existed in the there and then, the story terminating in the present when the protagonist fused with the narrator" (121).

The construction of a narrator that can balance past with present is both an essential component of a successful personal essay and the tool that enables the writer to feel that she has an ally in the writing process. In an article in the *Chronicle of Higher Education,* the personal essayist Vivian Gornick wrote, "This point of view could only emerge from a narrator who was me and at the same time not me . . . I realized . . . there was a narrator on the page strong enough to do battle for me . . . she was in control . . . I had created a persona" (B9). This persona allows us to make choices about how we see ourselves. The emotional and the cognitive converge. As Sharon put it in her journal, "The words and the emotions that come with them can never be separated. As the images become normalized, the quality and type of emotion may change, but the emotion never goes away . . . Each survivor's narrative is their life story; without it, s/he would be wandering helpless, fragmented, and alone. It is the emotional narrative that ties everything together and allows the healing and 'moving on' process to begin."

Writers understand from this process that concepts of a self are constructed, not a priori, that the labels that we assume from our interpretations of our experiences can be altered, and in the process we can temper the sense of isolation from oneself and others and promote integration. As Suzette Henke demonstrates, "In the very act of articulation, the trauma story becomes a testimony, a publicly accessible 'ritual of healing' that inscribes the victim into a sympathetic discourse-community and inaugurates the possibility of psychological reintegration" (xviii). We can move from victim to survivor to pilgrim, one whose work it is to lighten the loads of others as she lightens her own. Anne Hunsaker Hawkins observes that "the need to tell others often becomes the wish to help others" (25).

But how should writing teachers deal with personal material in a writing class? The benefits of self-disclosure do not negate the problems associated with it. For all the right reasons writing teachers worry about the ethical, moral, and legal issues inherent in this kind of pedagogy. In addition, the academic opposition to personal writing has a theoretical as well as a practical edge. Social constructionists argue that the job of the writing teacher is to prepare students to write for the academy and the professional sector after graduation. Personal writing, they argue, is an effete genre with little utility in the post-modern world. As Carolyn Ericksen Hill in *Writing from the Margins* explains, "To express oneself has been associated with pressing something out from an inside (often, an emotion-full subject presumably needed to release pressure), as opposed to indicating to others something 'objective' which is already outside oneself" (109). These arguments have a political cast. Some opponents of expressivist pedagogies argue that writing teachers need to help students learn to resist political orthodoxy, and only a more argument-centered pedagogy can accomplish this. But the most problematic, perhaps even ignorant, objection to expressionist pedagogies is a statement by Roger Rosenblatt, himself a memoirist, quoted in a *New York Times* article by Karen W. Arenson: "I don't think anyone ought to teach memoir writing to undergraduates, because they don't have enough to remember" (Arenson B8). I suspect my student Sharon would have a few words to say about this.

The kind of writing that Sharon asked permission to do is being produced in colleges and universities; high schools, both public and private; support centers for cancer, AIDS, and other illnesses; senior centers; any place that people gather to use writing to learn, grow, and heal. As Charles Anderson, Jeffrey Berman, Guy Allen, and others have stated, student writers will gravitate to their painful stories whether invited to or not. Charles Anderson articulates this process clearly and eloquently in his article in *Writing and Healing:*

> They go to the hardest places they know and write about the things they seem least able to understand—births and deaths, loves and hatreds, fears. I have witnessed writers struggling through texts of unimaginable difficulty, telling and retelling stories so harsh and broken that I have wondered how they could ever have survived the lives those stories tell me they have lived. I and the others in the class have worked with them, not on their lives, but on the stories of their lives, on the texts they bring to us, on the pages that hold the possibility of meaning and therefore of wholeness. I have watched those pages resist and submit, shift and change, grow luminous as watch dials at midnight. And I have seen writers change, come into being, and discover themselves. I have seen them get better . . . And I have come to know writing as a primary symbolism, a way we are and can be in the world, the material out of which we spin what Ernst Cassirer calls, "the varied threads which wave the symbolic net, the tangled web of human experience." (59)

Writers have been telling their stories all over the country while the pedagogy of the personal essay undergoes little scrutiny because many teachers are understandably too nervous to reveal what their students are actually writing about. Few intrepid souls volunteer their encounters with student self-disclosure; those that do often reflect highly polarized views.

In recent years therapeutic writing has become a topic of interest in both the popular and the academic press. Discussions of pedagogy for such writing, however, can still be fraught with professional peril, particularly for untenured faculty. In *Writing Relationships,* Lad Tobin states, "Most writing teachers know that therapeutic models can help explain and explore the teacher-student relationship, but because they find this . . . threatening they publicly deny it" (29). This relegates many classroom stories about this subject to the realm of academic urban legend. Fortunately, several recent books and articles investigate the relationship between writing and healing and have helped shed light on this subject, especially the work of Jeffrey Berman, Charles Anderson, Judith Harris, Suzette Henke, and Guy Allen.

Much of the difficulty in this pedagogy involves responding to texts that describe the writer's traumatic experiences. The purpose of this book is to discuss the relationship between trauma and writing—to study how we process difficult experiences and how writing can help us to integrate them—and to provide a pedagogy to encounter the difficult life stories that often emerge in the personal essay classroom. We will investigate the assertion that healing is an ambient effect of good personal essay writing; that is, many of the same techniques that produce effective personal essays also produce a therapeutic effect. The focus, however, is on producing good writing, which protects both student and teacher. Brief sections within the first and second chapters were previously published in my chapter in *Writing and Healing: Toward an Informed Practice* (edited by Charles Anderson and Marian MacCurdy). This book continues and deepens the study by providing a comprehensive view of the relationship between trauma and writing—a key element too often overlooked by composition teachers—locating that relationship within writers' texts, and providing a personal essay pedagogy that can be effective and safe for both teacher and student. It acknowledges James Moffett's observation that "unhealed wounds and undeveloped souls will thwart the smartest curriculum" (261) and provides a method for helping our students use the wounds they bring us to move beyond them and produce effective prose in the process.

Chapter 1 investigates what trauma is, how traumatic memories are stored and retrieved, and how writing affects them. Chapter 2 focuses on the traumatic image: how it affects us as writers, how we can link image to narrative, and how the revision process enables writers to find their subjects. It then discusses the teacher's role in this process. Chapter 3 presents one sexual abuse narrative that took the entire semester to emerge and shows how writing in stages became transformative for the writer. Chapter 4 investigates the effects of the study of trauma on an entire class, demonstrating how the process of writing and witnessing can benefit both individuals and a community, and chapter 5 investigates written responses to trauma in a professional writer's autobiographical text, demonstrating that the same issues maintain there as in student work. It investigates the relationship between writer and reader in such a text, building on the discussion of witnessing from the previous chapter, and it takes the subject of writing and healing into the international venue to look particularly at issues of justice, retribution, and forgiveness.

As we look at individual student cases we will discuss the particular pedagogical choices made in dealing with those texts and their writers, but here I offer a few of my primary principles to begin this investigation, all based on one major premise: Teachers are not therapists. While the work can at times look similar—we listen to students, we actively participate in the process of the construction of a therapeutic narrative, we can care about them as people—our job is to focus on the text, not the life, to help writers produce effective work. Having said that, sometimes the best way to focus on the text is first to listen with compassion and empathy to their stories and then respond by validating, not judging, the writer. Jeffrey Berman in his book *Empathic Teaching: Education for Life* argues that a relational model of education depends on empathic understanding (105), basing much of his pedagogy on Carl Rogers, who said, "A high degree of empathy in a relationship is possibly *the* most potent factor in bringing about change and learning (qtd. in Berman 99). Everyone needs to believe he has been heard to extend himself in relationship communication. Therefore, if a writer offers something of herself in a text, I may give the text a grade but never the life. Teachers are advisers, mentors, and role models. Listening with compassion helps to fulfill those responsibilities and creates the trust needed for the student to delve into a difficult topic. Sometimes, simply thanking the writer for trusting me enough to share his/her paper with me can demonstrate this respect and compassion. However, teachers are not therapists. While a therapist may listen and then counsel, teachers listen and, if appropriate, suggest counseling and other professional services—and then turn to elements of the text. The only occasion for me to intervene is to obey the law, which requires that I disclose any threats to health or safety. I always try to remember that only the survivor can determine what is perceived as trauma. What may cause one person merely to shrug heavily and move on might, for another, be a life-defining experience. When dealing with self-disclosure in student texts, we are committed to a pedagogy that empowers students. This means students make the ultimate choices about their texts, and we must be prepared for this. The grade may be affected by their textual choices, but these are still their choices. The following are a few ground rules that help guide me in the process of encountering student texts about trauma:

1. While students make the final decisions about their texts, it is my job to teach writing and to grade student texts. I can offer compassion and understanding and still give an essay a low grade. The elements of characterization, setting, narrative and thematic construction, voice, verb tense, and grammar are all critical to successful writing. The personal essay has a long historical tradition with its own aesthetic, which can help teachers focus on text when we most need to.

2. The pedagogy of the personal essay requires writing in drafts. All writing is a recursive act: The writing changes the writer. Therefore, encouraging—and reading—multiple drafts promotes effective writing. This is where most of the learning occurs.

3. I allow students to tell the stories that need to be told, but I do not mandate that they write about specific experiences. This does not mean that I do not offer topics, but if the choice to write about specific moments is student-directed, this can protect both student and teacher.

4. I model workshop protocols with students, including showing them how to respond with "I" statements: I really like this. You lost me here. I love this section, but I can't "see" this one. Can you provide further details here? How do you feel about this section? I do not mandate that my students workshop every paper. I allow them to serve as reader/editor without offering their own paper if they have produced a paper that is too personal to share. It is better to opt out of a workshop than not to write the paper at all. Once community is established in a class, most students have developed a relationship with at least one person with whom they feel comfortable sharing their work. I may also suggest readers, knowing the topics of all their papers.

5. I meet with every student in private conferences several times per semester, both to discuss how their writing can be improved and to find out what they feel and think about their writing. It's important for teachers to be prepared for the fact that when writers first encounter painful topics they may feel upset. This is normal and demonstrated by research. Research also shows that this phase should not last longer than a few hours, days, or weeks. Long-term depression, difficulty

coping, and/or the voicing of self-destructive thoughts are signs to refer the student to counseling.

6. Before reading student work aloud or using it in writing, I obtain written permission from the student. It is also important to protect the anonymity of the writer with pseudonyms unless the student specifically puts as a requirement that his/her real name be used.

7. I make every effort to be hopeful, positive, enthusiastic, supportive, and non-coercive. Teachers should never appropriate a student's text by assuming we know what the writer wanted to do or should do. This work is an opportunity for everyone to grow as writers and as people. But self-disclosure can only be encouraged, never required.

Working with students who write essays of self-disclosure is not for everyone. Some find this pedagogy compelling, fascinating, life-changing; others see it only as difficult, pain-inducing for both student and teacher, and even threatening to the established mission of higher education. Indeed, it can be all these things. Jeffrey Berman in his book *Risky Writing: Self-Disclosure and Transformation in the Classroom* found in a survey of his students in a personal essay class that "76 percent of the students found it painful to write one or more essays. Seventeen percent of these students found one essay painful; 32 percent found two essays painful; and 9 percent found five essays painful" (234).

However, pain can also be the precursor to health. Berman goes on to say, "Eighty-six percent of these students indicated that they were glad that they wrote on painful topics. They felt the experience was valuable because writing . . . made them feel better, brought them new insights, helped them to identify problems, helped them to master fears, and made them feel less isolated" (235). And most important, "The overwhelming majority of the students . . . believed that the ability to disclose personal information about oneself contributes to health and well-being . . . Nearly the same percentage believed that the course heightened their 'emotional intelligence,' which Daniel Goleman defines in his best-selling book as self-awareness, impulse control, persistence, zeal, self-motivation, empathy, and social deftness" (235).

These students have discovered what so many writers have noted. As D. H. Lawrence put it, "One sheds one's sicknesses in books, repeats and presents again one's emotions, to be master of them" (Zytaruk 90). Berman describes his students' commitment to this process: "Students wrote about their *lived* experiences. They told stories, offered their own interpretations and expanded and revised earlier accounts. They took responsibility for these stories and realized that they could change their lives by changing their perspectives" (150). Teachers whose lives are enriched by the personal informing the professional—and vice versa—have had experiences similar to this. We do not argue that all education should embrace this model, just that teachers recognize and understand its value and provide resources to assist those who seek them. As Jerome Bruner observed, "I cannot imagine a more important . . . project than one that addresses itself to the 'development of autobiography'—how our way of telling about ourselves changes, and how these accounts come to take control of our ways of life" (15).

Our students provide the encouragement, the motivation, the impetus to move forward because for them it is not "academic"; what we do matters. This process is transformational. The following is from Sharon's journal much later in the class: "My story helps me to function in this society as a person with a purposeful life. My story allows me to go back and read it or think about it and not cry wildly. My story allows me to pull myself out of the depths of despair. What the telling of my story is helping me to do is live on, whether or not anyone understands my story . . . The power lies within myself as well as within other survivors of sexual abuse to create awareness in our communities by putting words to the atrocities of abuse that have been committed against us so that other victims may recognize that they are not alone."

And perhaps this is the ultimate purpose of education—to help teach students to live on, even thrive, independent of others, to own their own pasts and therefore control their futures, and to move beyond themselves to contribute to the welfare of the broader community.

CHAPTER 1

From Traumatic Image to Narrative

If you bring forth what is within you,
What you bring forth will save you.
If you do not bring forth what is within you,
What you do not bring forth will destroy you.

GNOSTIC GOSPEL OF THOMAS

IN THE DECEMBER 3, 2004, issue of the *Chronicle of Higher Education* Dan P. McAdams argued in his article "Redemption and American Politics" that Republicans won the 2004 election because they provided a more compelling narrative for Americans than did the Democrats, a "narrative of redemption—a story about a . . . protagonist in a dangerous world who sticks to simple principles and overcomes suffering and hardship in the end" (14). He also asserts that George W. Bush's personal narrative follows closely the script of the redemptive self: a reclaimed sinner who gave up alcohol, found God, and is transferring his own narrative onto the political sphere. His destiny is to lead; America's destiny is to spread democracy and American values throughout the world. It is not rare in the current political climate to hear a politician or even a college president assert that God has chosen him for his public role. Their salvation becomes the country's or the college's. Bush's second inaugural address indicates that his vision of America's mandate is to spread democracy throughout the world. Whether or not this is an appropriate mission is not my point here. I am arguing that this vision springs from

Bush's personal-salvation metaphor—and now that metaphor has become manifested in a kind of evangelical public policy.

Americans love a hero, someone to transform all our doubts, fears, and struggles. Finding that hero in ourselves, creating our own redemptive narrative and transforming our own lives is far more difficult. Patricia Hampl states in her essay "Memory and Imagination" (180–90) that if we don't create our own life narratives someone else will do it for us. Too often teachers, doctors, lawyers, and politicians are quick to tell us how we should think, feel, and act. Even parents have an investment in their own redemptive narratives and often resist accepting, perhaps even hearing, their children's version of their lives. As Milan Kundera's character in *The Book of Laughter and Forgetting* so famously said, "The struggle of man against power is the struggle of memory against forgetting." Nothing less than our history is at stake, and therefore also our future. This has both personal and political ramifications.

In 1995 I attended a conference on trauma offered by Harvard University in Boston. We were sitting in the massive ballroom of the Copley Square Hotel with its crystal chandeliers and pale blue ceiling laced with puffy white clouds, when a thin, bearded man, an associate professor of political science from Brown University, walked to the podium. His hands were shaking as he looked out at us and began to tell the story of his sexual victimization many years before, perpetrated by an administrator at a summer music camp for children. Ross Cheit talked about how he came to remember and name the sexual abuse perpetrated on him when he was about nine or ten. He had completely forgotten these experiences. He had completed his academic work and got through his tenure challenge. It was only then, perhaps when it felt safer and he could plunge into the past without unraveling his present, that his intrusive symptoms began, and he realized he had a story he needed to tell, to himself and to others. The media accused him of bringing a false memory charge—until many others came forward to corroborate his story. Many of these survivors had always remembered their stories; they just didn't come forward until someone else did first. Cheit's courage validated their memories, and they could speak. Cheit himself not only felt vindicated, but also found that his professional life became driven by his social awareness—his research and teaching interests now involve marginalized populations.

Our stories are life defining and can be told only by us. There is nothing less than our freedom at stake—our freedom to define our lives for ourselves, to construct our own values based on our experiences and how we interpret them within our life context, to create a worldview consonant with those experiences. Memoirs and life narratives capture the imaginations of people all over the globe. Books such as *Angela's Ashes, Every Secret Thing,* and *Zlata's Diary: A Child's Life in Sarajevo* have joined *The Diary of Anne Frank* and *I Know Why the Caged Bird Sings* as significant accounts of personal trauma. Memoirs have appeared on best-seller lists and won the Pulitzer Prize, and their writers have become in demand on the talk-show circuit. Many of these popular life accounts demonstrate that trauma is, and has been for millennia, a large component of the stories that have become part of our collective knowledge, that define what it means to be human. As Bessel van der Kolk wrote in *Traumatic Stress,* "From the earliest account of an adolescent's experience of a catastrophic disaster, the eruption of Mount Vesuvius, in the *Letters of Pliny the Younger* (AD 100–113); through the autobiographical description of intra-familial abuse and societal violence provided by Maxim Gorky in *My Childhood;* to the powerful literary rendering of the Holocaust by Elie Wiesel in *Night* . . . authors have reflected on the formative influences of traumatic experiences" in their development as writers and as people (332).

One of the hallmarks of the past hundred years has been repeated instances of genocide, beginning with the Armenian Genocide in 1915 and continuing up to this day with the massacres in the Sudan. After the Nazi Holocaust the watchword was "never again," but Samantha Power points out in her ground-breaking book *A Problem from Hell* that our nation more often than not turns a blind eye to genocide. As Lt. General Romeo Dallaire, the force commander of the United Nations mission in Rwanda and author of the book *Shake Hands with the Devil,* said in a speech at Colgate University on February 15, 2005, "Eighty percent of humanity is deeper in the mud, the blood, and the suffering of indignity . . . and youth is a prime target of horror." We can see that principle operating even closer to home: Some have even argued that the violence in our inner cities is itself a kind of genocide.

On April 16, 1998, the *Ithaca Journal* carried an Associated Press story that described a project at Woodrow Wilson High School in Long Beach, California, begun by a then twenty-three-year-old student teacher, Erin Gruwell. The project got its inspiration after a discriminatory incident involving a drawing that seriously troubled the affected student. The teacher said it reminded her of Nazi propaganda. "The students stared blankly. 'How many of you have heard of the Holocaust?' she asked. Not a hand went up. 'How many of you have been shot at?' Every hand went up." This was the genesis of the

Freedom Writers, an English program at this high school where students tell their stories. One story printed in the newspaper was so horrific it sounds nearly unbelievable: The writer's father poured gasoline over the head of his own mother, the writer's grandmother, and lit her on fire. When the student saw her grandmother in the hospital the grandmother had blisters all over her body, her hair was burnt off, and her skin was black and hanging off of her. The grandmother, just before she died, said to her granddaughter, "My own son took my life—your daddy" (2B). Another student wrote about her father, whom she had never met: "My dad is only the first man in a long line of men who have deserted me. For years I had to go to therapy because my mom thought I was crazy, and she would have to give me up. She said I was out of control. I used to sleepwalk, and once I even went into the street and was hit by a car. I almost died. Then, after my mom fixed the door so I couldn't get out, I would go into the kitchen and get knives. I would slash my arms, legs . . . Not too long after that, I got voices in my head. My therapist finally figured out what was wrong with me: It was the depression I was going through from not knowing my father" (2B).

These writers are homeless kids, honor students, former gang members, and survivors of violence and sexual abuse—a representative sampling of American life. The Freedom Writers have branched out beyond their school boundaries, getting the attention of Miep Gies, who helped hide the Anne Frank family, and Steven Spielberg, the director of *Schindler's List*. Erin Gruwell published the story of this extraordinary class, including excerpts from their journals in the book *The Freedom Writers Diaries*.

We hear stories of trauma from our students. As Dan Morgan wrote in an essay in *College English*: "These students' topics and concerns, and their life experiences and points of view, reflect what has been occurring in our society at large. Our students write about violence and substance abuse and broken families because they're writing about what they have lived and witnessed firsthand, what they care mostly deeply about. Their crises, past or present, mirror the condition of our society, reflect what has become more and more ordinary" (324). In any given Personal Essay class I teach, over half of my students will choose to write stories that they would call painful or difficult, whether or not they define them as traumatic. I began this study of trauma when I realized that my students would write these stories whether invited to or not. My assignments in this class are always open-ended. Students choose which experiences they write about, yet invariably I will receive trauma narratives—stories of parents' or other relatives' alcoholism, illness, or death, as well as the students' own experiences of accidents, illness, and rape or other criminal violence.

Some stories concern narratives that to another might not seem traumatic but to the writer were painful enough to cause serious writer's block. For example, one student, a major in screenwriting, could not write clear details. His writing was fuzzy, convoluted, vague: everything that a screenplay should not be. Yet his writing also demonstrated brief moments of clarity, so I wondered what was impeding his progress. I suggested that he locate and write about a moment in his childhood that seemed important to him, some single moment that helped define how he looks at the world. He told the story of being awakened by a fierce argument between his parents late one night when he was eight years old. He had to go to the bathroom, and he waited for a chance to streak through the living room to get to the bathroom to relieve himself, but the arguing went on and on. He became more and more anxious, terrified of interrupting the fight, which would let his parents know that he had heard them. My student was from an Asian family where honor and "face" is paramount. For him, revealing himself to them while this terrible argument was going on was untenable. Finally he couldn't wait any longer, and he ran through the room past his stunned parents. Once he wrote this narrative his writing opened up, and details began to flow—he had found his voice. He knew immediately what had happened: He had locked up that story to be "loyal" to his parents and in the process hid from himself the person he really had been as a child: the product of a stressful, tense household. His own feelings had to be hidden—and with them his creativity. Remembering his childhood reality and telling his stories freed him to become the writer he had always wanted to be.

This is the crucial element for us as writing professionals: Healing is an ambient effect of good writing—and vice versa. In focusing on a detailed moment, the start of good writing, this student was able to discover his voice and his response to his past. The very same elements that produce a therapeutic effect also improve the writing, particularly attention to detail and locating and focusing on the core element of the essay. For this reason, in simply focusing on what makes for good writing, writing teachers are encouraging their students on the path to self-discovery.

Another student writer, whose work is discussed in chapter 3, wrote of severe parental abuse, yet, because she had attempted to normalize it for so long, she felt it was "no big deal"—and her writing was utterly flat in tone. Only after her peer editor became enraged while reading these stories did the author begin to connect the events and her emotions, which ultimately enabled her to dislodge herself from her past and to change her life. It is not unusual for trauma survivors to need external validation to name their traumas. Humans are amazingly adaptive; we adjust to even difficult experiences by attempting to normalize them. If that won't work, we can even leave them hidden in those corners of the mind that are pre-verbal until something or someone stimulates change or we are hit with an image that recalls our experiences.

Some may argue that the mission of higher education does not include attention to personal stories; however, as James Moffett argues in an interchange in the May 1994 *College Composition and Communication,* "We get good at doing something as a part of getting well and realizing our deepest being. I know, the university feels it shouldn't play doctor or priest, dirty its hands with therapy and its mind with religion. But if it has real-life students on its hands, its hands are already dirty . . . Unhealed wounds and undeveloped souls will thwart the smartest curriculum" (261). Robert Coles in his book *The Call of* Stories quotes from his discussions with William Carlos Williams, who was speaking of his life as a doctor and writer: "We have to pay the closest attention to what we say. What patients say tells us what to think about what hurts them; and what we say tells us what is happening to us— what we are thinking and what may be wrong with us. Their story, yours, mine—it's what we all carry with us on this trip we take, and we owe it to each other to respect our stories and learn from them" (30). As novelist John Barth stated in his essay in *Poets and Writers,* "All the world's a stage and our selves themselves may be said to be essentially the stories we tell ourselves and others about who we are" (21).

Invariably writers gravitate to their difficult stories, the ones that cause the most pain and confusion, in order to create a narrative that incorporates the experiences into the rest of life. Peter Taylor, who succeeded William Faulkner as the fiction writer at the University of Virginia, said in an interview in *Poets and Writers,* "My writing is a by-product of my own efforts to understand my own life; that's what it comes to" (Goodwin 31). And these stories may be emotionally powerful for the writer. Poet Robert Phillips demonstrates this with an anecdote about Thomas Hardy: " A woman was having tea with Mrs. Hardy and inquired, 'Did Mr. Hardy have a good day of writing?' Mrs. Hardy replied, 'Oh, I'm sure of it. I could hear him sobbing all afternoon' " (18). Phillips is even more specific in his article in *Poets and Writers:* I write to exorcise my demons . . . I write about the things I can't get rid of, the things that haunt me. I'm not talking about nightmares. I'm talking about life events and traumas that I wish I could get rid of, once and or all, to close them off between two covers and put them on a shelf, never to be thought of again" (18).

What Is Trauma?

Trauma is any assault to the body or psyche that is so overwhelming that it cannot be integrated into consciousness. The word "trauma" comes from the Greek *trauma* and means "wound," originally referring only to a physical wound but now understood as well to be a wound to the psyche. Ronnie Janoff-Bulman argues in her book *Shattered Assumptions* that trauma is an event that shatters belief systems about life, beliefs that help us all operate in the world—the assumption that the self is sufficiently competent to act, that people are generally good, that the world has meaning and is predictable. Trauma breaches the unspoken contract we think we have with life, that if we do what we are supposed to do we will survive.

When trauma hits, we often cannot absorb its meaning and at the same time still hold onto all of our core beliefs. As Susan Brison wrote in *Aftermath,* a book describing her recovery from rape and attempted murder, "Things had stopped making sense" (ix). The injury itself plus this conceptual disconnect is hard enough to manage. When accompanied by other factors, such as social isolation, repeated traumas, or horrific images, it can lead to delayed and uncontrollable, repetitive, intrusive phenomena such as nightmares and flashbacks. Michael Herr wrote in *Dispatches:* "It took war to teach it, that you were as responsible for everything you saw as you were for everything you did. The problem was that you didn't always know what you were seeing until later, maybe years later, that a lot of it never made it in at all, it just stayed there in your eyes" (20). Most individuals who have survived a traumatic experience will have some kind of stress response for a period of time after the event. We saw this on a large scale after September 11. Many Americans reported having trouble sleeping, concentrating, managing intrusive thoughts, and so on. However, as stated above, when accompanied by other factors, particularly repeated traumas or lack of social support, a more complex and potentially longer-lasting response called post-traumatic stress disorder (PTSD) can develop.

Pierre Janet in France in the late nineteenth century articulated a theory of trauma which is remarkably close to what we now call PTSD; however, his work lay fallow for many years as other psychological theories took precedence. Although the term "shell-shocked" was used during World War I, trauma was not recognized as a significant factor in our culture until thousands of Vietnam War veterans returned with symptoms that we now diagnose as PTSD. Finally, in 1980 the *Diagnostic and Statistical Manual of Mental Disorders,* third edition (DSMIII), the standard reference for medically acceptable diagnoses, included a new category of emotional/mental disorders. Before this edition, sufferers could be called hysterics or malingerers, or seen as nervous or even cowardly. Germaine Greer describes her father's experience in World War II with PTSD in terms that would have been common at the time: "When the [medical officers] examined men exhibiting severe disturbances, they almost invariably found that the root cause [lay] in pre-war experience, mostly "domestic": the sick men were not first-grade fighting material . . . The military proposition is [that it is] not war which makes men sick, but that sick men can not fight wars. The authorities compounded their distress by accusing them of fear. They were actually too tired and dispirited to feel fear" (qtd. in van der Kolk 33).

The denial of the reality of trauma in the twentieth century has had serious, large-scale consequences: As van der Kolk points out, during World War II in England, "despite the diagnosis of shell shock, doctors found it extremely difficult to distinguish it from cowardice. More than 200 soldiers were executed for cowardice; a notable fact is that only 11% of those who were condemned to death for desertion were actually executed" (49). What the DSMIII diagnosis and subsequent work with trauma has taught us is that people do not all respond in the same way to trauma. An event that could send one soul into torment may not have any long-term effect on another. Traumatic stress reactions depend on many factors: the nature and severity of the trauma, genetic predispositions, the amount of control the survivor may have had over the experience, and the social support network that exists for the survivor. Virtually everyone who experiences a traumatic event will have some stress responses. The responses' duration and intensity is what is so variable, and when those responses become complex and long lasting, the diagnosis of PTSD is often made.

PTSD is commonly understood to be a normal response to an abnormal situation, but this is only true in a very general sense. The way a culture responds to a trauma can have a powerful effect on survivors, a fact that we are just beginning to realize. The isolation and shame that accompany particularly traumatic experiences (rape, AIDS, incest, for example) can be as painful as the original trauma itself. Ultimately, the crucial factor is not so much the trauma but how it is handled. Family members and others can be so horrified by the trauma that they distance themselves from the victim, a phenomenon M. Symonds has called "the second injury" (qtd. in van der Kolk 27). Although social responses to traumatic experience have a profound effect upon the victim's ability to overcome its effects and to recover from PTSD, neurobiological factors governing memory and language need to be understood to make these social responses efficacious.

Trauma is no respecter of person, place, station in life, economic status, family status, age, occupation, or any other single defining element. As P.A. Resnick points out in *Stress and Trauma,* between 70 and 80 percent of the population will experience some kind of trauma over the course of a lifetime. Chris Brewin in his book *Post-traumatic Stress Disorder: Malady or Myth* writes that "In the U.S. Comorbidity Study, 35 percent of the men and 25 percent of the women reported more than one major traumatic event in their lives thus far . . . In National Family Violence Surveys, 28 percent of respondents reported at least one incident of violence in their current relationship" (8–9). And these statistics do not take into the consideration the incidence of trauma around the globe—from tsunamis, to war, to genocide. It is important to state that trauma responses exist on a continuum—from simple stress responses that fade relatively quickly to complex post-traumatic stress disorder that may be the result of multiple traumas. Genetics, personal history, and context all play an important role in how we respond to life's challenges. When trauma comes it affects every area of the individual's life. For example, in recent years researchers have studied the importance of normal development of narrative coherence in children—that is, the ability to organize narrative material into beginning, middle, and end. As the authors of *Traumatic Stress* indicate, "Current research among pre-school children exposed to violence indicates interference with the task, resulting in more chaotic narrative construction. Achievement of this developmental task is essential to subsequent competencies in reading, writing, and communication skills" (342).

Writing has been shown to alleviate stress or trauma responses for virtually all age groups. This may be why student writers often choose to write about difficult experiences even when such topics are not on the teacher's agenda. Ironically such writing can help students become better writers. Guy Allen, a contributor to the book *Writing and Healing: Toward an Informed Practice,* edited by Anderson and MacCurdy, has documented research with his own students that demonstrates that students, even at-risk students, who write personal narratives become better academic writers even when academic writing is not specifically taught. However, often writers struggle with getting started. I have discovered from my own work with students that the single most influential element in producing writer's block is some undisclosed trauma, of whatever magnitude. To investigate why this is and what we may do about this we need to understand the difference between normal memories and traumatic ones.

Traumatic Memory

Contemporary research has demonstrated that human memory systems are extremely complex, and since the technology to study the brain is relatively recent, conclusions are tentative, contentious, and inconclusive. However, a brief discussion of some of the major areas might help to frame the issues. Researchers identify two memory systems: declarative memory, also known as explicit memory, and nondeclarative, also known as implicit, or procedural, memory. Declarative memory refers to a conscious awareness of facts, events, and moments in time that are subject to verbal, conscious expression. As Brewin points out, declarative memory is supported by the cortex, the medial temporal lobe and the hippocampus, which is involved in working memory and the learning of temporal and spatial context (119). The cortex is the site of executive control, the guiding light of conscious awareness, and one of its major functions is to keep out of consciousness unwanted or irrelevant information. Another important function is to integrate new information into existing data. But trauma often contradicts pre-existing assumptions about the world, overloading the cortex and producing what Brewin calls "catastrophic interference" (120). Declarative memory is an active process of construction. Once an event or a piece of information is integrated into the general mental scheme, it will no longer be remembered as a separate entity but as a general part of the whole.

Nondeclarative memory refers to the learning of skills, abilities, emotional responses, unconscious actions, and conditioned responses (van der Kolk et al. 280–81). These memories cannot be consciously recalled—we ride a bike automatically once we have mastered the skill. Some researchers see nondeclarative (implicit) memory as a part of a separate "perceptual representation system" that identifies perceptual objects and is not involved with verbal narrative memory. Daniel Schacter in his book *Searching for Memory* has called traumatic memories implicit ones (161–91). Whereas explicit memories can decay over time, implicit ones tend not to. In fact, "studies of people's subjective reports of personally highly significant events generally find that their memories are unusually accurate, and that they tend to remain stable over time," van der Kolk argues in *Traumatic Stress* (281). That is, traumatic memories, as opposed to normal or even flashbulb memories, tend not to become distorted over time or even, for that matter, to fade. As Schacter illustrates, "When people in a 1984 study were asked to produce their three most vivid memories, hardly any of the recollections involved events of national importance; they tended to be highly personal events with great emotional significance" (201).

Whereas people seem to assimilate memories of ordinary events over time and individual details usually are not remembered, memories of emotionally charged events—happy as well as traumatic—can become indelible and qualitatively different from non-emotionally charged memories. When distortion occurs—and it can—it is most likely to involve specific details. When any emotionally charged experience occurs, stress hormones flood the brain, and those hormones help to encode the images and the emotions together into memory. This process occurs for all memories that carry emotional weight, as McNally points out in *Remembering Trauma* (62), and this is why we usually remember such experiences so vividly. It is also important, however, to point out that loss of recollections for traumatic events is also well documented. Researchers have been studying the relationship between traumatic and normal memories, and while this area is still hotly debated, most researchers agree that normal and traumatic memories appear to have some differences.

As Schacter and others have described, declarative memory consists of mental constructs with which we make sense of the experiences of our lives. Familiar experiences are easily assimilated into the psyche without much conscious awareness, while frightening experiences may not fit into existing cognitive frameworks or, indeed, may resist integration altogether. Some experiences are so terrifying that they are stored quite differently in the brain and are therefore not available for conscious recall. Instead, they leak into the conscious mind unbidden, usually in situations that are reminiscent of the original trauma. This process has a neurobiological component. The brain has three primary divisions: the brainstem and the hypothalamus, which is associated with internal regulation; the limbic system, responsible for maintaining balance between the internal world and the external; and the neocortex, which helps us to analyze and interact with the external world.

Trauma produces something called "iconic memories," mental pictures that can be stored deep within the brain in certain parts of the limbic system, where they are linked to the emotions with which they were encoded. Traumatic memories are sensory; that is, the body reacts to them even when the conscious mind is not aware of the cause of such reactions. This is because these iconic memories are stored in parts of the brain that not only retain these memories but are responsible for attaching emotional weight to them. For example, the hippocampus, a seahorse-shaped organ which aids in logging in short-term memories, will register exactly where on a wooded path you saw a rattlesnake, but the amygdala, an almond-shaped organ that helps register our emotions, will make sure you remember seeing the snake because the image of it and the fear it generated will be encoded within that organ. The surge of adrenaline that signifies fight or flight helps to imprint these responses, neither of which goes first through the cortex, a pattern with survival and therefore evolutionary benefits because it saves much-needed time in the event of danger. The disadvantage of that system is that traumatic experiences are encoded as images and emotions together in the brain and cannot be retrieved independently of each other. The emotional power of traumatic, iconic images helps log them into the part of the brain that is nonverbal, which is why survivors use language such as, "I was speechless with terror," or "I was struck dumb," because they literally were. This does not mean that survivors do not remember their experiences or cannot put words to them. It does mean that the iconic nature of the traumatic image often takes precedence over language, which can make it difficult to both "feel" the image and construct a narrative about it at the same time. (See van der Kolk et al. for discussions of traumatic memory.)

This iconic nature of emotional memory also maintains for happy memories, as mentioned above. David Pillemer includes many examples of emotional memories in his book *Momentous Events, Vivid Memories,* and while most are negative, he also offers examples of happy events leading to long-lasting memories as well—for example, a romantic moment, a flash of insight. These memories are almost always image-laden as well, which leads him to postulate the existence of two separate memory systems, one we are born with and the other we develop during our pre-school years. In the former system memories are expressed through images, behaviors, or emotions, whereas in the second memories are encoded in narrative form. He has also observed that when survivors describe frightening experiences, they often shift automatically into present tense, as this example he offers indicates:

> We heard this "Pop, pop, pop, pop, pop, pop, pop, pop, pop." All of a sudden Chris *says,* "Jesus, it's gunfire." And I *look* and I *see* the dirt kicking up all around us, and I see the windows shatter, the car in front of me, I *look* around and I see Larry Semme, the security officer in the—in the Toyota following me, in a Land Cruiser, with his long frame, and I can *see* the bullets hitting his car and the windows shatter there, and then I *see* his long frame lean out with a pistol and he *returns* fire to up above, and meanwhile, Chris has said, "Back up Eddie." He *backs* up. We're so close to the car in front of us that we *have* to back up to get around, and there's so little room to get around that we *side-swipe* all the way down. The car that was close in front of us had two dead and three wounded. The car behind me had ten bullets through it. Our—ours only had one. (Qtd. in Brewin 92–93)

Pillemer believes that this kind of language is not a simple recounting of an experience but is more a reliving of it, which is why the tense shifts to present. Indeed, I have found with student writers that when gripped by a particularly important experience, present tense enables them to get back to the details of the moments more readily. I often suggest present tense to writers who are having difficulty writing "in the moment," and it usually helps. If they wish they can switch into past tense for subsequent drafts, but present tense does seem to facilitate recall and that sense of immediacy.

The memories jogged by this kind of process appear more like flashbacks than narrative memory. Flashbacks are disjointed fragments of memory replete with sensory detail, which includes sounds and smells as well as visual and auditory sensations. Survivors often feel thrown back to the time of the traumatic event, even smelling original smells and feeling temperatures or pains that they felt at the moment of the trauma. As Jonathan Shay writes about combat trauma, "Traumatic memory is not narrative. Rather, it is experience that reoccurs, either as full sensory replay of traumatic events in dreams or flashbacks, with all things seen, heard, smelled, and felt intact, or as disconnected fragments. These fragments may be inexplicable . . . [and include] terror, uncontrollable crying, or disconnected body states and sensations" (172). Judith Herman in her book *Trauma and Recovery* calls these "frozen memories," a term similar to Janet's "fixed ideas." Herein lies one of the paradoxes of trauma: While flashbacks are intrusive, compelling, and to easy to recall, traumatic memories can also be very elusive. Brewin explains it this way: "As events begin to increase in emotional intensity central details are retained for longer, often in the form of visual image, and peripheral details are worse recalled. But there seems to be a point at which the intensity of the emotion interferes with the clarity of recall, with the result that memories become fragmented and disorganized" (102–3). In other words, trauma memories are both difficult to recall and so easy as to crowd in when they are unwanted. They can be accessible to narrative recall and so frightening and powerful that they surface in bursts of sensory images that appear to be happening in real time as they are recalled.

In the past few years, scientists have been focusing on the relationship between emotion and cognition in an attempt to understand better how the two systems interact. Cahill and McGaugh were among the first researchers to discover that emotionally charged memories are more persistent than neutral ones because the stress hormones released at the time that the experience occurred helped to lock the memory into the brain. (See my chapter in *Writing and Healing* for a fuller discussion of this research). *Science News* reported on a study by neuroscientist Bryan Strange of University College London that demonstrates that this vivid recall can also block memories of what happened just before the emotionally arousing experiences occurred. The stress hormones from the adrenal glands cause the amygdala to create long-term memories of the emotional experiences, and those memories persisted even after a delay of several weeks. However, what occurred just before the emotionally charged experiences was less likely to be remembered, which means that the charged memories lost their context and appear separate from the rest of life. This can help explain why writers are often compelled to write about their traumas yet find this such a cognitive as well as emotional challenge (*Science News* 293)

The Memory Wars

Trauma has become an important topic—particularly since September 11, 2001—as we begin to understand its effects on individuals and culture. However, it has also become a contentious issue, given the media attention to what has been termed "false memory syndrome." The false memory controversy was mostly precipitated by a few cases of "recovered memories" of satanic cult abuse on the part of incompetent therapists. The overwhelming

percentages of documented amnesias for childhood sexual abuse are responses to corroborated events, as Ross Cheit, a childhood sexual abuse survivor and political science professor at Brown University, stated in the lecture
he gave at Harvard Medical School in 1995 discussed earlier in this chapter.
Cheit himself discovered only as an adult while on a family camping trip in
Canada that the images that flooded him on his trip were scenes of his childhood sexual abuse by a summer music camp administrator. Cheit found this
man, who, it turned out, had abused other boys as well, and brought him to
justice all those years later, clear evidence that some childhood traumatic
memories can be "repressed" and then "recovered."

Interestingly, as McFarlane and van der Kolk have noted in *Traumatic
Stress,* the "issue of delayed recall was not controversial when Myers (1940)
and Kardiner (1941) gave detailed descriptions in their books on combat neuroses; when Sargent and Slater in 1941 reported that 144 of 1,000 consecutive
admissions to a field hospital had amnesia for their trauma; or when van der
Kolk noted it in Vietnam combat veterans" (566). Van der Kolk has argued
that as long as men were found to suffer from delayed recall of atrocities committed, this issue was not controversial. "However, when similar memory
problems started to be documented in girls and women in the context of domestic abuse, the news was unbearable; when female victims started to seek
justice against their alleged perpetrators, the issue moved from science into
politics" (566). As van der Kolk points out, once the media entered the picture, the science was gone.

While it is true that incompetent therapists can construct false narratives
for clients, implanting specific images is another matter unless the therapists
involved step far outside professional protocols. Both Jennifer Freyd and
Bessel van der Kolk have argued that traumatic memories have such a
high image content that implantation is quite unlikely. Van der Kolk and
McFarlane point out in *Traumatic Stress* that the issue of false memories has
become so "heated" that Elizabeth Loftus, a leading laboratory researcher on
false memories, omitted from her book, *The Myth of Repressed Memory,* her
own study published in *Psychology of Women Quarterly* which demonstrates
that sexual abuse can indeed produce memory loss (567). In addition, memory researchers have claimed that false memories can be implanted by referring to those lost-in-the-mall studies where a child is told that he was lost
while shopping and he begins to repeat this story as if it were true. But, of
course, this is not a "trauma" of great magnitude, nor is it image-based, as
most traumatic memories are. It is true, however, that context for memory

retrieval can have a bearing on which memories we choose to bring to consciousness and which we allow to stay buried.

Most researchers into the nature of traumatic memory see key differences between normal and traumatic memories. First, as Daniel Schacter argues, all memory is constructed, not a faithful representation of what was experienced. Berliner and Briere state in their chapter in the book *Trauma and Memory* edited by Williams and Banyard that all memories are a combination of what was encoded when the event occurred, the base within which the experience was integrated, the way the experience was interpreted, the accuracy of retrieval strategies, and the context for recall (7). Normal memories are mutable because once information is coded into a meaning scheme, the individual bits of data are no longer important, and indeed are often forgotten. Traumatic memories retain their imagistic quality precisely because they are not coded into a meaning scheme. They are too overwhelming for that. That's the definition of trauma. This does not mean, however, that traumatic memories are always indelible. Lenore Terr has shown in two 1983 journal articles that both adults and children can misremember certain details of a trauma. Berliner and Briere state that a "significant proportion of adults who report a trauma history also describe a period of time when they did not recall the experience . . . The rates of reported forgetting range from approximately 20% to 60% depending on the study. Three studies of adults with documented childhood sexual and/or physical abuse histories provide confirmation that some survivors appear genuinely not to recall the events" (6). Some memory researchers, such as Elizabeth Loftus, assert that if traumatic memories are "forgotten" that this is caused by the same mechanism that produces forgetting of normal memories, and they continue the argument by asserting that survivors would be better off if this forgetting occurs because then they would not be plagued by the traumatic images any longer (qtd. in Williams and Banyard 117). That does not, however, appear to be how this process works.

It appears that whether the memories are buried (that is, repressed by some process of denial that pushes them away) or "forgotten" (that is hidden by dissociation and unable to be remembered because the trauma was never integrated into consciousness), the trauma will still have an effect on the survivor with the presence of emotional and/or physical symptoms that intrude into life. Williams and Banyard offer a study by Briere and Conte in which "59% of 450 women and men survivors had some period of their lives during which they had no memory for their abuse. They found that this group also had higher current levels of psychological symptoms (116). One of the most convincing studies (described in chapter 9 of *Trauma and Memory*) is that of Linda Williams, who relied on officially documented histories of child sexual abuse. She studied 129 women from a large U.S. city who had been treated as children at a city hospital emergency room for sexual abuse. The girls, ranging in age from ten months to twelve years old, had reported sexual abuse perpetrated by a person who was at least ten years older than they were. Approximately seventeen years later, the women were interviewed in a private office by two women trained in conducting interviews on sensitive subjects and who were blind to the details of the women's histories. Of the 129 women interviewed, 49 did not appear to remember the incident, and 12 reported some period when they had forgotten the event.

In addition, the researchers attempted to determine which of the women had had ongoing psychological symptoms as a result of the sexual abuse. They used a Trauma Symptom Checklist, a forty-item measure of emotional problems that has been found to distinguish between sexual abuse survivors and nonvictims. It identifies such problems as depression, anxiety, sleep disturbances, and sexual problems. Women who appeared not to remember the abuse were more likely to be younger at the time they were abused and to have been abused by someone they knew. The researchers found that although those with memory problems may not be doing worse than those with continuous recall, they also do not seem to be clearly doing better. This is contrary to some discussions, which assert that having no memory for traumatic events may lead individuals to do better than survivors with continuous recall. Those who do not remember the abuse may show effects of abuse at levels comparable to abused women with continuous recall, yet they may have difficulty in obtaining appropriate therapeutic intervention (Williams and Banyard 124).

Linda Williams reports in her 1995 article in the *Journal of Traumatic Stress* that "memories of child abuse reported by adults can be quite consistent with contemporaneous documentation of the abuse and should not be summarily dismissed by therapists, lawyers, family members, judges, or the women themselves" (670). Even when conscious memory is missing, the physical, mental, and emotional effects of traumatic abuse can be felt. Bessel van der Kolk was speaking of this when he said at a 1995 Harvard Conference on Psychological Trauma, "The body keeps score." That is, the body has imprinted within it the results of that abuse, which can range from physical changes in the brain to biochemical reactions that affect behavior.

Several groups have a stake in the issue of traumatic memory, among them survivors, psychiatrists and other mental health professionals, neuroscientists and memory researchers, and stakeholders in the criminal justice system. It is not difficult to see how these disparate groups can approach such a complicated topic from different perspectives, particularly when we add the fact that expert witnesses make considerable money convincing juries that they are right. In general, mental health professionals who work with survivors on a daily basis are more likely to apply experiential induction to this issue, while the pure researchers draw tentative conclusions based on experiments that can only simulate a traumatic experience given the ethical problems in imposing a trauma on experimental subjects. The confusion is compounded by the fact that traumatic memories appear both indelible and forgettable.

Elizabeth Loftus, a leading laboratory researcher on memory distortion, may be able to shed some light on this discrepancy. Jennifer Freyd in her book *Betrayal Trauma* includes a narrative written by Loftus in which she describes an incident of sexual abuse when she was six and which she recalled when she was in her forties:

> The memory flew out at me, out of the blackness of the past, hitting me with full force . . . I saw Howard the baby-sitter who used to sit next to me on the sofa and rub my arm, using the back of his hand against the smooth skin, his fingers following the gentle curve from wrist to elbow and up for a second, then back down . . . One night, after my younger brothers had gone to bed and after Howard had rubbed my arm for a while, he took my hand and led me into my parents' bedroom. He took his pants off, pulled my dress over my head, and removed my underpants. He lay down on the bed and pulled me on top of him, positioning me so that our pelvises touched. His arms circled around me, I felt him pushing against me, and I knew something was wrong. Embarrassed and confused, I squirmed off him and ran out of the room. After that, there is only blackness in my memory, and total darkness with not a pinhole of light. Howard is simply gone, vanished, sucked away. My memory took him and destroyed him . . . Ten hours later I was . . . exhausted but sleepless, too tired to pull myself back into the present or to dream about the future, too absorbed by that scene in my parents' bedroom when Howard the baby-sitter

betrayed my trust, stole my innocence, and put an indelible impression, a bad, black memory into the place where only good, warm, happy memories should be. (Freyd 29)

As Freyd argues, "Elizabeth Loftus' description illustrates the paradox of traumatic memory: how the survivor can have a memory of the event that is 'indelible' yet so blocked that it causes the perpetrator to 'vanish'; a memory that was forgotten yet flies 'out of the blackness of the past'" (29).

Loftus herself has used the term "repression" to explain this phenomenon: "Repression is one of the most haunting concepts in psychology. Something shocking happens, and the mind pushes it into some inaccessible corner of the unconscious. Later the memory may emerge into consciousness" (qtd. in Freyd 14). This implies a deliberate putting away of a memory. Other researchers use the term "dissociation," which implies that the memory was never placed into normal memory contexts in the first place. Part of the reason for this apparent discrepancy is the distinction between amnesia and "knowledge isolation," in which the information is not completely lost to consciousness but is isolated, not integrated into our life narratives. Loftus remembered that indelible image but had no place to put it, nowhere it could reside that made any sense of the experience—and this is a hallmark of the traumatic image. What becomes the most significant element for survivors is not simply the initial event but its aftermath—and with small children who have no one to help them integrate the experience it can be split off from the rest of normal memory. While the traumatic images are still alive, the survivor has no current context for them, and they can remain caught in the past. Although this does not generally produce total amnesia for an event, amnesia can occur, especially, Freyd argues, with the trauma of incest.

This is a contentious area, since some memory researchers such as Daniel Schacter argue that repeated events are more likely to be remembered than isolated single events, making it difficult to believe that amnesias for repeated sexual abuse could occur. Many trauma researchers, however, such as Judith Herman in *Trauma and Recovery* and Jennifer Freyd in *Betrayal Trauma*, argue that repeated sexual abuse is more likely to cause amnesia than single events because it is most often at the hands of a caregiver or trusted adult. This makes living in the environment impossible unless the child completely dissociates from the event. In fact, recent research has corroborated this theory. In the DSM IV field trials, van der Kolk reports that "hypernesias are more common after one-time traumatic events, particularly in adults, while chronic amnesias tend to occur after repeated traumatization in childhood" (*Traumatic Stress* 173). Drawing on the work of Briere and Conte, Herman and Shatzow, and his own research, van der Kolk states that amnesias for traumas appear to be "age-and dose-related: The younger a person was at the time of the trauma and the more prolonged the trauma was, the greater the likelihood of significant amnesia" (285).

The working hypothesis for many trauma specialists is that amnesias are not caused by repression, which implies motivation and some kind of volition, but by severe dissociation, a splitting off into areas of the brain material that is either too threatening to allow into conscious awareness or has no historical context and meaning schema. Therefore, the material was never integrated in the first place. It was not repressed, which connotes a vertical construction; it was put aside, hidden, which implies a horizontal construct. Dissociation is in many ways a natural process of survival as opposed to the conventional concept of repression, which implies an unwillingness to allow images or thoughts into consciousness. This definition of repression can seem to place blame on the victim, which is one outcome of Freud's constructs after he repudiated his *Aetiology of Hysteria* (in which he argued that "hysteria" is caused by abuse). He saw a natural process as a neurosis, and we still are fighting this same battle today. To be fair, Freud's use of "repression" was at times ambiguous. Often he used it to mean a pushing down of information, but at other times he seems to have used it in the way that Janet did—as a form of dissociation. This ambiguity extends to our day and is part of the reason why the "repressed memory" question is so problematic.

Attempts at a "Unified Field Theory" of Trauma

Brewin is one of many researchers attempting to provide a memory theory that will account for the various inconsistencies and confusions surrounding traumatic memory. Brewin has postulated what he calls the "dual representation theory." Two memory systems are in operation—what he calls the *verbally accessible memory* system (VAM) for memories that are integrated with other autobiographical memories and can be retrieved at will, as other normal memories can, and *situationally accessible memory* system (SAM) named for the fact that flashbacks are triggered by the physical or emotional context in which the survivor finds himself. The SAM system contains information that may not be part of the survivor's conscious awareness—for example, images, sounds, smells that were so briefly encountered that they were not yet consciously perceived and therefore have not been made a part of the verbal system. Also a part of the SAM system are the physical responses to trauma—rapid heartbeat, sweaty palms, and so forth, which enable flashbacks to carry emotional weight. Brewin offers his research studies, which appear to support this hypothesis (114). He also offers information that links his theories to current thinking about the effects of stress on the amygdala and the hippocampus.

Declarative memory is initially enhanced by the release of stress hormones, which ensures that we will remember exactly where on the wooded path we saw the snake. However, prolonged stress associated with highly elevated levels of stress hormones tends to impair the functioning of the hippocampus and can even shrink it in size (van der Kolk et al. 231). This, of course, has negative effects on declarative, verbal memory and may explain why some trauma survivors have a hard time concentrating on a task. The amygdala's functioning improves, however, with the additional stress hormones, which is consistent with survivors' developing highly conditioned emotional responses. Brewin argues that his dual representation system accounts for why survivors can develop verbal memories for trauma but can also find those memories inadequate, vague, and incomplete. While flashback memories are not exactly nondeclarative in the usual sense of the term, they are a perceptual form of memory that arrive unbidden and appear to be unchanging and temporally without a context, since the experiences they refer to happened in the past but the memories describe events that seem to be in the present. As Brewin says, "All these features are suggestive of an image-based non-hippocampally dependent form of memory that is unable to encode information about past versus present" (124).

We can see this kind of memory trace in Ross Cheit's description of his experience: "I woke up thinking about him [the abuser]. I woke up thinking about a man I hadn't thought of in twenty-four years . . . It was like he was in the room with me. I could picture him. I could hear his voice. I could remember him quite well. And it was very compelling" (qtd in Freyd 7). This kind of experience does not appear to be produced by normal forgetting and remembering, as Elizabeth Loftus and Frederick Crews have proposed, the latter in articles in the *New York Review of Books*. If normal forgetting were operating, we would expect that the more distressing the event, the more it would be remembered. However, just the opposite has been documented in a large study of traumatic events cited by Brewin. With respect to child abuse, "we would similarly predict that the less violent or threatening the experience, or the less the events were interpreted as sexual at the time, the easier the abuse should be to forget. Almost every study that has examined the influence of threats and violence has found the opposite, with greater forgetting being associated with more violence, with more threats of harm, and with a trend toward greater use of force" (163–64). In addition, McNally has written that we are more likely to remember an event when the "context for remembering resembles the context for encoding" (40). Ross Cheit's memory of his abuse was reactivated when he was on a summer camping trip; the abuse occurred during summer music camp. The similarities between those two settings helped to kick in his long-dormant memory. As Brewin argues, the sensory nature of traumatic experiences is contained in a "separate knowledge system that is accessed automatically in response to similar sensory stimuli" (qtd. in Lepore and Smyth 143).

The central issue that experts—and the media—have been grappling with is how survivors can appear both to remember traumas so clearly and yet also have amnesias for either parts of the trauma experience or in some cases all of it. Dissociation produces both vivid memory traces and memory gaps, one of the paradoxes of trauma. Brewin's dual-representation theory appears to account for this apparent contradiction. Brewin offers Emily Holmes's suggestion that dissociation which occurs during a traumatic event blocks encoding of the memory in the verbally accessible memory system (Brewin's VAM), so that the person has fewer conscious memories; but this blocking does not prohibit encoding in the situationally accessible memory system (SAM), since that encoding can be a subcortical process (175). As Brewin points out, "The perceptual, image-based SAM system is thought to be mainly responsible for the intrusion of visual trauma memories and is inhibited by the existence of detailed memories in the VAM system. According to the theory, therefore, anything that blocks encoding into the VAM system (such as a disturbance in consciousness) should have two quite separate effects, *making the trauma harder to recall deliberately and making spontaneous intrusive images more likely*" (175, italics added). Brewin goes on to argue that "whether the memories are recovered in the form of fragmented images or as whole autobiographical memories depends ... on the degree of conscious processing that the events originally received" (176). It is important to remember that traumatic events often do not permit the kind of conscious rumination—at the time of the event—that would allow for this processing. This is why individuals often feel so out of control in the midst of a trauma—not only can they do nothing to prevent the event, but they also do not have the time to organize their thoughts and feelings about the experience until after it has been en-coded in the brain.

Medical science may be able to provide some biological markers to add to these theories. Bessel van der Kolk has been conducting positron emission tomography studies of patients with post-traumatic stress disorder and offers some of his results in *Traumatic Stress*. One study (Rausch et al.) demon-strates that when people with PTSD are exposed to stimuli similar to their original traumas "there is an increase in perfusion of the areas in the right hemisphere associated with emotional states and autonomic arousal. More-over, there is a simultaneous decrease in oxygen utilization in Broca's area—the region in the left inferior frontal cortex responsible for generating words to attach to internal experience. These feelings may account for the observa-tion that trauma may lead to 'speechless terror,' which in some individuals interferes with the ability to put feelings into words, leaving emotions to be mutely expressed by dysfunction of the body" (van der Kolk et al. 193).

Van der Kolk points out that problems with using language to identify feelings can begin early. Cicchetti et al. have demonstrated that "maltreated toddlers use fewer words to describe how they feel and have more problems with attributing causality than do secure children of the same age. Secure children spend more time describing physiological states, such as hunger, thirst, and states of consciousness, and speak more often about negative emo-tions, such as hate, disgust, and anger. Not knowing how and what one feels may contribute to the impaired impulse control seen in abused children" (van der Kolk et al. 194). This study is significant because it indicates that language can be a crucial skill in expressing and processing negative emotions. Our culture tends to underestimate the power of emotion to influence behavior. Our schools, our criminal justice system, even some therapy modalities prefer to see cognition as dominant over emotions. This view, that volition can and will can curb negative emotions, is not necessarily an accurate representation of the effects of trauma. The neuroscientist Joseph Le Doux argues that emo-tion itself can be seen as a memory, and he maintains that it should be treated as a memory process rather than as a process that simply affects memory (van der Kolk et al. 269–88).

In another PET scan study, van der Kolk and his associates collected vic-tims' own imagistic narratives and then read them back to the participants. When the narratives triggered autonomic responses and flashbacks, a brain scan was made. Neutral scenes were used as a control. During exposure to these narratives, subjects demonstrated heightened brain activity in the right amygdala and other related structures. Activation of these areas was "accompanied by heightened activity in the right visual cortex, reflecting the visual re-experiencing of their traumas that these patients report. Perhaps most significantly, Broca's area 'turned off.' We believe that this reflects the tendency in PTSD to experience emotions as physical states rather than as verbally encoded experiences. Our findings suggest that PTSD patients' difficulties with putting feelings into words are mirrored in actual changes in brain activity" (233). Most trauma survivors remember their traumas. They do not have complete amnesia for the events; however, they often have trouble connecting the events with the emotions that accompanied them. Van der Kolk et al. argue that this occurs because the iconic nature of the image and the verbal recounting of the event are not integrated into a part of the brain that can "read" them together. The goal in effecting healing is to combine the images and the emotions they generate with thought processes, and this can be done only through activation of the verbal system. As van der Kolk said, "A sudden and passively endured trauma is relived repeatedly, until a person learns to remember simultaneously the affect and cognition associated with the trauma through access to language" (167).

Traumatic Image and Remembering

The emotional intensity of trauma produces fragmented, imagistic memories that are difficult to pull together into a coherent narrative. Clinical treatment involves helping survivors to remember each image, connect it to the next image, and string them together to produce a narrative that helps to reduce the sense of fragmentation and separation from oneself. Clinical psychologist Edna Foa evaluated the rape narratives of fourteen female sexual assault survivors at the beginning and at the end of treatment. After a course of therapy that required the survivors to describe what happened in detail again and again until symptoms subsided, the researchers discovered that "decreases in fragmentation over the course of therapy predicted improvement in PTSD symptoms" (qtd. in McNally 135). Narrative fragmentation was defined as repeated phrases, speech fillers, and unfinished thoughts that interrupted the narrative.

Tom Williams describes the therapeutic process involved in working with survivors of trauma: "For a therapeutic intervention to be successful one must get the story of the trauma in precise detail. For example, it is helpful to know the details about environmental conditions, particularly smells, articles of clothing, and other situational cues. It is important for them to tell you about the trauma scene as clearly and vividly as possible . . . The more they tell the story . . . the less intense the emotions become" (80). As Susan Brison observes in *Aftermath*, "Saying something about the memory *does* something to it" (xi).

This technique may at first be difficult to accomplish because it involves re-experiencing the emotions generated by the original trauma, something most survivors have carefully avoided; however, it is just those images that can help the survivor heal from the trauma. Once the images start to come, so do the feelings that have been suppressed. Williams makes sure to tell his clients that "people do not die from crying, and that once they start crying they will stop" (80). This is crucial to say because many survivors have spent years avoiding their feelings precisely because they feared being overwhelmed by them, an understandable fear given the power of the traumatic image. In addition, Freud defined therapy as a process of abreaction and catharsis, abreaction being a re-experiencing of the moment of the trauma leading to a catharsis. Therefore, survivors fear that the therapy process will lead to collapse or an overwhelming experience of being lost inside the past. However, contemporary trauma therapists emphasize the integration of past and present, which moves clients beyond the catharsis Freud posited and helps them to trust that the therapeutic process allows them to feel the past without being consumed by it.

Williams offers an excerpt from two interviews with a Vietnam War veteran. In the first, the veteran speaks blankly about being shot, burned in a field, smoked out by the enemy in an ambush. No emotions are shown; the vet shows no connection to the events described. In the later description he begins to allow emotional content to enter his speech. Williams argues that only after the images and the emotions can be connected can healing occur, and the best way to accomplish that is to help the survivor describe the event with as much imagistic detail as possible. Carolyn Agosta and Mary McHugh describe a similar technique: "You encourage her to talk about what happened in detail. As she experiences a safe place to discuss her rape, she begins to feel the emotions of that violent encounter; then she may begin to recover her memory . . . As this occurs, her fear level will heighten, she will become more in touch with her pain, and she will experience relief" (244).

As Brewin described in his explanation of VAM and SAM systems, survivors are flooded with images and sensory impressions because the hippocampal system allows for some recognition of the event, but the amygdala has so emotionally weighted the memories that they have not been integrated with knowledge in the cortical system. This "may contribute to a sense of unreality surrounding the event" (182), which keeps it split off from the rest of life. The goal is integration into the verbal system, which can pull the memories into the cortical areas where they can be integrated into the person's overall mental and emotional framework. As Brewin argues, " 'Denial' consists in the refusal of the trauma victim to consciously dwell on the traumatic experience and to initiate the process of interleaved learning. The existence of unchanged neocortical knowledge structures may be why certain traumatized people describe being able to 'live in the past' and to pretend that the event never really happened" (182). To use Brewin's language, "detailed memories in the SAM system that signaled the continuing presence of danger are matched by detailed memories in the VAM system that locate the danger in the past. When the person encounters trauma reminders, these VAM memories are accessed, preventing inappropriate amygdala activation and the accompanying return of fear" (181). Both narrative, verbal memories and procedural, sensory ones are crucial for integration to take place.

In *Lucky*, her memoir of her rape as a nineteen-year-old college student at Syracuse University, Alice Sebold describes the moment she tells her teacher, Tobias Wolff, that she must miss class because she just saw her rapist again and must call the police. Wolff took her by the shoulders and said, "Alice, a lot of things are going to happen, and this may not make much sense to you right now, but listen. Try, if you can, to remember everything" (106). Wolff, the author of his own memoir, *This Boy's Life*, understood the imagistic power of narrative. As Sebold wrote, "He knew . . . that memory could save, that it had power, that it was often the only recourse of the powerless, the oppressed, or the brutalized" (106).

Much of the power of Toni Morrison's Nobel Prize–winning novel *Beloved* comes from its images as a trauma narrative. Paul D., a former slave, who has survived having his neck in irons, his feet burned, and his friends hanged, is asked a question that triggers his past traumas, and they come up as iconic images, not narratives, with over-powering emotions stuck to them: "A shudder ran through Paul D. A bone-cold spasm that made him clutch his knees. He didn't know if it was bad whisky, nights in the cellar, pig fever, iron bits, smiling roosters, fired feet, laughing dead men, hissing grass . . . neck jewelry, Judy in the slaughterhouse . . . ghost-white stairs . . . Paul A's face . . . or the loss of a red, red heart" (235). Each of these images represents a significant moment, most of them traumatic, which flew unbidden into Paul D.'s mind when he was asked a question that in itself was traumatic. His painful experiences are linked together because each one feels similar to the next, like gray pearls on a string. We sense our painful memories even if we cannot verbalize them into a narrative. We seek a way to make the unknown known.

Image to Narrative

Re-experiencing sensory details encoded during extreme life moments is at the core of trauma recovery. Traumatic memories lack verbal narrative and context; instead they are "imprinted in the brain in the form of vivid images and sensations," as Judith Herman has said in her ground-breaking book *Trauma and Recovery* (38). When victims speak of the moments of their trauma, they do not produce clear narrative lines but instead describe pictures and sounds that remain encoded permanently in their minds. I broke my finger once by closing it in the car door. I do not remember even this relatively mild trauma as a consistent narrative. Instead I remember seeing the gray seatbelt caught in the door; I picture yanking on it with my right hand; I remember seeing my left middle finger deeply grooved, bent, and blue. I do not remember opening the door and pulling my hand out of the door after I injured it. I remember not a narrative but moments within that narrative.

Many times, however, writers come to their subjects with what I call the story of the story; that is, the way they think the story was, not the way they really felt it was. They are separate from the emotional truth of their experience because their cognitive and affective responses were not unified. Sometimes this process is exacerbated by writers believing someone else's version of the story—a parent's, a sibling's, or a teacher's. Sometimes it happens because the emotional impact of the event would be so difficult to absorb, particularly if the trauma happened in childhood, that the survivor cannot grasp it. Often this means that the survivor can only experience emotional reactions as somatic states without being able to understand what he is feeling and why. The survivor may not even know his own emotions, many times because we locate ourselves within another's interpretation of the world to maintain connection.

Charles Anderson borrows from film critics and Lacanian scholars the term "suture" to denote "the process by which we, as viewers of a given scene or as participants in a particular discourse, move toward and are fastened into the subject position. Because meaning is essential to human beings and is dependent upon being located within the discourse of an other, the process of suturing ourselves or allowing ourselves to be sutured into the discourse of another is all but irresistible . . . Suture inserts us into discourses that appear to give our lives coherence, wholeness, and meaning, but in that process, they also wound and break us, separate and alienate us, pacify us, and expose us to losses so severe that we can easily cease to be" (61). When we accept an imposed meaning schema driven by our affiliations rather than connect with the images we carry within and the emotions those images generate, we are creating a cognitive dissonance so great that we may have to split off our emotions to exist.

It is important to remember that the same thing that helps us recover from traumatic experiences—describing images in detail—produces writing that is alive with sensory description. Indeed, trauma theory can offer the writing instructor/coach important insights into how to help writers produce the sensory images so necessary for effective personal essays. Most beginning writers do not move seamlessly into the defining images that shape their experiences, and they instead often provide labels of emotions rather than pictures—"I felt sad, I felt angry, I felt excited"—without connecting with the images that powered these emotions. They also can lean on clichés and weak intensifiers that can dull the impact of the experience. The personal essay teacher's job is to help the writer move beyond the story of the story and the labels this generates in order to reach the level of direct experience. This can often be accomplished through classroom exercises including visualizations, which will be discussed in the next chapter. Once writers cease depending on these labels, the images and the moments they convey can come through. Only then will the writing provide effective details instead of a list of labels such as the following: summer camp was a time of growth, military school was a lesson in independence, the death of a grandparent taught them about the process of death, divorce taught them responsibility and provided them with double birthday presents.

Wilma Bucci in her article "The Power of Narrative" demonstrates that labels—that is, prose that does not convey concrete images—cannot have a healing effect. She postulates what she terms "referential activity," a process for symbolizing emotional experience while retaining access to the "analogic components of the feeling state" (106). In other words, verbalizing an emotional state must convey a sense of the affect. These referential connections are the most productive when direct, specific, and concrete images are being described verbally; they are less productive for abstract concepts: "Thus high RA [referential activity] is reflected in language that is concrete, specific and clear, that captures a quality of immediacy in the speaker's representations, and that is likely to evoke vivid and immediate experience in the listener, as well" (Bucci 109). Bucci offers the following example of low RA prose: "I love people and I like to be with people. And right now I feel very bad because I can't be with them and do the things I would like to do. But I'm looking forward to a happier and healthier future and—I don't know what else to say. What else can I talk about?" (109).

As Bucci points out, this speaker is talking about emotions but is unable to connect her words to the emotions that underlie them. Bucci has developed systematic procedures for describing qualities of language style: "The methods of scoring RA include qualitative rating scales and objective measures based on quantifiable linguistic features. These measures have been validated by . . . experimental and clinical work"(110). The RA rating scales measure concreteness, imagery, specificity, and clarity of speech. Bucci adds two more elements to the scale: ET (emotional tone) and AB (abstraction dictionary). The emotional tone word list consists of diction that demonstrates the emotional state of the speaker and is likely to produce an emotional reaction in the listener. AB words are abstract nouns that indicate intellectual concepts based on logical reflection and evaluation. Bucci has put together a computer dictionary (called CRA) to measure RA, which reflects the style rather than the content of the speaker's words. The high-CRA list includes words people use when they describe images and events (such as prepositions) and other words representing spatial relations ("in," "out," "outside"). A low-CRA list includes words that generally represent logical relations and functions, such as quantification. The referential cycle Bucci usually finds "would begin with emotional arousal indicated by high ET [emotional tone], leading to a narrative of an incident, a memory, or a dream, which appears as an RA peak. This would then be followed by concomitant increases in ET and AB [abstract words]. The CRA peak is essential for the cycle. High ET and AB utterances without a CRA peak indicate activation of subsymbolic and verbal symbolic representations, without connections between them; thus the dissociation that is the focus of treatment is allowed to continue unchanged" (114).

In other words, Bucci argues that for healing to occur, speech must integrate concrete images and their related emotions into the concepts that they can produce. A 1994 study by Pennebaker and Francis asked college students to write their thoughts and feelings about coming to college and examined the effects of that writing on the students. The experimental subjects were classified into three subgroups: those showing health improvement, those who remained unchanged, and those who became worse. Bucci attempted to discover the factors that influenced these outcomes. She discovered that the initial writing session produced words high in emotional tone (ET) and CRA and low in the quality of abstraction (AB):

> Subjects in this initial session were describing episodes representing emotion schemas, with both imagery and related emotional components. The second day is characterized by some decline in CRA and ET, and an increase in AB, as the subject begins to reflect on the stories and experiences he or she has reported. On the third day, these improved subjects show concomitant increases in all measures, indicating insights about emotional material expressed in concrete and specific form, not intellectual insight alone . . . This pattern corresponds to the optimal pattern of a therapy session . . . This pattern is not seen in the other groups. The unchanged group shows relatively low CRA and ET, while AB follows essentially the pattern of the health-improvement subjects. The subjects who became worse are clearly differentiated from the other two groups by high AB across all three writing sessions, and by ET consistently below the levels of the other students, as well as by CRA that never rises above the standard score mean. The measures indicate that this group begins by warding off emotional experience to a considerably greater extent than the other two, and consistently remains within the abstract verbal mode, rather than using language first to access emotional experience and then to represent it in symbolic form . . . Emotion was aroused by the task, but they were unable to symbolize this adequately (117).

I have offered this material to demonstrate that researchers are finding ways to describe the process by which writers produce both effective prose and therapeutic benefits. When the writing connects the emotions with the images, healing occurs—and so does good writing. Particularly interesting in Bucci's system is the fact that AB begins to rise after ET and CRA peak, meaning that abstractions and intellectualizations of experiences follow when the emotions produced by the experiences have been expressed. In "Language, Power, and Consciousness: A Writing Experiment at the University of Toronto," an article in *Writing and Healing: Toward an Informed Practice*, Guy Allen argues that his students' academic writing improves once they learn to write effective personal essays. According to Allen, empowerment, confidence, and community can all be built up in the personal essay class and can positively affect writing ability; similarly, Bucci's work indicates that once writers can find the words to express their emotional lives, intellectual growth can follow. What David Bartholomae calls "a corrupt, if extraordinarily tempting genre" (71) can prove liberating to the intellect as well as to the emotions. But this process can work only if writers gain access to the imagistic reality of their memories, which is why writing professionals need to understand this process to help students move beyond labels into image and narrative.

The following story illustrates this problem with labels. One semester break I participated in a symphony performance of Haydn's *Missa Cellensis.* Just as I stepped up to sing my first solo, I looked out into the stone cathedral where we were performing—this huge open space big enough to land a small airplane in. I stared up at the stained glass windows that framed us on three sides, their panes finely cut jewels with the late afternoon light burning through them; I heard the symphony playing the introductory bars perfectly in tune; and I realized that I was not paralyzed by pre-singing panic as had happened occasionally in the past. I understood why Middle English poets loved the image of light behind stained glass. I thought, "Music doesn't get any better than this." Instantly I was horrified. How could I have described one of the peak experiences of my musical life with such a cliché, a media cliché at that, one that conjures up Madison Avenue images of beer and male bonding? But of course I hadn't described my experience; I had labeled it. And this label separated me from my direct experience.

Trauma survivors rely on the mind's capacity to cope. We cannot, however, both process an experience and cope at the same time. Therefore, survivors often have difficulty expressing the very images that can help them the most, but they can be aided in this process by techniques to reconstruct image. In *Trauma and Recovery* Judith Herman quotes Jessica Wolfe describing her approach to the trauma narrative with combat veterans: "We have them reel off in great detail, as though they were watching a movie, and with all the senses included" (177). Once the images are expressed, a full narrative can be constructed, but the story must begin with image. As Herman says, "A narrative that does not include imagery and bodily sensations is barren and incomplete" (177). The reason for this is the survivor has had to numb the emotions to cope. As Susan Brison writes in *Aftermath,* "The inability to feel one's former emotions, even in the aftermath of trauma, leaves the survivor not only numbed, but also without the motivation to carry out the task of constructing an ongoing narrative" (50). Connecting to the image, on the other hand, can reactivate the emotions that are necessary for healing to occur. The same process applies to the personal essay. The personal essayist holds not a mirror up to nature but a motion-picture camera. I suggest to my students that they imagine a film camera in their hands that is recording all that they saw, heard, and touched when the moment they are describing occurred. Such a camera will not record a voice-over or a narrator pasted on later; it will record the scene in the same way that a play conveys dialogue and details of setting: as they unfold. In fact, initially it helps writers see narrative as a series of separate images linked by persistence of vision—the method animators use—not as a series of abstract concepts about the event. Once this process begins, interesting and sometimes unexpected changes can occur.

First, writing about traumatic experiences seems to offer health benefits. James Pennebaker, a leading researcher in the therapeutic effects of expressive writing, has conducted extensive studies showing that writing about trauma improves immune system functioning. He describes them in his book *Opening Up:* "People who wrote about their deepest thoughts and feelings surrounding traumatic experiences evidenced heightened immune function compared with those who wrote about superficial topics . . . The effect . . . tended to persist six weeks after the study. In addition, health center visits for illness dropped for the people who wrote about traumas compared to those who wrote on the trivial topics" (103).

Second, the writing process itself, the actual process of constructing stories, is instrumental in the therapeutic effects of writing, as shown by Pennebaker: "Using our computer analysis as a guide, we realized that the people who benefited the most from writing were constructing stories. On the first day of writing, they would often tell about a traumatic episode that simply described an experience, often out of sequence and disorganized. But day by day, as they continued to write, the episode would take on shape as a coherent story with a clear beginning, middle, and end. Ironically, participants who started the story with a clear, coherent, and well-organized story rarely evidenced any health improvements" (103).

Pennebaker describes his research methods in his essay "Telling Stories: The Health Benefits of Narrative," published in the journal *Literature and Medicine.* Volunteers were divided into two groups, a control group and an experimental group. The control group was asked to write on trivial topics such as daily activities, weekend plans, and descriptions of the lab room the participants were writing in. The experimental group was given the following instructions: "In the next four days, I would like you to write about your very deepest thoughts and feelings about the most traumatic experience of your entire life. In your writing I would like you to really let go and explore your very deepest emotions and thoughts. You might tie your topic to your relationships with others, including parents, lovers, friends, or relatives, to your past, your present, or your future, or to who you have been, who you would like to be, or who you are now. You may write about the same general issues or experiences on all days of writing or on different traumas each day. All of your writing will be completely confidential" (4).

Pennebaker states in his article that 98 percent of the participants said if given the choice, they would participate in the study again (4). The subjects of these essays include rape, family violence, suicide attempts, drug abuse. Pennebaker tracked health center visits and found that "those who had written about their thoughts and feelings drastically reduced their doctor visit rates after the study compared to our control participants" (5). Pennebaker has had similar results with many different populations, from college students to psychiatric prison inmates, leading him to the following conclusion: "The act of converting emotions and images into words changes the way that a person organizes and thinks about the trauma. Further, part of the distress caused by the trauma lies not just in the events but in the person's emotional reactions to them. By integrating thoughts and feelings, then, the person can more easily construct a coherent narrative of the experience. Once formed, the event can be summarized, stored, and forgotten more efficiently" (8).

In his earlier work, *Opening Up,* Pennebaker argued that inhibition causes many of the negative effects of unexpressed trauma. Inhibition is physical. When survivors actively hold back their thoughts and feelings, they have to exert significant effort that the body finds taxing and that has a negative effect on long-term health. When writers are not emotionally connected to the experience, or when they have written incomplete narratives, the writing is less effective both therapeutically and aesthetically.

Writing about trauma removes the experience from the inarticulate parts of the brain and puts it in contact with the more cognitive areas, allowing the impression of control over the trauma, even if that control is only linguistic. Rita Charon comments on the therapeutic quality of narration: "As in psychoanalysis, in all of medical practice the narrating of the patient's story is a therapeutically central act, because to find the words to contain the disorder, and its attendant worries gives shape to and control over the chaos of illness" (1898). Isabel Allende wrote in *Paula,* her book about the death of her daughter, "My life is created as I narrate, and my memory grows stronger with writing" (qtd. in Schacter 93). Invariably, the immediate response to writing about trauma is sadness, even tears, followed by a sense of relief to have the story on paper. While the event does not change, perception of it does. As I mentioned earlier, it is not the trauma but how we handle it that counts—and writing about trauma, constructing our own narrative, seems to provide a sense of control over the event rather than having it continue to control us, as Brison understands: "By constructing and telling a narrative of the trauma endured, and with the help of understanding listeners, the survivor begins not only to integrate the traumatic episode into a life with a before and after, but also to gain control over the occurrence of intrusive memories" (Brison 54). Brison knows firsthand the power of narrative to help survivors "master" the trauma through the telling and attempts to provide some answers for how this is possible: "Whereas traumatic memories . . . feel as though they are passively endured, narratives are the result of certain obvious choices (e.g., how much to tell to whom, in what order, etc.). This is not to say that the narrator is not subject to the constraints of memory or that the story will ring true however it is told. And the telling itself may be out of control, compulsively repeated. But one can control certain aspects of the narrative, and that control, repeatedly exercised, leads to greater control of the memories themselves, making them less intrusive and giving them the kind of meaning that enables them to be integrated into the rest of life" (54).

Pierre Janet, who in the late 19th century had already developed both the theory of dissociation and the theory of the subconscious, argued that the healthy response to stress is to mobilize action. And he viewed active memory itself as an action, the action of telling a story. In other words, telling our stories becomes an act of taking control. The psychologist Dan Adams, who has argued that life stories play a crucial role in cognition and behavior, says, "The unfolding drama of life is revealed more by the telling than by the actual events told. Stories are not merely 'chronicles', like a secretary's minutes of a meeting, written to report exactly what happened and at what time. Stories are less about facts and more about meaning. In the subjective and embellished telling of the past, the past is constructed—history is made" (qtd. in Schacter 93). The point here is that the events themselves are not the most significant contributor to the trauma. First, traumatic memory, like narrative memory is, as Brison states, "articulated, selective even malleable, in spite of the fact that the framing of such memory may not be under the survivor's control." And even more important, "There is a gap between the event (which may be described in countless ways) and the experience of it" (31).

Events are experienced by means of sensory, bodily sensations and impressions, but these are all influenced by the social and cultural context—that is, the environment within which the survivor finds herself and how that environment affects her ability to interpret and integrate the trauma. As Brison argues, "Contexts are just as much in need of elucidation as events" (34). Trauma drastically affects the meaning systems of the survivors. Healing means rebuilding a relationship to the world. If this isn't done, old patterns repeat themselves, and writers tend to offer clichés, long-accepted ways of internalizing the experience, and the details necessary for effective writing are missing. The process by which we help writers to connect with their emotions—by finding the images that lie inside their memories—can move them beyond the clichés and into the uniqueness of their responses to their moments, beyond the concepts about the experience to the experience itself. Only after we integrate our emotions with the memory of our experiences can we begin to question our interpretation of our experiences and the contexts within which they reside. Self-awareness and integration are the byproducts of the process of producing effective writing.

Our culture has a polarized response to trauma: On the one hand we are mesmerized by confessional stories that land people on talk shows; on the other, as a culture we shy away from opening ourselves to the difficult stories of acquaintances and friends because we have not been taught how to respond appropriately. However, simply listening and responding honestly can have a positive effect on those working through trauma. And although the integration process can be difficult, often painful, trauma offers opportunities for growth and positive change as well. We become more empathic to others as we better understand our own life experiences and how they affect us. Richard Tedeschi and his colleagues use the term "posttraumatic growth" to describe the growth and learning that can be created after a crisis. But this is most likely to happen when others support us in this enterprise.

I can offer an example of the integration process prompted by an experience from my own life and teaching. My students in Personal Essay write a paper on their relationship to their physical bodies. They can write about any aspect of their bodies—a time their bodies worked really well, such as the great sports "win," or a time they didn't work all that well, or they could write about an illness or an accident when they first realized they were not immortal, or a time they felt really physically alive. They asked me for an example of what I would choose if I were writing the paper. I thought for a minute and decided that if I were writing this assignment I might write about sliding down the sidewalk on my sled when I was six. A woman pulled into her drive-way without noticing me, and I slid under her car on my sled as her car was moving. The students asked for details: What part of the car did I pass under—between the wheels or behind them? I hadn't thought about this be-fore. In fact, until that moment I rarely thought about the experience. I was silent, then said, "I remember smelling a muffler, so it must have been behind the four wheels." All of a sudden I felt claustrophobic. I re-experienced what it felt like to be flying under that car and realized that the reason I never could hide under beds as other kids could was because of that car. It was the sensory image of the smell of that muffler that did it, and that image was extra-verbal, that is outside verbal recall. I was able to recognize an incipient claustropho-bia because I had integrated my affective response to the accident with my cognitive one.

This technique can be used in many contexts. One young man had had writer's block since the beginning of the semester, and nothing we tried helped. We had completed an exercise—to write about a happy moment and then a sad moment. The sad moment had weight for him, but he avoided writing about it. He finally decided to try and came back with an essay that surprised him. He wrote about the day he, his brother, and a friend inflamed their young male aggressive tendencies by creating an implement of destruc-tion akin to a Star Wars light saber—a stick with an axe on the end. Their peer-driven bravado caused them to kill a ground hog, which so traumatized them that they never again played in the fields together. It was this incident that my student didn't want to write about yet had to write about. Once he did, his writer's block ended, and he became one of the best writers in his class. More important for him, however, was the understanding this experi-ence had created.

It is crucial to remember that no one but the writer can determine what material might be perceived as traumatic. Nor is it essential that the experi-ence be defined as a "trauma." What matters is if the difficult experience pro-duced a stress response, and this—or a complex trauma response—can result from surviving an attack, being in a car accident, or fighting in a war. It also can come from separation from parents, or living with a depressed parent, or being in a household with marital tension. The depth of the response is de-pendent on the intensity of the experience, prior traumas, genetic make-up, and social context. Most people will have some kind of response to a trau-matic event, but that does not mean full-blown post-traumatic stress disor-der, which is a medical condition—evidenced by intrusive thoughts, sleep

disturbances, inability to concentrate, and other well-documented signs—
that needs treatment. Both young men mentioned above evidenced their difficult moments with writer's block, which was dissolved by writing about
their experiences, but neither one suffered from PTSD. However, their responses still interfered with learning. As Lepore and Smyth argue in *The Writing Cure,* "There is abundant evidence that the inhibition of thoughts, feelings,
and behavior requires physiological work, which can result in low-level autonomic arousal. Also it has been noted that such arousal, if persistent over a
period of time, can undermine biological mechanisms of adaptation and increase heath risks"(9).

This is why James Pennebaker's work that demonstrates improved immune system functioning in college students is so significant. In their article
titled "Emotional Expression, Expressive Writing, and Cancer" in *The Writing
Cure,* Stanton and Danoff-Burg demonstrated that cancer patients appeared
to have fewer physical symptoms and medical appointments for cancer-
related symptoms when writing (44). Emotional expression produces positive physical and emotional benefits for cancer patients since writing is a
meaning-constructing event. Daiute and Buteau argue in the same volume:,
"Narrative writing is a site of personal meaning making because it is a symbolic process by which individuals control cultural tools, including language
and values, for social and personal purposes"(58). The same authors also
argue that constructing narrative has benefits for young people: Writing narratives about one's life is an activity involving the presentation "of self in social context, as well as an emotional release. Young people can use this context
to connect program-based social values with their own experience and imag-
inative processes"(58). They define the healing function of writing as "the integration of social-cognitive and emotional life which influences some aspects
of living in a stressful environment that might be under a person's control"
(70). They argue that our educational assumptions too often prevent teachers
from allowing students to write narratives about conflict or trauma, which is
problematic since the research indicates that students can benefit from such
writing.

Of course, educators find this material discomfiting. This is, after all, a
writing class. How can we advocate a process that sounds as much like therapy
as it does composition? In spite of the opinions of scholar/writers such as
Jane Tompkins, who argues that we need a more holistic approach to higher
education to allow into the conversation the emotional issues that affect how
we see the world, most of us in higher education are not prepared for such

directions. However, writing teachers are particularly vulnerable to the eruption of personal experiences into educational contexts, just by the nature of what we do. Our students will write about painful subjects whether we ask them to or not. Some will produce such material even if we tell them that it won't be counted for the grade. The reason they will write about such subjects is because trauma is all too often an intimate part of their lives, and all they need is the real or perceived opportunity to express it.

In 2003 in the United States 12.6 million American families faced hunger (*Ithaca Journal*, November 20, 2004, 3A). More than 10 million children in the United States live at or near the poverty threshold (*Ithaca Journal*, May 23, 2002, 2A). School shootings have become so commonplace that gun checks are routine for many high schools. Urban violence has even arrived in homespun upstate New York in cities such as Syracuse and Rochester. The sixth graders of Enrico Fermi School in one of the poorest neighborhoods in Rochester have lost classmates to stray bullets launched during drug disputes. The students are producing a booklet, organized by the University of Rochester Medical Center and titled *Children's Visions and Voices,* as a response to the violence. Former surgeon general David Satcher wrote in the foreword, "I am always amazed at what we learn when we take the time to listen to children. Without their perspective we cannot see the full scope of community issues that need our attention" (*Ithaca Journal*, March 24, 2004, 4A,). Homicide is the leading cause of death of children in the US. Many children in psychiatric treatment centers are thought to be survivors of abuse and/or neglect. Yet in spite of the fact that in the past decade there were thirteen controlled studies on psychopharmacological treatment of children with Obsessive Compulsive Disorder and thirty-six on the treatment of ADD/hyperactivity, van der Kolk et al., the authors of *Traumatic Stress,* point out that as of 1996 there was only one controlled psychopharmacological study on the treatment of PTSD in children in the entire world literature (568).

The American Academy of Pediatrics has recently recommended that physical punishments are ineffective and dangerous for children. In spite of the fact that scientific research has demonstrated this for a while now, the resulting furor over this issue is evidence that many parents in our culture automatically associate physical punishment with discipline, an attitude that can turn a spanking into abuse. Children too often have no clear advocates, especially since we tend to deny the effects of trauma and violence on children. The *Ithaca Journal* ran a story on September 5, 2001, with the headline, "Children feel pain as much as adults" (3B). The story reported a new policy issued jointly by the American Academy of Pediatrics and the American Pain Society: "Doctors should do more to relieve youngsters' pain from injuries, illnesses, and medical procedures . . . Doctors have not done as much as they should to relieve that discomfort for several reasons, including a misconception that youngsters don't feel pain as adults do, the statement says." I can attest to this "misconception": Until a relatively few years ago baby boys were circumcised without any anesthesia because it was thought they were too young to feel pain. When my daughter was born in one of the best hospitals in upstate New York, my hospital room was two doors down from the room where baby boys were circumcised. Day-old newborns were naked, strapped to a board, and cut with no anesthetic. I can attest to their screams that went on for hours. When I protested, I was told this was standard protocol because these babies are crying from anger, not pain because they can't feel pain yet. Any mother can tell you otherwise. Our culture tends to minimize the effects of pain and trauma, especially on children.

Jeffrey Masson, Judith Herman, and Bessel van der Kolk have suggested that the psychiatric profession seems to be playing out an instance of repetition compulsion in denying the significance of trauma to children's lives today since the same kind of denial occurred at the beginning of the twentieth century. When medical doctors first began their studies of what they then termed hysteria, a gender-based term that in itself signified bias, it was seen by the profession as the primary cause of psychological difficulties. Freud was familiar with the work of Pierre Janet, who first developed the hallmark of PTSD—his theory of dissociation—as well as the theory of the unconscious. In 1885 Freud studied with him and Charcot at the Saltpetriere in France, a hospital where theories of dissociation were formulated and studied. In 1896, with the publication of the *Aetiology of Hysteria,* Freud thought he had discovered the source of the psychological Nile: that all "hysteria" was caused by sexual trauma of some kind. Within just a few years, this over-generalized analysis was abandoned, along with any relationship between trauma and emotional and physical symptomology, although Freud maintained an ambivalent relationship with trauma for the rest of his career. It was replaced by Freud's reliance on repressed wishes and fantasies. In other words, the victim became the perpetrator.

Freud abandoned his seduction theory most probably because he and his colleagues could not believe abuse could be happening in upper middle-class culture. Indeed, as Jeffrey Berman in *Empathic Teaching* argues, it must have been a stretch for Freud and his colleagues to believe that "so many of them [female patients] who came from respectable Viennese families could have been telling the truth" (116), but some historians of psychoanalysis also argue that Freud's seduction theory may have begun to negatively affect his career. In any event, since Freud soon became more famous than Charcot and Janet, the study of trauma was relegated to the dustbin of medicine. It took two world wars, two major instances of genocide attached to those world wars and countless others, the dropping of two nuclear warheads, a Vietnam "conflict" that produced thousands of traumatized soldiers, multiple massacres around the world, and soaring documented cases of sexual and physical abuse and neglect before our culture could begin to see what the oft-quoted comic strip character Pogo already knew: "We have met the enemy and he is us."

Certainly Freud's "talking cure" remains a cornerstone of therapy, but when Freud replaced his sexual seduction theory with his theory of repressed oedipal wishes, the move proved detrimental to the treatment of trauma. His theories of childhood fantasy eclipsed the importance of direct experience, leading to the "blame the victim" mentality we are still fighting today. (For a discussion of Freud's repudiation of his seduction theory and development of his theories of fantasy, see Jeffrey Masson's *The Assault on Truth*.)

A study of the famous "Dora" case demonstrates Freud's reliance on a patriarchal relationship between therapist and patient, one that challenges the veracity of the patient. Briefly, Dora (a pseudonym) was a young woman of eighteen brought to Freud by her father for analysis. Her symptoms included *petite hysterie,* a suicide attempt, and physical symptoms, including stomach problems, cough, and other signs of malaise. She stopped therapy abruptly after three months. Freud wrote his recollections of the case and published them in 1905 with the title "Fragment of an Analysis of a Case of Hysteria." In Lakoff and Coyne's ironically titled book *Father Knows Best* they argue that this case outlines a treatment methodology which cannot help but create a power differential between patient and therapist that can become abusive.

Dora lived with her parents and brother. Freud and Dora's father were well acquainted. According to Freud, the father was dominating and the mother suffered from "housewife's psychosis." (She spent her time on household activities and therefore was not involved intimately in her children's lives.) The father was being treated for syphilis and apparently the mother, too, who had contracted it from the father. Dora believed that she had also contracted the disease, which she blamed for her various symptoms. The father was nursed by a neighbor, the wife of Herr K, while the mother stayed out of the sickroom. Dora took care of Frau and Herr K's children. It became

obvious to her that the Ks were having marital problems, and that after the
father's recovery Frau K and he were having an affair. Dora complained to her
mother, who said that Frau K had saved the father from suicide, thereby justi-
fying the affair. Herr K began to press himself on Dora. He lured fourteen-
year-old Dora to his office by telling her his wife would be there, but in reality
he asked his wife to stay away. When Dora arrived to a darkened office, shades
drawn, Herr K, reports Freud, "came back and suddenly clasped the girl to
him and pressed a kiss upon her lips" (qtd in Lakoff and Coyne 18). Throughout her fifteenth year, Herr K sent Dora flowers almost daily. Then at sixteen,
while she was staying at the Ks house by a lake, Herr K "had the audacity to
make a proposal." He told Dora, "You know I get nothing out of my wife."
Dora "slapped him and ran away" (18). Her "hysterical symptoms" grew.

Here we have a case where a young girl of fourteen is being used as a decoy
to prevent the dysfunctional family structure from breaking apart. Dora was
angry with her father for the affair and for leaving her to the wiles of Herr K.
According to Lakoff and Coyne, "Freud accepted as his therapeutic task to
'bring Dora to reason,' to persuade her that her father and the Ks were not
responsible for her problems. The father referred to Dora's ideas as 'phanta-
sies,' and while Freud accepted them as *historical* truths he took pains to indicate to Dora (and the reader) his contempt for her historical, as opposed to
genetic (intrapsychic) reality. What Dora claimed (he says) may well have
happened, but her responses to it were neurotic" (74).

Any attempt on the part of the patient to define her problems as having
been a product of a historical reality are denied by Freud in favor of placing
the responsibility on Dora herself for her inability to deal appropriately and
effectively with her own reactions—that is, her failure to bring them into
alignment with the expectations of her environment. In other words, we have
blamed the victim. This stance toward Dora was present even as recently as
1974 with Kurt Lewin's comments published in *Psychoanalytic Review:* "One
could well imagine such a girl [as Dora] leading men on, frustrating them,
and finally destroying them altogether . . . Hell hath no fury like a woman
scorned" (qtd. in Lakoff and Coyne 7). This kind of attitude helps explain a
study of clients treated at the Menninger Clinic which found that, as Lakoff
and Coyne explain, "patients receiving simple supportive treatment fared as
well as those receiving psychoanalysis" (135).

While Freud's emphasis on "the talking cure" underlies current therapeutic methods, many clinicians no longer believe his specific methods are efficacious for dealing with trauma. Indeed, some see them as retraumatization of

the client; particularly problematic can be the power imbalance set up by conventional Freudian psychotherapy. One of van der Kolk's studies demonstrated that the capacity to find comfort from the presence of another person was more powerful than the trauma history itself as a predictor of being free from intrusive images (198). Therefore, a trusting relationship between therapist and client is crucial to recovery. Currently, the goal is integration of the unclaimed parts of experience into the entire structure of the self and into the larger community, and one of the important steps in this process is creating a narrative that reflects the emotional reality of the experience. As Judith Herman in *Trauma and Recovery* demonstrates, the three primary goals for healing from trauma are establishing a safe environment, integrating affective and cognitive realities, and establishing a community to re-join that can accept the survivor's integrated psyche. Chris R. Brewin in *Post-Traumatic Stress Disorder: Malady or Myth* argues that what happens after a trauma is as important as the original trauma in determining if a person will develop post-traumatic stress disorder. Two of the most significant factors that affect how someone will respond to a trauma are ongoing life stress and social support. Silence and isolation are antithetical to recovery, and writing has been demonstrated to break that silence and help create a narrative that can be repeated to others. As Brewin argues, "During the narrative the attention that is paid to detailed, emotion-laden images (flashbacks) results in the information they contain being re-encoded into the VAM system. Here, all those details are classified for the first time as belonging to the past, so that they are less likely to trigger further flashbacks when trauma reminders are encountered" (219). This is why the survivor then has the impression of control over that which we cannot control—the past. Van der Kolk points out that as early as Janet trauma professionals thought that the "power of traumatic images cannot be tempered until they have been translated into a personal narrative" (285).

Recent research has shown that certain illnesses as well as traumas respond positively to writing, particularly asthma and rheumatoid arthritis. In a randomized, controlled study published in 1999 in the *Journal of the American Medical Association* and summarized in *Arthritis Self-Management,* the authors divided 112 patients with either asthma or RA into two groups: Those in the experimental group wrote about an emotionally stressful experience for twenty minutes on three separate days while those in the control group wrote on emotionally neutral topics. At the end of the four-month study, the experimental group showed a 28 percent improvement in symptoms as demonstrated by levels of inflammation and pain. Other research indicates that avoidance and thought suppression is related to slower recovery from PTSD (Brewin 59), and excessive emotional suppression and control has been implicated in cancer (Lepore and Smyth 101.) After September 11, James Pennebaker said that expressing emotions is a key to preventing a longer-term trauma response. The journalist Jamie Talan asked Pennebaker what we can do to deal more appropriately with our trauma responses. As Talan wrote:

> [Pennebaker] has spent years studying trauma—including the 1995 Oklahoma City bombing of the Murrah federal building—and found that people cope remarkably well in the first few weeks after a trauma. The reason: Everyone is talking about it. But then, around the first month, something happens and people stop talking. The mind is shutting down, people are self-protective . . . He remembers that weeks after the 1989 San Francisco earthquake, T-shirts popped up saying, "Thank you for not sharing your earthquake experience." "It's not that people have stopped thinking about it, they just can't take in any more information," Pennebaker said. And this is precisely the time when people are most at risk for a stress reaction, including physical illness. His writing research showed that people who wrote about their personal traumatic experience for fifteen minutes a day for four days had a more profound change in physical and mental health than those who wrote about superficial events in their lives. "Putting traumatic experiences into words has effects on blood pressure, immune function, progression of disease, sleep and depression," Pennebaker said. "Writing allows us to organize the trauma and move past it." (Talan 8A)

The key to this process is control, control of the time and the place this process occurs, and most important, *if* it occurs. Indeed, if a student reveals to me a very recent trauma, I do not suggest that she write about it and instead recommend that she go immediately to the counseling center, as should be done for any case of deep trauma that has never been heard by anyone other than the survivor. Teachers should *never* ask students to write about specific topics. Writers need complete control over this process every step of the way. Nor should writing about difficult experiences be an expectation of the class—implicit or explicit. Life is full of experience. Whichever ones resonate the most for the student will probably inspire the most, but writers may not wish to approach their deepest experiences—happy or sad—until they are ready, and we need to ensure that their choices belong to them. Having said this, however, in my experience, writers will go to those moments that are stuck in their minds, and we need to know what we will do when this happens. For this reason, writing teachers perhaps more often than other educators find themselves in the position of having to decide how to deal with this material when it arises, because it will. In the next chapter we will study particular student texts and discuss appropriate protocols.

Narrative is the chain that links our moments together, but image is what we see in the dark of night, what we wake up with from dreams, what we remember when we recall those we love. It is image that burns itself into our minds whether we want it to or not, and image that can free us from a past if we can look straight at the pictures that live behind our eyes and communicate them to others. Language is a key element in this process of integration since it is a large component of what we need to exert control over our lives. With language we can express our past experiences and the emotions those experiences generate. With it we can build community. For better or for worse, the writing classroom has emerged for some teachers and students as a natural environment for this work. In the telling of their stories to themselves and ultimately, if they choose, to each other, these writers re-create themselves and their worlds. As Maya Angelou wrote in *On the Pulse of Morning,* "History, despite its wrenching pain, cannot be unlived, but, if faced with courage, need not be lived again."

CHAPTER 2

The Phoenix in the Box

Terrorists, Trauma, and the Transformation of Writing

We don't just want our writing to come out right, we want to come out right.

JAMES MOFFETT

M OST WRITING TEACHERS remember when the field of writing instruction was in the boiler rooms of education. Writing instruction was done by literary critics or by graduate students who wanted to become literary critics. Then increased student need and the development of our own intellectual currency via theoretical as well as practical approaches to the study of writing helped writing instruction become respectable. But not all areas of writing were admitted into the academy's inner sanctum. And indeed the theory wars continue today. Those of us who suspected that writing could be a redemptive act spoke in whispers and certainly didn't include such conversations in our tenure files. Recent conferences, however, (for example, the Association for Expanded Perspectives on Learning conference in June 2002 on writing and healing) and a flurry of books about writing and healing is evidence that those of us whose professional lives include investigations into the therapeutic effects of writing are finally emerging as a force within the academy.

And it's a good thing, because we cannot assume that the children and young people that we see looking back at us in our classrooms have pristine pasts unhampered by traumatic moments that can affect education. Trauma and its attending effects—the results of violence, sexual abuse, and neglect—are far more common than any other psychiatric condition in America today.

September 11, 2001, demonstrated to Americans the vulnerability we all face in a violent world. The event began a national conversation about trauma and healing that could not be accomplished by two world wars, institutionalized racism, the Vietnam "conflict," the bombing of the federal building in Oklahoma City, and countless tragic school shootings that hit us where we are the most vulnerable—our children. Indeed, this tragedy has begun to democratize trauma. And the Iraq War, with its indefinite, perhaps porous, boundaries and thousands of dead and dismembered soldiers and civilians, is a daily reminder of the consequences of violence—especially since the military must deal with PTSD in many of its soldiers and we all fear the possibility of civil war. Fewer of us now respond as did Bartleby the Scrivener: "I prefer not to."

Since September 11 the news media have demonstrated an interest in what promotes healing after trauma and the power of the traumatic image. Of course, the reasons for this preoccupation are clear: According to a special PBS radio broadcast on March 6, 2002 titled "State of Mind," 9 million people said they felt less able to deal with life after 9/11. Former Surgeon General David Satcher offered that 25 percent of our population felt very stressed. However, these concerns are only extensions of what many children face every day. Environmental conditions, social and family stress, and urban violence pose serious hazards to many children today. According to Daiute and Buteau in their article in *The Writing Cure,* one-third of the injury deaths of young people in the United States are caused by violence (53). What does the word "healing" mean in this context? As Lucille Clifton said to a room of educators and clinicians at an Association of Poetry Therapy Conference in 1996 about the children they work with, "Every day some of those children are bearing something you could not bear . . . Every day something has tried to kill [them] and has failed."

I teach in Ithaca, New York, just three and a half hours from New York City. Many of my students live in New York, or their parents work in the city. In the wake of September 11, we were overwhelmed with stories of those who were lost. I began collecting newspaper clippings that dealt with the traumatic effects of 9/11. As the months wore on, the pile grew: stories of those who survived and the writing they did immediately afterward, stories about the rise in the incidence of nightmares across the country, stories about grief in the workplace, grief among children, grief among family members, stories about PTSD and what to do about it.

Some articles talked about the value of poetry: USA Today.com posted poetry by its readers at www.life.usatoday.com. Poets were in high demand, both for their poetry and for their words about the efficacy of poetry to heal during difficult times. Former U.S. poet laureate Robert Pinsky was quoted in the *Ithaca Journal* on September 26, 2001, saying, "TV's tremendous immediacy and ubiquity fill one set of needs; poetry's intimacy and universality fill others" (4B.) On October 1, 2001, the poet Adrienne Rich spoke at Ithaca College on the value of poetry: "Art takes us into the interior where we connect with other human beings." In an answer to a question regarding the nature and value of cathartic art, she responded, "How can we connect with the outside if we cannot connect with the inside?"

These questions about and hopes for the capacity of the arts to heal arose out of painful need. Many of us watched on TV as that second hijacked plane crashed into the second tower, creating a conflagration that transformed the entire World Trade Center complex into a pile of rubble, taking close to 3,000 lives with it. Not only do we have the fact of the atrocity to absorb but we also have the image of that plane playing over and over again in our minds. As the artist and author Art Spiegelman said, "The whole thing was so visual that it hit that part of your vortex in ways it could pull something out of you. But on the other hand, the reverberations are so deep, people just go in and out of traumatic shock" (*Ithaca Journal*, September 25, 2001, 4B). This does not mean that something is wrong with us. Indeed, it may mean that something is right with us, that we are responding in predictable ways to an unpredictable situation. The events of 9/11 provide a communal example to illustrate both the power of the traumatic image to affect us months after the event and the myriad ways individuals react to that image.

As previously discussed, trauma is most commonly defined as a normal response to an abnormal situation; however, the frequency of rape and other violent crimes has forced us to modify that definition. We must admit that trauma is all too common in contemporary America, but this does not lessen its impact, nor does it blunt the power of the traumatic images that are a hallmark of trauma. Those images are permanently encoded as emotions and images together in the brain and cannot be retrieved independently of each other. While these images are noncognitive, and therefore not easily accessible, they have deep emotional presence. They pop up sometimes unbidden when we smell, hear, see, or touch something that takes us back to the time the traumatic event occurred. It is these images that must be accessed if a story of the trauma is to be told, but these images are hard to verbalize because they are encoded into a part of the brain that combines image and emotion, as described in the previous chapter. This process is even chemical. Experiments show that when high levels of adrenaline and other stress hormones are circulating through the bloodstream, memory traces are deeply imprinted into the brain (Cahill and McGaugh). We will remember the image of that plane crashing into the World Trade Center for the rest of our lives because it is burned into our midbrains. However, the image does not have to retain its original horrific quality. As painful as it is, eventually the immediate terror can fade, leaving behind a sadness that becomes integrated into the rest of life. This chapter investigates how this process happens and how writers and teachers can help it along.

When a trauma first occurs, we are speechless; we have no words. The shock is so great, we simply stare and cannot take in the reality of what has just occurred. The closer we are to the trauma, the more intense the shock. Poet laureate Billy Collins, when asked on September 11 for his response, said, "Nothing, I can say nothing." Emily Dickinson knew this nothingness:

> Pain - has an Element of Blank -
> It cannot recollect
> When it begun - Or if there were
> A time when it was not - (339–40)

We cannot think. Our minds and emotions are anesthetized. Then, with the passing of each hour, our bodies remind us that we need feeding; our minds begin to ask questions and reach out to other minds; our hearts begin to bleed; and the tears come. At that time we turn to community—to family, friends, and fellow citizens—for support, love, assistance. After September 11 we all saw and perhaps participated in the outpouring of help from firefighters, police, EMTs, doctors, blood donors, and those giving time, money, warm socks, and love and support to those aiding the recovery process. When we act, we defeat despair. When we lean on each other, we are all stronger. Action is the first defense against trauma.

As time passes after trauma, we begin to share our thoughts and feelings with each other as well as our actions. For centuries poetry, that intensely focused form, has in its beauty of language helped give our grief an order, as Emily Dickinson's poem "After great pain" shows:

> After great pain, a formal feeling comes -
> ....
> This is the Hour of Lead -
> Remembered, if outlived,
> As Freezing persons recollect the Snow -
> First - Chill - Then Stupor - then the letting go - (170)

Ben Jonson's poem written after the death of his young son is just as sharp with grief today as it was when it was written in 1616 and has provided the comfort of the commonality of loss for many: "Here doth lie / Ben Jonson, his best piece of poetry" (619).

Yet in spite of loss, most of us do learn to love and hope again. We do heal, perhaps with scars, but we do heal. What helps us to move past the images that are burned into our brains, the grief that makes love such a danger, the fears that made two of my students not want to sleep in their rooms on the tenth floor of the West Tower residence hall the day after the September 11 attack?

Those of us who have been doing this work know firsthand that writing can be redemptive, but now the general population is beginning to catch on as well. Hundreds of people who recorded what they saw and experienced on September 11 shared their fears and grief with thousands, maybe millions of other people by virtue of the Internet. The September 18, 2001, issue of the *Wall Street Journal* published the stories of two survivors of the September 11 tragedy: One 2,500-word essay was written by an investment banker for the May Davis Group which was on the 87th floor of the WTC's Tower 1: "My name is Adam Mayblum. I am alive today. I am committing this to paper so I never forget. SO WE NEVER FORGET" (B6). He wrote his essay the day after the attack and posted it on the Internet; within a few hours Mr. Mayblum had replies from as far away as Brisbane and the *Times* of India, which reprinted his essay. Another writer, Neil DeGrasse Tyson, an astrophysicist at Princeton, witnessed much of the destruction from the streets of his Manhattan neighborhood. He, too, posted his written responses on the Internet and was receiving calls from the *New Yorker* and ABC news: "All I could understand was that the written word somehow humanized what was going on. It's easier to do if emotions are 90% of what are coursing through your mind. I was simultaneously emotionally charged and wounded" (B6). Tyson has captured exactly a description of the effects of trauma: We are simultaneously emotionally charged and wounded, and writing begins the process of integrating those internal, preverbal wounds with the verbal parts of the brain, the cortex, so we can have access to them to get them outside of us and out to the world. By talking and writing we begin to create a community with others. Through our writing, we begin to feel less isolated by the trauma, and therefore less helpless, and so we begin, ever so slowly, to heal. We realize that writing is a verb as well as a noun. We can learn to integrate our traumas into the rest of our existence and go on, as these writers are attempting to do, by sharing their stories with the world. Adrienne Rich wrote these prophetic words in 1993: "When the landscape buckles and jerks around, when a dust column of debris rises from the collapse of a block of buildings on bodies that could have been your own, when the staves of history fall awry and the barrel of time bursts apart, some turn to prayer, some to poetry: words in the memory, a stained book carried close to the body, the notebook scribbled by hand—a center of gravity" (115–16).

Therapeutic Writing in the Academy

In "The Solace of Literature," published on October 5, 2001, in the *Chronicle of Higher Education,* Carolyn Foster Segal discussed how she handled teaching an upper-level American literature class the day after 9/11. She asked a student, "Could reading bring solace now?" The student responded, "Maybe not reading, but perhaps writing could bring solace. And then later others will be able to read it and look back" (B8).

September 11 showed us that trauma is a part of our immediate world. Our public conversations began to reference the effects of trauma far more often than ever before. Jeffrey Berman in *Empathic Teaching* offers sobering statistics demonstrating that counseling centers at many colleges are showing dramatic increases in the numbers of students who use their services. Berman quotes Robert Gallagher, past president of the International Association of Counseling Services, who conducts an online annual survey of counseling directors: "In 1988 [Gallagher] began asking colleagues in the National Survey of Counseling Center Directors if they noticed the same increases on their campuses. '56% of the respondents said yes. I have asked this question in succeeding years and each year the percentage of directors reporting this trend has gone up until the last few years where it has leveled off at about 58%'" (294). Clearly, we all need to be more prepared for the students that face us in our classrooms today. But what do we do when our students choose to write trauma narratives and show them to us?

The academy has historically rejected such subjects, so we have little experience in dealing with such material and even less in the way of safe and effective protocols. We do not teach teachers how to encounter student references to personal trauma, and therefore we are understandably at a loss. Lucia Perillo in her article in the *Chronicle of Higher Education* lets us know from the title of her essay, "When the Classroom Becomes a Confessional," that for her personal trauma is not an appropriate subject for the college classroom. Perillo described a classroom situation prompted by a poem written by an older female student about sexual abuse. The class was speechless and awaited the teacher's response. The teacher treated the poem as she would any other work:

> I launched my standard patter about structure and shape and specific-ity of image. A minute into my comments, however, I realized that a black cloud had descended on the class. A young female student cut me off and stood up to deliver an impassioned speech about the cour-age the writer had demonstrated and how she ought to be applauded for sharing her experience.
>
> After she sat down, the class looked my way accusingly, no doubt wondering why I wasn't the one to say these things. I tried blustering a bit about the difference between poetry's therapeutic and aesthetic uses, but before I could even make the terms of that distinction clear, I realized that no one was listening. Not to applaud the act of confes-sion flew in the face of everything my students had learned from pop-ular culture. Trailing off into inaudibility, I had the feeling that we had all somehow astral-traveled to Oprah Winfrey's studio. And I was the bad guest, the expert who'd been brought in for the audience mem-bers to attack. (A56)

This is an unfortunate moment for everyone in this class: The teacher felt trapped into either turning her classroom into a therapy session or becoming "heartless," as she put it; the writer's self-exposure risked negative judgments not only of her poem but also of her; and the class was derailed because no one was prepared for the virtually inevitable: the moment when art is used to express and perhaps transcend pain.

This chapter outlines a pedagogy that enables writers to delve into their difficult moments if they choose and demonstrates how teachers can partner with their students in this process. The very first step that a teacher must take is to discuss with students the possibility that difficult material may be the subject of a student's work and what to do if that happens. This is not to mandate or privilege the writing of such material; students must freely choose their topics, and that means they must not feel pressured either to write about or to avoid painful subjects. Students may share this work in a workshop, read it aloud if they choose, or keep their silence and submit only to the teacher, but whatever the choice, available options must be discussed so appropriate protocols are in place, and no one is surprised by what may occur. Perillo and her class were totally unprepared for this student's poem to be read, which compounded the problem.

Another difficulty is the fact that the teacher felt compelled to talk about the aesthetics of the piece when the students were looking for validation for the writer's bravery. I have made it a practice in commenting on a piece that describes a difficult experience first to validate the writer before going on to a critique. This is not to turn the writing classroom—or a given essay—into an occasion for therapy but is simply a moment to recognize each other's humanity. If we cannot model that, we will not be effective teachers. Jeffrey Berman wrote, "More important than my technical comments on student essays are the affirming, validating ones. Effective teaching is affective learning: Intellectual and emotional development are complementary" (199). Once I have modeled this approach, students generally follow my lead. As Jeffrey Berman states, "If the teacher responds sensitively and appropriately, so will the class" (57).

Only after that do I begin commenting on the essay itself. But this can be difficult as well. What do we do when students write first drafts of narratives that demonstrate a predictable grasp of clichés and confusions, such that we are not at all sure what the essay is even about? How can we help writers, including ourselves, to avoid writing what I call the story of the story—what we want to believe happened, or what others want us to believe happened—and learn to unearth the emotional, imagistic truth of our experiences?

What follows is part of the first draft of an essay turned in to me in a Personal Essay class by one of my strongest writers, a young woman with excellent writing skills and a great deal of intuitive understanding of writing. The topic of the essay was the following: "Write about a person or a place that had a helpful or a harmful effect on you."

> The house is brown stucco. A family with a very young daughter and a large black lab lives on the first floor. The husband is a co-owner of a

nightclub with his younger brother. Their entrance is at the front of the house, with a huge porch. To the left of the porch is a small concrete pathway, wide enough for one person. It's bordered by a chain link fence on one side and the house on the other. Inside the fence is a beautiful garden and an idyllic house with vines enveloping the windows. Every time I have ever looked at that house, I have wondered which room belonged to a boy named Nick. He lives there with at least his mother; I met Nick in summer camp, when he put a dollop of red oil paint on his nose and I took his photograph. Although it's not good to have 'favorites' as a counselor, I did. He was one of them. I have never seen him go in or out of the house, but I know he lives there because Matt told me.

Matt lived on the top floor of the big brown stucco house. To reach his old apartment at the end of the narrow pathway, you swing a right and go up the rickety steps of the back porch. Then, you jimmy open the screen door and the sagging wooden one and begin tromping up three flights of gloriously worn steps, gray wood, a little bowed in the middle from years of tromping. The staircase has white walls and white banisters with gray-blue accents. As you ascent the stairs, on each level of steps is a square window.

The window on the first level has a yellow circle sticker on it that says, "IN CASE OF FIRE: THIS ROOM CONTAINS A CHILD." The window on the second level is broken, with a small sickly yellow plant on its ledge. The window on the last set of stairs is bare. The odd thing about this apartment is that at the top of these stairs is a landing. And the apartment door, to the left. And next to the apartment door is a window, inside the building, from Matt's apartment to the stairwell. We never really understood that window, and it was usually half-covered by stacks of cookbooks or cases of beer.

The landing at the top of the stairs threaded into a hallway, past the indoor window at a right angle, ending at a door twenty feet away. This was the second third-floor apartment inhabited by a writer named Emily whom I never met, but who complained about loud sex next door and hated it when Matt smoked in the hallway and had permanent writer's block; however, in the end she gave Matt a couch which he still has, and she recommended an excellent list of books to him. For some reason, Matt's apartment was detached from his bathroom; Emily's was not; hence, Matt ran the constant risk of being discovered in a questionable state of dress, and the uncomfortable dash to the bathroom or from the bathroom after a late-night shower was a regular occurrence for him and me. His bathtub was an ancient porcelain giant on four stubby legs that didn't drain well, with a blue shower curtain he held shut with clothes pins. He had an entire shelf of Ivory soap within reaching distance of the tub, because it was cheaper than shampoo and more versatile. There was a small rectangular mirror with a bright green frame above the sink, which we both looked at sometimes when we brushed our teeth. The ceiling was growing a small garden of mildew, but when I suggested that he buy a mildew-remover, Matt spent some of his last money on a product that took the ancient paint off the ceiling as well as the mold. The floor of the bathroom was linoleum the color of eggshells.

I will skip over the next few paragraphs because they are more of the same: descriptions of the rest of the bathroom where the cat's litter box is located, etc. We pick up the essay on page 3:

Although the apartment was small, it was home to a wild cat named Tenacity. I was there the day Matt brought her home from the SPCA as a kitten. She would live there almost two years before running away one day to explore life at large in the city. Matt still hasn't gotten a cat to replace her, and that was two years ago. Matt loved his cat, even though at first it was strange love because he was grooming her to be wild. He delighted in driving her to frenzy over the smallest things. Slowly, she developed her own psychosis without Matt's strange games. He loved her terribly.

Matt moved into the apartment shortly after he broke up with a serious flautist girlfriend he had lived with for almost a year. He moved out of the apartment when he fell in love with Sarah and they moved in together. I was heartbroken when I discovered that he was leaving. I couldn't explain the feeling—I was living in Boston, and he was overjoyed to be living with Sarah. The apartment was certainly too small for two people to coexist comfortably for any sustained amount of time. And yet, I questioned. Maybe it was the coming home from a Tequila party at four a.m. memory of the apartment; the memory of

Monte wanting to sketch me there; the memory of sleeping more soundly in that bedroom than I did in my own; it was *something* that I knew I would miss.

As I drive by the building today, I cannot help but feel the sudden urge to pull over my car, and run down the alley, up the porch steps, through two doors, up the three flights of stairs. But Matt never locked his door. And what if the new inhabitants of the place didn't either? What could I do at the doorway to this place I so often sought, but open it slowly at first, and cross into the bedroom to sit and ponder when Matt was coming home?

When I read this paper, the second assignment in the class, I was aware of the wealth of descriptive detail included: the Ivory soap, the mildew, the steps bowed in the middle. Yet it was also clear that Lauren had not yet grasped her topic. The essay was organized in a kind of descriptive chronology: What would we see if we walked down the front path, up the porch, into the house, and up the stairs to Matt's room? However, the essay has no core, no awareness of *why* we are reading all of these descriptive details. While it is clear that Matt's apartment is important to Lauren, we don't know why. Is it their relationship, it is the place itself, or is it something beyond this person or this place that gives it its power?

Here is one of the hallmarks of responses to repeated stress or trauma: They surface when we least expect it. They worm their way into our lives such that we do not know we are reacting to them. The one key is the passion, the energy that our emotions can bring to our writing. This setting and the person she associated with it were important to Lauren, and that was clear from the loving descriptions. An artist once suggested to me the following advice regarding creativity: "Follow the energy." Where does Lauren's energy most show itself in this piece? For me, it was in the next-to-the-last paragraph: "the memory of sleeping more soundly in that bedroom than I did in my own." So when Lauren and I met for our conference after class, I told her that while I loved the description, I wasn't sure why it was there. And then I asked her why she slept in Matt's bedroom more soundly than she did her own.

Lauren, a light speed quick study, immediately said, "Oh, I know what's missing. Home is ridiculous." And she began to speak of exactly why she slept more soundly at Matt's than she did at home. The next week she turned in the following rewrite:

It's four a.m. and quiet. "This is my favorite time to be on the road," he says, as we weave our way down East Street and hang a right at the stoplight. He takes a last drag on his American Spirit cigarette and flicks the butt out his barely open window. Outside, it's gray and still, a little snow dusting the ground. I nestle into the side of the car and let the sound of the tires crushing road salt lull my eyes closed until we come to a stop. I shimmy out the door into a snow bank breaking the thick crust with my Doc Martins in a mad jog for the back door.

In the daylight, this house is brown stucco. A family with a very young daughter and a large black lab live on the first floor. Their entrance is at the front of the house on the sprawling porch. To the left of the house is a concrete pathway wide enough for one person. It's bordered by a chain link fence on the other side that looks in to a beautiful garden and an idyllic house with vines enveloping the windows . . .

Matt and I scamper down the small pathway on the side of the house and ice nearly trips me, but Matt sees it in time, and he grabs my hand with his sinewy one, his graceful pianist fingers digging into my palm, and I do not fall. Matt is a concert pianist-rock star who can play exquisite Debussy but would rather play tortured five-chord songs of his own composition. He pays his bills by teaching, but every month he swears he's leaving soon to go to New York. He cannot afford shampoo, but his dream of 'the band' in the city is what keeps him locked in a stuffy room five days a week, listening to 78 painful renditions of chopsticks. He also delivers pizza, but only on the weekends, and only when he is tight for money. . . .

I fling open the door to his apartment, and take a running leap onto his bed, a clean two rooms straight ahead. On this early winter morning, everything is so dim, and the house is cool, but I know the color of his sheets without looking, because Matt owns several identical sets, enjoying the stability of this constant. For the first time, I realize how sweaty I am from our night of dancing, and I touch my stringy hair. Matt puts his hand on my head and says, 'Baby, look at the ice on the window,' and I do. It's stretched out into hundreds of lacy curls, and the closer I get to it, the more intricate it becomes. Matt has affectionately called me 'Baby,' ever since our second date, when dropping me off three houses down the street so my parents wouldn't see his car, he asked me if that was okay. He doesn't call other women that, just me, when we're alone. 'I feel sticky,' he says, 'I'm headed to the shower.'

For some reason Matt's apartment is detached from his bathroom; Emily's is not; hence, Matt runs the constant risk of being discovered in a questionable state of dress, and the uncomfortable dash to and from the bathroom after a late night shower has become a regular occurrence for him and me. His bathtub is an ancient porcelain boat on four stubby legs that doesn't drain, with a blue plastic shower curtain held shut by five wooden clothespins. He has an entire shelf stacked full of Ivory soap within reaching distance of the tub, because it is cheaper than shampoo and more versatile. There is a small green rectangular mirror above the sink, which we both look at sometimes when we brush our teeth. The ceiling is growing a small colony of molds, but when I suggested that he buy a mildew-remover, Matt spent some of his last money on a product that took the ancient paint off the ceiling as well. The floor of the bathroom is linoleum the color of eggshells. . . .

The apartment . . . goes straight back in a style sometimes called a 'railway' apartment: kitchen, sitting room, bedroom, large closet/cramped storage room where Matt kept Tenacity's litter box. Wild Tenacity was the last piece Matt needed to complete his home. I was there the day Matt brought the kitten home from the SPCA. She lived there almost two years before running away one day to explore life at large in the city. Matt has yet to replace her, and that was a year ago. He loved her even though at first it was a strange juxtaposition of wild Matt and a defenseless kitten. He delighted in driving her to frenzy over the smallest things, but as time wore on, she developed her own psychosis to complement his.

When Matt returns, golden hair dripping, I am ready for a shower myself; I come back to see that he is already a lump in bed, lights off, gently snoring. I creep across the floor, dripping footprints, and see Tenacity at the window, nose to the glass because it's snowing out. It was in this room that I spent many evenings counting the large red second hand on his bedside clock until ten minutes before we had to race up the hill to beat my curfew. It was to this room I fled after the screaming at home began to penetrate even the darkness of my closet. I sought this room when my mother's wild tears in the garage grew to be too much and when my father's prolonged absences from our dinner table killed my mother's ability to cook at all. I slept more soundly in that bedroom than I did in my own.

Matt and I spent two years dancing to the *Buena Vista Social Club* sound track. During that time, we had one fight. It was in his car. It lasted no longer than ten minutes, after which he cried the rest of the way home. Two days later, I brought him a post card of a surreal view and left it on his bed. He still has it, hanging in the living room of his new apartment. I began to date Tyler, a bass player with a fantastic overhand pitch. Shortly after that in the car one night, at the stoplight in front of Maxi's, Matt whispered, 'I love you,' for the first time. 'I'm sorry,' I said, realizing, as I went to bed later that evening, how much I had wanted to hear him say those words, and how differently I felt about them when he said them.

Matt had moved into his apartment following a messy breakup with a serious flautist girlfriend he had lived with for almost a year. He left this apartment when he fell in love with Sarah and they moved in together. I was living in Boston and did not know of his departure until several weeks after it was final. The old apartment remained vacant for less than a week, but being cheap and in a good location it was soon occupied.

As I drive by the building today, I fight the urge to pull over my car, run down the alley, up the porch steps, through the two doors, up the three flights of stairs. Matt never locked his door. What if the new inhabitants of that place don't either? What could I do if found myself standing at the door to this place I so often sought, open it slowly at first, cross in to the bedroom, and sit to ponder when Matt was coming home?

Now Lauren has an essay. The theme is the sense of peace, acceptance, and love that being in Matt's room brings to her and the poignancy at the end of the essay upon her recognition of the loss of this peace. The details provide the evidence that demonstrates her theme. Why was this so hard to write in a first draft? Why was the key sentence, the one moment when the veil is lifted from herself and she can see exactly why Matt and his apartment mattered to her, not immediately apparent when she first sat down to write? Why was it so hard for her to write "It was to that room I fled"?

It is remarkable how well we all adjust to our difficult experiences. We adjust so well that most of us do not understand their impact on us, regardless of how many car accidents, serious illnesses, and family conflicts we endure. In a senior honors course I taught called Trauma and the 20th Century, only one student self-identified on an initial questionnaire as having had any experiences they might call traumatic. (She had lost both her parents.) We expect trauma to mean genocide, war, murder, or other life-threatening event, and we hesitate to compare our experiences to such horrendous ones, but in reality any painful experience can provoke a stress response. Only after our class began to read, talk, and more importantly listen to each other, did others begin to recognize the effects on them that their difficult experiences had. Everything from parental alcoholism to a Down syndrome brother, parents with bipolar disorder and depression, serious accidents, psychiatric disorders, and family feuds was represented in that one class of students who did not initially see their experiences as traumatic. Our traumas become commonplace. We underplay their effects on us to allow us to plod along without threat to our worldview. And this is not simply a semantic distinction. These students did not understand how these experiences affected them. The label is not what's important; the effects are. They were so afraid of being seen as weak, or unable to cope, that they, as we all do, minimized these effects and did not "give the devil his due," both sealing themselves off from these significant moments and inhibiting their own creativity. Passion is, after all, not selective. Whatever has the most energy provides the most power.

In *Worlds of Hurt: Reading the Literatures of Trauma* Kali Tal discusses the centrality of personal myths in our lives. She offers Daniel Goleman's suggestion that personal myths take the form of " 'schemas'—assumptions about experience and the way the world works" (Tal 116). Such schemas, which function as coping strategies to organize the world in predictable ways, usually operate at the level of the unconscious, and as such they skew our interpretation of events. As explained in chapter 1, a traumatic event can threaten our worldview, causing us to reevaluate the way we see the world and perhaps those in it that are closest to us. Goleman holds that "a distorted awareness" is traded for a sense of security, a tradeoff that he calls an "organizing principle of human existence" (Tal 116). Tal herself writes, "Grand revision of a personal myth must always spring from a traumatic experience, for the mechanism that maintains those foundational schemas will automatically distort or revise all but the most shattering revelations" (116). She then cites Chaim Shatan, a psychiatrist who works with trauma survivors, who describes this challenge to our belief systems as the "basic wound" that creates a new more adaptive worldview.

But no one is looking to have her worldview shattered. First, as I mentioned earlier, we cannot both feel our traumas and cope with life at the same time. Traumas are often locked away from conscious, narrative recall for survival reasons: If we felt them fully and immediately, we might not make it through. Keeping our traumatic images away from consciousness may at times be a mercy of nature. Second, our traumas may be off-limits for adaptive reasons: We may prefer hiding even the most egregious problem from ourselves, if possible, so we can get on with the business of "getting and spending" as Wordsworth wrote, because if we don't, we will have to do the hard work of recognizing just how troubling the given trauma is to us, doing something about it, and integrating our new actions and worldview into our lives. This is painful, disruptive, and time consuming. Who would choose to do this hard work if he could avoid it? Denial isn't a character flaw. It is a common modus operandi of human beings—until the denial compounds the original trauma and the resulting pain forces change. It is a truism of trauma that it is not the original trauma but how it is handled that counts. When a rape survivor, for example, has appropriate supports—from the legal system, friends, family, and/or partner—she can more easily adjust her world to this glaring threat to her security. But when any one of those areas is perceived as threatening, integration may never come.

So it is little wonder that Lauren absorbed her family's traumas and quietly attempted to escape them. Matt and his apartment became a hideout from the *angst* she found at home. Indeed, it is not Matt himself that Lauren wants—witness her deflation when he finally tells her he loves her. But Matt and his apartment provide a peace, a sense of love that she cannot find in the chaos of home. She thinks his love is the source of this peace, which is why she wanted to hear him say those three words, but once he does it becomes clear to her that she wants his presence and his support, not his adoration.

Once Lauren completed her paper she understood the role Matt played in her life. She also became painfully, furiously aware of the level of dysfunction in her family and its impact on her. It is not that she had no knowledge of this before. Of course she could see how unhappy her parents and siblings were. But she maintained the illusion that life could go on as it had, that she could escape it all, that her home life had little or nothing to do with her, in spite of her deep love for her family. This created a cognitive/emotional split that helped drive her out of her home. Once she wrote her paper and recognized the effect this conflict had had on her, the agency that writing provided gave her the impetus to push against the family dynamic, a not-uncommon effect of text creation. Suzette Henke argues that, "Because the author can instantiate the alienated or marginal self into the pliable body of a protean text, the newly revised subject, emerging as the semifictive protagonist of an enabling counternarrative, is free to rebel against the values and practices of a dominant culture and to assume an empowered position of political agency in the world" (xv–xvi).

Lauren chose to speak with her parents about her perceptions of home. Not only did she feel empowered by her action, but she also found that this provided an opportunity to form a more transparent relationship with her parents, which has indeed occurred. Of course, this might not happen with all families. Transparency can produce rejection as well as acceptance, but Lauren felt confident that she had her parents' love, and this would allow for the kind of transparency she needed to forge. Lauren's new draft demonstrates the importance of revision—re-visioning—to her essay and to her life. Adrienne Rich wrote, "Revision—the act of looking back, of seeing with fresh eyes, of entering an old text from a new critical direction—is for us more than a chapter in cultural history: It is an act of survival" (1137). Lauren knew that Matt was important but she had no conscious idea why—until she connected emotions and images, speech and affect. And this often does not occur on the first try. The import of some events is buried within the conceptual framework we create to maintain the structure in our current lives. Lauren lived with her family, which made it difficult to challenge its assumptions. She had the courage to tackle the topic, but it took her some time to home in on what she needed to say. As Brison writes, "After gaining enough control over the story to be able to tell it, perhaps one has to give it up, in order to retell it . . . to be able to rewrite the past in different ways" (103).

Narrative provides a framework within which we can entertain relationships with our past, yet it also, as Brison says, "facilitates the ability to go on by opening up possibilities for the future through retelling the stories of the past. It does this not by reestablishing the illusions of coherence of the past, control over the present, and predictability of the future, but by making it possible to carry on without these illusions" (104). An excerpt of Patricia A. Foster's *Just Beneath My Skin: Autobiography and Self-Discovery* was published in the April 15, 2005, issue of the *Chronicle of Higher Education*. In it, Foster says, "The truth is that often I don't know what I know until I see it revealed on the page.

I don't mean that hidden events emerge in the act of writing or there's a sudden recall of memory. Nothing like that. It's that by writing imaginatively, motive and meaning take shape, sneak out into the light to expose themselves, dancing alone in the spotlight. Perhaps it's because writing about the self gives you a point of view" (B2).

This is what happened with Lauren. She already knew her home life was problematic, but she had not yet put together its effects on her relationships outside the family. Writing her essay gave her the opportunity to step back and look at herself and her responses in a new way, in the process constructing both an essay and a life that worked better. In an essay in the *Chronicle of Higher Education* Carlin Romano writes, "Stories shape reality for us and are made, not found . . . stories make the familiar and ordinary strange again . . . [Narrative's] etymological roots hopelessly mix the notions of telling *(narrare)* and knowing *(gnarus)* that scholars strain to unravel" (B12). In the telling we begin to know. In the telling we construct a reality that makes more sense of our lived experience. In constructing a narrative we reconstruct our lives; in revising our narrative we step outside our traumas for the moment and revise them, then invite others in to witness our construct.

The Teacher's Role

Working with writers in this way makes many faculty understandably nervous. The line between therapist and teacher, they fear, is breached. We leave ourselves open to being drained by our students, even to being sued by them. A former colleague of mine used to ironically describe three piles that her students' essays would fall into, like the three bowls of oatmeal Goldilocks found that morning when she entered the bears' house—not enough pain, too much pain, just the right amount of pain. These concerns are appropriate. Writing and literature teachers, however, are usually the first ones to hear of their students' traumas, and unclaimed trauma is one of the most common causes of writer's block. If we wish to be effective teachers, we acquire the tools to help us.

Jeffrey Berman argues in *Empathic Teaching* that teachers will learn "along with their students, that traumatic knowledge creates the opportunity for posttraumatic growth . . . that their students want them only to listen to their stories rather than to intervene in their lives . . . that students who are encouraged to pursue an education for life will achieve new breakthroughs of understanding for themselves and their classmates" (375). As I have discussed in *Writing and Healing,* we can respond constructively to students' trauma narratives without becoming their therapists (193–95). I wish to emphasize what I stated earlier in this chapter: My first job is to validate my student writer and then to talk about the text. I may thank him for trusting me with his story. With an experience of sexual abuse I may praise the writer for having the courage to write the piece. If the essay recounts a death, I may simply say I can imagine how hard the experience must have been for the writer. These are moments to establish common humanity. However, the cardinal rule is although we validate the writer, we work with the text, not the life, so we move on to the discussion of the work itself.

I begin with what worked for me, the parts of the essay I particularly appreciated, what I enjoyed. I attempt to play off the writers' successes. Next I move to the places that I got lost. I told Lauren that while I loved the descriptive details, I couldn't figure out why they were there. Which ones were the most important and why? I couldn't locate a theme, the focus that should link all the details together. I did not tell her she didn't have one, just that I couldn't locate it. And then I focused on the sentences that intrigued me—moving quickly to the pivotal one—"I slept more soundly in that bedroom than I did at home." The sentence seemed important, but I didn't know why—and then I asked her the question that helped her to recognize consciously what she already knew emotionally—why was this so? What was it about Matt or his apartment or her bedroom at home that made this true?

The teacher's role is to offer what she sees—or does not see—not what is or is not in the student's mind. We cannot tell if a writer has not reached an emotional truth. We can only tell if *we* couldn't from reading the text. And that's what we point out. As writing professionals we look for all the elements of a personal essay that make it work: descriptive detail that leads somewhere, demonstrating moments rather than relying on voiceovers to tell them, unity of focus that enables us to locate what holds the essay together, careful setting and character construction, and so on. We have at our disposal all the elements of the personal essay to rely on. We must remember that we do not have more insight into the student's life than the student. But we may have insight into what makes a text work and what inhibits it. We can provide feedback and ask questions about the text, but it is the writer's responsibility to make sense of it all. Of course we may choose to listen as they talk about difficult moments in their lives, as I did with Lauren. But my appropriate response is as active listener, not therapist. It is also important to note that themes often evolve in a beginning writer's drafts. If we begin by demanding a theme before writers have focused on which experiences they want to write about and eventually why, we can shut down the ability to find those moments. Having said that, an essay without a unifying principle becomes an anecdote or a moment that has no significance to the reader; therefore, this element of the personal essay must be encountered at some point, but I have found that it will appear as essays evolve and the writer gets more distance from the event in the process.

It is obvious that the teacher's role in this writing process skirts the line between therapist and writing instructor. Just asking the questions that can lead to text improvement may encourage the writer to open the door to a therapeutic encounter. In an article published in the *Journal of Advanced Composition,* Wendy Bishop follows up on Donald Murray's argument that all writing is autobiography: "If all writing is autobiography, a life in writing must of necessity consider writing as a process of self-discovery and the writing classroom as a site of such exploration" (505). She goes on to argue that "the analogies between writing instruction and therapy have something to offer me and something I need to offer to the teachers I train" (514). In support of her argument she offers the view of Lad Tobin: "We cannot create intensity and deny tension, celebrate the personal and deny the significance of the personalities involved" (qtd. in Bishop 505).

Alice Sebold's memoir *Lucky,* about her rape as a nineteen-year-old college student, illustrates these principles particularly well. The semester she was raped, Sebold was taking a writing workshop with Tess Gallagher at Syracuse University. Sebold had not written anything about the rape except for a few journal entries, so she decided to write a poem about the experience:

> It was awful. As I recall now, it ran five pages, and rape was only a muddled metaphor that I tried to contain inside a wordy albatross that purported to be about society and violence and the difference between television and reality . . . Gallagher was kind.
>
> "Let's talk about the poem you've given me, Alice." And she listened. She was not bowled over, not shocked, not even scared of the burden this might make me as her student. She was not motherly or nurturing, though she was both of these things in time. She was matter-of-fact, her head nodding in acknowledgment. She listened for the pain in my words, not to the narrative itself. She was intuiting

what it meant to me, what was most important, what, in that confused
mass of experience and yearning she heard in my voice, she could
single out and give back.

"Have they caught this guy?" she asked, after listening to me for
some time.

"No."

"I have an idea, Alice," she said. "How about you start a poem with
this line." And she wrote it down. *If they caught you* . . . (98)

Sebold then included the complete text of her poem. I offer here only the
first two stanzas and last two lines:

If they caught you,
long enough for me
to see that face again,
maybe I would know
your name.
I could stop calling you, 'the rapist'
and start calling you John or Luke or Paul.
I want to make my hatred large and whole.

If they found you, I could take
those solid red balls and slice them
separately off, as everyone watched.
I have already planned what I would do
for a pleasurable kill, a slow, soft ending.
. . . .
Come to me, Come to me.
Come die and lie, beside me. (98–99)

Sebold then continues with her narrative. "When I finished this poem I
was shaking . . . Despite its wobbles as a poem, its heavily Plath-influenced
rhymes, or what Gallagher later called 'overkill' in many places, it was the
first time I'd addressed the rapist directly. I was speaking to him" (99–100).
Gallagher was not afraid to deal directly with Sebold's experience because she
knew, from the first draft, which was bereft of the focus and details necessary
to poetry, that those elements would only be present in the poem when Alice
herself was present in the poem. In this piece Sebold allows herself to begin to

take control of her experience by giving herself permission to express hatred for her rapist. Gallagher's encouragement and acceptance was critical to this process. But how does this mesh with the current educational/pedagogical context?

Personal Writing in the Academy

Living in the academy post-postmodernism has burned into us that context is everything, that we are written upon at least as much as we write. We have been told the author is dead, that we do not have an authorial self because we cannot have a self in a world that presses on us like a book flattens dried flowers. This presents clear challenges to composition pedagogy. David Bartholomae, for example, in the article in *College Composition and Communication* mentioned earlier, called the personal essay, "sentimental realism." He went on to label it a "corrupt, if extraordinarily tempting genre" ("Writing with Teachers" 71) because it makes students "suckers and . . . powerless, at least to the degree that it makes them blind to tradition, power, and authority as they are present in language and culture" ("A Reply to Stephen North" 128–9). Bartholomae argues that the personal essay provides the illusion of an autonomous self, giving the erroneous impression that young writers actually *have* a self when their primary job should be learning the language and methodologies of the academy ("Writing with Teachers" 71). (This argument seems rather effete since we have yet to see a writer refuse to collect book royalties because he does not believe he has a self to collect them.)

Peter Elbow, on the other hand, argues that he wants to help students "see themselves as writers," to help them "take some time for themselves away from others' demands" ("Being a Writer" 73). His goal is to "cultivate in the classroom some tufts of what grows wild outside" ("Response" 90). Elbow is aware that the writing classroom is often not a place of discovery for young writers but a scene of humiliation and defeat. His goal is to use a natural urge for self-expression to demonstrate to them that language can empower. Elbow has often been misinterpreted as favoring a solipsistic view of writing, but this is an imposed reading of his work. Indeed, as Fishman has argued, "Elbow . . . hopes to increase our chances for identifying with one another and, as a result, our changes for restructuring community" (651). Elbow states clearly in *Writing without Teachers* that "writing is a string you send out to connect yourself with other consciousnesses" (77). McCarthy, in her section of the Fishman/McCarthy article, attempts to bridge the gap between social constructionists and expressivists by arguing that "expression is fulfillment as well as clarification, that we do not know where our expressions are going until we complete them" (660).

In a special issue of *College English* focusing on personal writing Victor Villanueva argues that the writing of autobiography can be an epistemological tool, a way of examining our subject position: "I find it hard to reconcile a theoretical position that argues that ways of seeing the world are contextually constituted and linguistically mediated, even linguistically formulated, with a methodological position that strives for—and most often claims to achieve—objectivity. There must be room for elements of autobiography, not as confession and errant self-indulgence, not as the measure on which to assess theory, not as a replacement for rigor, but as a way of knowing our predispositions to see things certain ways, of understanding what it is that guides our intuitions in certain ways. This is the autobiographical as critique" (51).

These positions affect not only our pedagogy but also our scholarship. Scholars can provide the "story of the story" as well as student writers, which is why Gesa Kirsch and Joy Ritchie argue that "it is not enough to claim the personal and locate ourselves in our scholarship and research. In doing so, we risk creating another set of 'master narratives,' risk speaking for and essentializing others, and risk being blinded by our own culturally determined world views" (8). They urge us to follow Adrienne Rich's suggestion to women, to "investigate what has shaped their own perspectives and acknowledge what is contradictory, and perhaps unknowable, in that experience" (9). When we can examine our contexts and our responses to those contexts, we can better understand the institutions—and the people within them—that have framed our lives. In this way the goals of the social constructionists and the expressivists are similar.

These theoretical and pedagogical issues reflect the more practical concerns faced by writing teachers in both high school and college: How can we best prepare our students for the writing tasks ahead of them in college and in life? As writing professionals are well aware, theory wars exist in our discipline just as they do elsewhere, and the polarized and polarizing arguments presented by some have not provided much clarity. Some teachers and scholars, however, have attempted to pull together pedagogies that acknowledge, even honor, the role of expressivism in the writing classroom while instituting techniques that enable writers to become aware of their contextual subjectivities. Bruce Horner in his essay "Students, Authorship, and the Work of

Composition" has attempted to offer a line of breadcrumbs to lead us through the contentiousness of the social-constructionist-versus-expressivist arguments and offers alternatives to these polarized views. Barbara Kamler, in her book *Relocating the Personal: A Critical Writing Pedagogy,* presents a pedagogy that attempts to both help students immerse themselves in their narratives and recognize the context that helped produce that narrative.

Kamler recognizes the many benefits of expressivist pedagogies; however, she is concerned that the focus on voice alone does not take into account the important element of context, which so influences that voice, and she uses some of Tim Lensmere's arguments to demonstrate this: "Lensmere argues . . . to assume a stable preexistent self that can be expressed in writing is to assume that language itself is simply a tool for that expression, a neutral vehicle for making and expressing preexistent meaning—rather than a site of struggle where subjectivity and meaning are produced . . . It is to ignore . . . that writers are not isolated individuals pursuing personal meaning but are embedded in social relations of gender, race, class, and sexuality that influence the work of writing and creating a self . . . Voice is the starting point, the basis for the collective work to be done" (38). Shifting the emphasis to story as a metaphor for feminist theory and pedagogy "allows a more textual orientation than voice, a closer attention to what is written (rather than she who has written)—to the actual text—and the contexts in which it is produced . . . Stories are specific rather than abstract, they . . . do not tell single truths, but rather represent a truth, a perspective, a particular way of seeing experience and naming it. Stories are partial, they are located rather than universal, they are a representative of experience rather than the same thing as experience itself" (45–46).

As we have seen, the key element in the process of healing from trauma is producing a narrative that can be examined, refined, and revised, all of which creates distance from the original trauma and a sense of control over the narrative. It also ultimately enables us to *choose* how we will respond to the trauma, as opposed to feeling caught in its maw. This subjective shift from victim to survivor that narrative construction helps generate is crucial to the recovery process, and this is similar to the process that Kamler presents in her pedagogy: "I am interested in the ways a writer's personal experience can be represented in text, in the shifts of subjectivity that are made possible through rewriting and re-imagining the text" (47). She argues that emphasis on text can:

- Allow a clearer separation between the writer's life and the experience she is writing about
- Make the labor of the writer more visible, less naturalized, and therefore more accessible to the learner
- Treat stories as a learned cultural practice, so that the process of production and the stories produced can be unpicked, examined, and analyzed rather than just celebrated or studied for the right or wrong voice. (46)

Kamler then uses T. Threadgood's arguments to demonstrate the dynamic nature of writing: "The significance of this conception for writing is that it opens up the 'personal' to change . . . It allows us to imagine the possibility of rewriting the multiple and contradictory subject positions we occupy and/or bringing into being new positions to sit alongside the old. It allows 'the possibilities of resistance, not determinism, and of new, transformed selves'" (47–48). The act of writing changes us; we are not the same people we were before.

Kamler offers the text of a widow in her writing workshop who experienced this kind of transformation:

> Bella entered the writing workshop a woman in grief. Her husband had died thirteen months earlier, and she continued to mourn his absence . . . Each week in workshop Bella cried easily . . . I suggested she consider writing about her husband's death, as the act of writing might help and certainly would not be more difficult than her present pain. To confront death by constructing a narrative of dying, however, is to break a cultural silence that refuses death as a part of life. Bella not only agreed but seemed physically transformed when she returned with her story the following week. The black circles under her eyes had lightened and her white-streaked hair was pushed back with a dramatic flair as she read her text aloud to the group:
>
> > . . . He went to bed. I gave him his sleeping pill and as every night before falling asleep he said, "Darling another day together— thank you." We kissed and soon he was asleep . . .
> >
> > When I woke up some time later, Sam was laying across my bed—he could not move or talk, he just looked at me with wide opened eyes. I tried to shift him but could not do it. A nurse arrived and we put him back in his bed. He was conscious and rest-

less. The doctor ordered a Valium injection, which calmed him down, and he fell asleep.

When he awoke on Saturday morning, he was conscious and responded to requests but did not speak any more . . . I knew that he was dying and that I could not do more than stay with him. I was calm. I knew that this was the end and that these moments would stay with me as long as I lived. I needed to remember every one of them, every breath, every change. I lay next to him fully dressed and watched him. I called his name. He opened his eyes— he could hear me. His mouth was dry and I put some soothing lotion on it. I listened to his breath, felt his pulse, touched his body. I lost sense of time and space. I felt removed from everything and everybody. There was only Sam and I. I remember his breath becoming slower, the silences becoming longer and then it stopped. Sam was dead.

I touched his face and kissed him. He was warm and soft. I do not remember crying. I stayed alone in the room until he was taken away. The last I saw of Sam was the long plastic black bag in which he was carried out . . . I was left alone . . . I vaguely remember the funeral. I felt and still feel that part of me died with Sam. (56–57)

As Kamler writes, emphasizing narrative allows for "a clearer separation . . . between the writer's life and the experience she is writing about. What the writer produces is a text, a story, that comes from her but is *not* her" (177). She then quotes from J. Summerfield, who refers to the context of college campuses: "We ask students . . . for their texts, not their lives. The distinction is crucial; the discourse is not the event. It is not real life" (qtd. in Kamler 177). Lauren and others show us, however, that these are not innocent requests. Asking questions about text—how an experience is developed, what is included, what omitted—is likely to lead to the writer's critiquing the life as well.

This process can become problematic in a first-year writing course when young people are already confronting hosts of changes—living away, sometimes for the first time; learning to accommodate to college academic standards; developing a social environment in a new context, and so on. This is why much of the contentiousness of the academic debates regarding personal narrative writing involves how to handle first-year writing courses: Are they opportunities for students to find their "voices" and construct life narratives or are they entry into the embattled world of higher education and beyond? Some compositionists use the personal in the service of the academic; that is, the personal becomes evidence within an academic argument. Others attempt to merge the goals of expressivism and social construction into a united pedagogical vision. While this may be possible, in some departments the task is akin to the discovery of unified field theory in physics.

Another way to manage this problem is to provide an upper-level personal essay course that has as its explicit goals developing a voice and engaging that voice in discussion of personal, social, and cultural contexts. This removes the strictly personal narrative from first-year writing and allows writers time to become acclimated to academia in the process. The first-year essay can certainly use personal narrative both as a separate genre and to provide context and support for an academic argument, but it leaves until later the fuller development of the personal essay, which can provide the depth and time that genre needs. It is crucial to note, however, that writing teachers in classes at all levels must be prepared to encounter student essays on painful topics—whether or not we assign those topics.

In his essay "Opinion: Ethical Issues Raised by Students' Personal Writing" published in *College English,* Dan Morgan describes the many essays he receives in his first-year writing course that focus on intensely personal experiences in a class that does not request them. He has received essays on parental abuse, domestic violence, rape, abortion, even murder, leaving him to wonder about his role in the writing/revising process. Does he ignore the content and focus on the writing skills? These essays are supposed to be arguments for something. Morgan describes a paper on parental abuse that involved an alcoholic father who was guilty of "throwing the writer across the room when she was three and a half, whipping her with a belt and kicking her for twenty minutes. Her brother took her into the bathroom to help her clean up, and they sat there for an hour as he applied ice to her face . . . until the father said it was time to go to church . . . A pattern of physical and mental abuse characterized her childhood. And what was the point of her paper? She is concerned that kids, especially teenagers, don't get enough discipline, and that parents have been denied the means to administer needed discipline these days" (320).

Morgan wonders what his role should be: Does he attempt to "nudge a student toward rethinking the traumas of her life? Or should the teacher focus on writing issues such as paragraph unity and sentence structure? . . .

What *is* the nature of our 'contract' with students exactly?" (320). This teacher is in a tough bind: He did not request a personal essay; he requested an argument, and his student provided one, even if the argument is more, he suspects, what I call the story of the story, rather than the emotional truth of the events. If this were a personal essay class, he could ask her to concentrate on the images, focus them until they were laser sharp. In the process, the images could conjure up emotions that might lead her to re-examine her interpretation of events, if indeed she felt this was appropriate. But this teacher feels himself stuck commenting on paragraph unity and sentence structure rather than the concept of the essay, leaving him frustrated and confused regarding his pedagogical role because, as he wrote, "students will write about what they want to write about" (322).

This is because the process of writing mirrors the therapeutic methodology for trauma survivors outlined in Judith Herman's *Trauma and Recovery.* Narrative construction based on traumatic images and the descriptive details that result from those images produce both evocative writing and a therapeutic effect. Writers often speak of the freedom and power that their writing brings. Poet Gregory Orr in an article in *Poets and Writers* states:

> The personal lyric says to the self: Translate your crisis into language— bring your disorder over to poetry's primal ordering powers) especially story, symbol, and incantation) and we will make a poem. This poem will dramatize your situation as an unfolding interplay of disorder and order—a model of your crisis, but with this crucial difference: The power relationship between disorder and order is reversed. Instead of your self being overwhelmed by disorder, we will have in the poem the opposite situation—your self as poet mastering what threatened to master you, ordering the disorder of love or loss of fear or joy into the drama of a poem. The same self that was destabilized by the disorderings of experience is here, in the poem, restabilized by taking charge through imagination and making a coherent model of its crisis. The poet thus creates what Frost calls "a momentary stay against confusion." This existential crisis might not necessarily be in the immediate life-moment of the poet. It could be in the more distant past—say, a memory of trauma or suffering—in which case we might identify with Wordsworth's statement that poetry is "emotion recollected in tranquility." I would substitute the term "safety" for "tranquility" and note that in Wordsworth's definition the poet's self is

circling back from a safer future moment to engage some earlier, emotion-based disordering experience. Whether we favor Frost's or Wordsworth's formulation, we have a similar project: using language and shaping imagination to master a confusing situation or emotion and order it into the dense and complex pattern of meaning we call a poem. (18)

Orr goes on to state that as efficacious as the lyric poem is, some experiences cannot be captured by the lyric alone. He tells us of the defining event of his life—his brother's accidental death in a hunting accident when Orr was twelve and Orr was holding the gun. He then recounts a string of traumas—his mother's death two years later, his older brother's accidental death at four (Orr was three at the time) caused by swallowing pills, of his country doctor father's addiction to amphetamines, the well-kept family secret that his father at the age of eleven had accidentally killed his best friend in a hunting accident, and Orr's own experiences of violence at eighteen as a civil rights volunteer in 1965 in Mississippi. As Orr said, "When I wrote lyrics, I was safe on the peaks of being: moments of intensity that rose up out of the surrounding wilderness. But to write the narrative of memoir, one has to connect up the peaks with a path. It may be that the peaks are moments in which the mystery of being can reveal itself to the poet, but the valleys between the peaks, the rough wilderness you must cross to get from one peak to the next—these reveal the mysteries of becoming, of how a self is transformed into a person" (20).

Orr understands that the lyric captures a moment in time, but narrative links those moments together into a story that helps the writer feel some control over past traumas. This process has physical as well as emotional benefits, as mentioned earlier. But that process of constructing stories must be emotionally honest, that is, it must go back to the images that contain the emotional reality of the experience. One young woman in my class wrote about an acquaintance rape, or so she thought. Melissa had mentioned in her journal that she had been raped a couple of years ago. Although she had written about it already in a women's studies class, it still was traumatic for her. In fact, Melissa had trouble falling asleep at night and often put on a Disney video to push away her feelings so she could sleep. She knew that she still had unfinished business with this experience and so asked if she could write about it again. I agreed and suggested that she try going back to the images she sees when she does not censor her mind, since that's usually where the energy is in traumatic memories. She agreed with this methodology. One day she came to see me looking shaken, near tears, and handed me a paper to read. I asked her what made this version of the story so different. She said, "It's not about rape. I wasn't raped. I remembered it as rape, but it wasn't. The paper is about the abortion I had. I can't think about it. I didn't want to remember it. He really liked me, really wanted to be my boyfriend, but after the abortion, I wouldn't see him, speak to him, wouldn't have anything to do with him. It's only now that I see it wasn't his fault. I blamed him for the abortion, hated him for what I had to do." As she wrote in her paper:

> I wanted him out of my life. I wanted this whole experience out of my life, and getting him out was the only way I could do that . . . He was the enemy. He was the cause of all my pain . . . I want him to be bad. I still do . . . I never once thought about how he might be feeling. Not once. I felt that my pain was worse than his, so why should I feel sympathy for him? I never realized this until now.
>
> I have written about this experience before, but [it] couldn't have been more different. I wrote about it for a woman's studies class my sophomore year. We had been talking about women's issues like date rape and abortion in the class . . . I was left utterly confused. I was left with more questions than answers. I had spun a whole new twist on the experience and I almost enjoyed it. I had given myself a loophole. I had validated the abortion once again.
>
> This writing experience was different. By the time I wrote this I almost didn't feel the need to validate myself. Every single day of class reminded me of my own trauma, and I got used to it . . . But after writing about it this time I have realized something brand new. The abortion itself wasn't that traumatic. The thoughts and feelings and the anxiety that surrounded it were more painful than the actual event.
>
> I still usually watch TV before I go to bed, but it doesn't have to be Disney, and sometimes I even turn it off. I am not too scared to think about what happened anymore. In the past couple weeks I have been thinking about it when I go to bed and when I wake up, and it is enlightening. I find something new every time I go there. I find another piece of myself.

Here we have an example of the relationship between memory and context. Melissa interpreted her experience in a way that conformed to the subject matter she had studied in her women's studies class—sexual assault—because it exonerated her, created, as she put it, a "loophole" large enough for her guilt to slip through. All she had to do was alter the facts a little. But she knew somewhere deep inside that she had created this fiction to protect herself. Hearing about trauma and learning its results gave her permission to delve into this experience again and peel away the protective construct. She learned that she is not a freak to have reacted as she did, that many trauma survivors turn away from their traumas any way they can, which is exactly what dissociation is. The greatest surprise for her was discovering that her anxiety was much worse than the event she had been running from: the abortion itself. As I said earlier, it is not the trauma but how it is handled that counts.

She ended up writing a paper that was completely different from the first, in both form and content. Where the first used what I call "the talking head"—that is, was narrator, not image driven—the second put her in the moment in present tense. She immediately realized that the first version was "the story of the story," that is, how she wanted to remember what happened; it did not preserve the emotional truth of her experience, or even the factual truth. She never was raped. Both she and the man allowed the situation to go further than either of them intended, resulting in a pregnancy. She was just as responsible as he was. In addition, she realized that he was upset for her and wanted to help her, give her money, go with her to have the abortion. He genuinely cared for her, but she projected her pain onto him, rejecting him and his attempts to help her. In her mind it became a date rape, and she never wrote about the actual abortion itself, which what is what generated the trauma. She allowed the class context to alter her narrative—not hard to do because she had been avoiding connecting with the images and the feelings they generated. This is a classic example of context affecting memory, which is what can happen in cases of false memory. Only after looking at her list of images did she become aware that she had never dealt with the abortion. Once she wrote about it, she realized that the young man was not the enemy, that she had projected her anger and pain onto him to avoid the guilt she felt for having had the abortion. She watched those Disney movies to try to keep the truth of her guilt at bay. Once she realized what the true trauma was, healing could then begin. After she wrote her second draft, she told me that although she was still upset by the experience, it did not frighten her to think about it any more. She is now able to go to sleep without being afraid.

Another student had a similar experience of re-evaluating her responses to her past. Kathleen had written a paper that described sexual abuse by her teenaged brother when she was five—an event that ended with her feeling inadequate. She ran from him, the only appropriate response at the time, only to have him fling after her that she wasn't good enough. "I wouldn't have been good enough anyway," she wrote. "I repeated it over and over again as I trudged down the stairs. I wouldn't have been good enough anyway. I'm not good enough. I'll never be good enough at anything." As is common in cases of sexual abuse, she blamed herself more than the perpetrator, and that blame translated into a lack of self-confidence. She was only five, and this was her brother, a person she loved yet had also learned to fear. The paper then described a relationship with a female teacher that helped her develop confidence in herself. The paper was well written, but after we discussed it in conference we both decided that it was incomplete. It leaped from the abuse scene to her freshman year in high school. It needed a second scene to function as a bridge to the scenes with her teacher. After writing the new material, which showed her giving up after a challenge, she came to me and said, "I never realized until I read my papers over again that I run when life gets hard. I learned how to do that as a five-year-old." Suddenly Kathleen's behavior made sense to her, which was the beginning of being able to change it if she chooses to.

Even complex, medically challenging issues can become less threatening through the writing process. Jonathan is a natural born writer. He encounters all writing assignments with creativity, passion, and utter competence. The first essay he wrote in the class was about a high school girlfriend who had been a childhood victim of incest and had so sexualized herself that her relationships with boyfriends became sexually obsessive. Jonathan tried to help her but only got caught himself in the process. The paper was well written, but it had holes in it that did not take long to find. Jonathan finally realized, several drafts in, that the real subject of his paper was his obsessive-compulsive disorder that got diagnosed in high school. The following is from his process statement:

> This has been, by far, the most time-consuming writing assignment I have ever worked on, and that includes the twenty-something-page story about the crazy man who sold voodoo dolls to a bloodthirsty contingent of townfolk I wrote in seventh grade. . . . Clearly the most important part of the process was transforming this essay from an

essay solely on my ex-girlfriend . . . into a paper that focuses more in-
tensively on my experiences with OCD.

Indisputably, the largest hurdle to writing this paper was simply
allowing myself to write about OCD. When my OCD went into remission (that is how I think about it), I was ecstatic. I was sleeping eight
hours a night, I wasn't afraid that I was a bad person; in short I felt
normal again. Because of this I was in no way interested in revisiting
my OCD. My mother repeatedly asked me to visit another psychologist to "gain strategies to deal with the OCD." When I would refuse,
and she would press me, I would become almost belligerent. "*MOM,*
my OCD is not here right now. You have *no* idea what I went through.
I'm not going to do anything that could disrupt the balance and bring
it back. I *refuse* to see a psychologist. I *refuse* even to think about it.

That being said, it is either a testament to the natural pull of the
cathartic process of writing, or to my complete idiocy and hypocrisy
that I decided to revisit my OCD via the written word. I'd like to think
it was the former. Based on my response to my mother's repeated suggestions that I see a psychologist, it is easy to see why the paper at first
did not discuss my OCD. I was afraid (and not unconsciously so) that
by bringing OCD to the forefront of my brain, my symptoms would
reappear. Happily, that was not the case. If anything, writing this paper
has made me feel more confident that I will experience no relapses.

We learned in class about how writing about trauma moves it into
the cognitive part of the brain. I believe that this is especially important with something like OCD. The trouble with OCD is the uncer-
tainty. You don't know if your thoughts are representative of who you
are or not. By putting them on paper, I can recognize the basic absur-
dity of the thoughts . . . By having it all on paper, I feel like I have more
control over it than I did before. That does not mean that I think writing is some kind of panacea for OCD sufferers, just that it does more
to help than it does to harm. I am glad I wrote the paper.

We need here to return to the important issue of the teacher's role in this
process. First, as Anderson, Kamler, and I, among others, have suggested, the
safest and clearest line for us to follow is to comment on text, not life. I asked
Melissa, who wanted to write about her "rape" but found herself blocked, to
ignore the previous narrative she had written (which was vague, without details) and instead to go back to the images that the moment produced to find

the specific details that drive personal essays. I suspected she had written an incomplete narrative, one that focused on something other than those core images. I had focused on the text, while knowing that it would also lead back to the life. The question I asked Lauren about her story had the same effect. She had offered something to the reader that seemed important—she slept more soundly in Matt's bedroom than in her own—but she had not created any context for this statement. The rules of the road for writing professionals allow this question. However, I knew that the answer would lead back to Lauren's life; I knew she would have to go back to the emotional memories that connected her to a difficult part of her life in order to figure out the answer to my question. In making the choice to ask this question I knew I was moving into complex territory, just as I had done when I asked my screen-writing student discussed in chapter one why he had such a hard time going to the bathroom the night his parents were arguing. These are not innocent suggestions and questions. We ask them to improve the text, but we know that the students will link their writing to their lives, which will then be re-evaluated in this new context.

Jonathan was a particular challenge because although his writing was excellent, he remained unhappy with the essay because he suspected that he was hiding his OCD behind his girlfriend's sexual compulsiveness. He needed the time, the space, and the trust in himself, in me, and in the writing process to go down the road that he had sworn to his mother he would never travel again. I read many drafts of this paper, until Jonathan made the decision himself to connect his girlfriend's compulsiveness with his own. It is essential to allow students the control over what they write because the very nature of writing is to take back that which was taken away—our autonomy. The writing process is recursive; as our texts change, we change, and vice versa. Sometimes it is difficult to tell which comes first. But we do know that the catalyst can be a class writing assignment, a selected reading for the class, a teacher's not-so-innocent question—and this takes us into complex territory; however, my first dictum—never mandate a topic—allows students to choose their own and protects both student and teacher. I have never had a student choose to venture into difficult territory who was not ready to make the journey. Some have discovered that they would like some professional help along the way, and I myself have referred students to our college counseling center for this purpose, but the process was initiated by the student.

It is also important to state the obvious: This is hard work for the teacher. Some nights at three in the morning when I have finally finished reading and grading a set of personal essays that have included the usual number of pieces on deaths, suicides, accidents, and other ills of humankind, as well as essays on nontraumatic topics—the ratio is usually three to one in favor of the former—I am struck by deep sadness at the thought that these beautiful children had to encounter such terrible moments in their lives. But I also know that tackling these subjects will enlighten them—make them lighter—as well as help them to become better writers. And I too am a part of this process. The students and teacher become change agents for each other. I grow as a person and as a teacher as well. Yesterday was graduation, and as each student walked by me—the young woman who wrote about incest, another who tackled the death of a pet caused by her mother's carelessness, the young man who wrote about his surrogate mother's cancer—I knew that their joy at their accomplishments and my pride in them for their hard work is the deepest reward possible.

In their article in *The Writing Cure* Daiute and Buteau argue that assigning painful topics, while going against common practice, can have great benefits for children: "Asking children to write about conflicts or any specific issue like painful experiences might seem inauthentic or controlling. The wide range of representations that children make in response to the prompts for social conflict narratives offers evidence to the contrary. Moreover, . . . teachers [can] provide referrals for any extreme expressions . . . This study indicates that . . . children can sustain and use narrative writing for personal gains" (71).

Daiute and Buteau also argue that teachers can safely assign specific topics, but I virtually never stray from my position of not doing this, since I believe it protects the autonomy of both student and teacher. I do model listening for the students since I offer support in office hours when students discuss their difficult experiences with me to help guide their writing on their chosen topics. But I do not attempt to act as therapist, only as teacher and mentor, if appropriate. Friendship can only emerge, if ever, after the student is no longer in my class. Even then, for me graduation is usually the dividing line between strictly professional and more personal relationships between teachers and students. This distance puts the locus of control in their hands, once again, which is crucial for them as writers and as survivors. Jeffrey Berman in *Empathic Teaching* puts it this way: "I never tell students more about themselves than they already know. They are the ones who interpret their own lives . . . I do not rescue them; they rescue themselves" (374).

It is also crucial to recognize that we may be the first to hear some of our students' stories. Child sexual abuse, rape, physical abuse, incest, even child violence against animals—these are all stories that are unfortunately all too common. Just exposing such stories to the eyes of a sympathetic other can provoke healing. Elie Wiesel discussed this phenomenon on an epic scale with a story he told in a television interview and which was published by Judith Harris in her book *Signifying Pain:*

> Elie Wiesel narrates his experience of liberation from a concentration camp where he was a child. He recalls that children in the camps had already had the wisdom of old people because they had been exposed to the polar extremes of human savagery. When the liberation came, Wiesel recalls, an African-American sergeant was confronted with the stench, the corpses, and emaciated forms of what were once living men and women. The sergeant cursed and cursed. He screamed and cursed all of humanity, as well as the perpetrators, for tolerating the savagery there. Wiesel said that the children wanted to thank the sergeant, to lift the man up on their shoulders in a hero's fashion, but they were far too weak and kept falling back to the ground. The sergeant did not give up, however, and tossed himself in their arms, trying to be light. Wiesel recalls the man's frolic in the midst of the tumbling children; he wanted to levitate himself for them, he wanted to do what a savior would do: to fly. Wiesel's testimony is beautifully symbolic; the liberating angel opens and attempts to revitalize the children again, both physically and spiritually to restore their strength. (65)

It is important not to overestimate a teacher's role, but it is just as important not to underestimate it. Although our students have probably not been incarcerated in concentration camps, some of them have been in mental prisons, some have been physically or sexually abused, and others have had their lives mangled by alcohol or drug abuse—and sometimes we are the first to hear of it. The heartbreak of the trauma can be comforted by the joy of liberation a witness can provide.

As noted earlier, Judith Herman identifies three fundamental stages in the recovery process: establishing safety, reconstructing the trauma, and regaining a sense of community. A writing teacher is often involved in all three aspects of this process once a writer decides to write about her trauma: The teacher helps to establish a safe environment in the classroom, he can offer exercises and support to aid in verbalizing images and constructing a narrative based upon them, and the workshop environment can help offer a productive community within which the writer can operate. But before all this, a teacher's support, encouragement, even love, offered sometimes by simply listening, can provide the impetus for writers to confront their stories and ultimately revise their lives as well as their texts. Sometimes only when we can look through another's eyes can we look at ourselves anew. This is the core of revision—not simply to fix specific problems but to re-imagine the concept. Suzette Henke observes in *Shattered Subjects* that "life-writing encourages the author/narrator to reassess the past and to reinterpret the intertextual codes inscribed on personal consciousness by society and culture" (xv).

It has been several years since James Pennebaker first began his research into the relationship between writing and healing; recently a number of books have been published that pick up the important work that Pennebaker has been doing. *The Writing Cure* is a collection of essays written by psychologists investigating what promotes healing and how it works. The authors argue from the results of their studies that writing about stressful events evidenced more beneficial cognitive effects than controls, and that writing can facilitate cognitive restructuring, not simply a cathartic outpouring (Lepore and Smyth 108–9). They go on to say: "Expressive writing can change people's perceptions about their responses to a situation . . . it integrates thoughts with feelings . . . People writing expressively about traumas subsequently perceived those experiences as more controllable" (110–11). And this is the hallmark of writing about trauma: As said earlier, we begin to perceive that we have control over the uncontrollable—the past—and in the process we begin to feel "easier in our harness" as Robert Frost wrote about freedom. Forming a narrative allows trauma to be "summarized, stored, and forgotten more easily " (Pennebaker and Seagal 1248) because writing about stressful experiences reduces intrusive thoughts—which have a negative impact on working memory, making learning harder. It also allows us to organize those thoughts into a narrative we can then put away and pull out on our command rather than being at the mercy of our intrusive memories.

Catharsis alone is not enough. Cognitive re-structuring is an essential component to the recovery process, and art facilitates this work: "Because art demands a certain amount of detachment . . . artistic activity perhaps accelerates the therapeutic process" (Harris 31). In their chapter in *The Writing Cure*, Lutgendorf and Ullrich demonstrate that writing about emotions and facts together is what produces the healing effect. The authors instructed undergraduates to write about "(a) their deepest emotions about an unresolved stressful or traumatic event, (b) their thoughts and emotions about a stressful or traumatic event, or (c) the facts about a news item involving trauma . . . Students were asked to write at least twice a week for at least 10 minutes over the course of a month . . . Participants in the cognitions and emotions group reported more positive growth from the trauma than the other two groups" (182). This indicates that simply writing how we feel—sad, happy, angry, those labels that make for ineffective writing—will also be ineffective in producing a therapeutic effect. Good writing makes good psychology. Put in the reverse, as said in chapter 1, healing is an ambient effect of good writing. Given that writers often gravitate to writing about their challenging life experiences, when teachers focus on descriptive detail, a focused theme, character and setting development, and especially a consistent voice, students will progress cognitively, educationally, and psychologically.

Because traumatic memories are weakly organized, their activation requires little stimulation, while efforts to repress them require much effort. Wegner and Smart argue in *The Writing Cure* that survivors attempt to keep painful thoughts beyond the reach of consciousness. However, while these traumatic thoughts and images are not available for cognitive work, they are highly accessible and often intrude into consciousness, especially when given any opportunity (143). This explains why so many students go immediately to their stressful experiences when we ask them to write personal essays. Not allowing them to write what they need to will only inhibit their writing ability and require them to exert further effort inhibiting these memories. As challenging as this process may appear to writing professionals, the positive benefits are well documented: "Effective expressive writing about traumatic events leads to an altered relationship to those events such that they become assimilated as legitimate facts of ourselves and no longer need to be held at bay as threats to our psychosocial coherence" (Booth and Petrie 169). Melissa can sleep at night without that Disney movie.

Lutgendorf and Ullrich argue from their research that cognitive restructuring is an essential component of psychological resolution. The first requirement is experiential involvement:

> Individuals who were more involved in the disclosure reported greater reduction in negative mood by the end of the disclosure compared to a nondisclosure group. Intrusion of trauma-related ideation decreased in the disclosure group over the course of the study as compared to

controls . . . Resolution implies coming to terms with the event in a way that allows integration or assimilation of the stressful material. Greater involvement in the disclosure and greater evocation of negative mood during the first disclosure session contributed to greater insight by the end of the intervention . . . These findings also indicate that the quantity of disclosure, as measured in number of words by itself, was not sufficient to produce beneficial cognitive and affective change. In fact, continued high word counts by the third disclosure session suggested a lack of resolution. It may be possible to be very expressive about the same distressing material over and over again without changing the cognitive schema or affective distress related to the event. Emotional arousal during disclosure was not a strong predictor of resolution, suggesting that emotional arousal without cognitive processing might not contribute to a better understanding of an event. Rather, experiential involvement accompanied by some affective arousal may be key elements in disclosure leading to trauma resolution. (181)

This research is critical to our understanding of the relationship between writing and healing. As we saw with Melissa, simply writing about an event without first beginning with the affect connected to the experience will produce few positive results. Connecting the emotions with the images is what produces a healing narrative—and a well-written one. I argue in "From Trauma to Writing: A Theoretical Model for Practical Use" in *Writing and Healing: Toward an Informed Practice* that the key for writers is to concentrate on the images called up by whatever experience they wish to write about because those images are paramount to memory and to narrative. If the images are traumatic, they reside in the parts of the brain that are deeply attached to the emotional centers of the brain. Calling up the images will call up the emotions. When we begin to put words to those images we are using the parts of the brain that create narrative, and we begin to create a sense of control over those memories. They no longer control us; we can move them around, manipulate them, call them up when and if we wish because they are now a part of our consciousness.

I discuss the experience of a student I called Tina, who wanted to write a paper on visiting her grandmother at her home but who was drawing a blank: "The piece was vague and unfocused because she could not locate herself in the setting for the paper. We tried a visualization exercise in which she listed as many pictures as she could remember from that house and discovered to her surprise that even though her grandmother had died when she was ten, she could remember whole rooms, even down to running her fingernail along the grooves in the couch, playing with the doilies that covered each tabletop, and noting the half-empty bottle of Canadian Club on the counter. Her final essay was grounded in both an emotional and a physical reality that she had thought was unknown to her" (174).

I had asked Tina to close her eyes, put herself back into her grandmother's home and try to see, feel, hear, touch what was in the room. She produced a list of pictures of her grandmother and her home that enabled her to move past the block she had had. Her resulting essay, detailed, clear, and powerful, was also clear on what had caused her writer's block to begin with. I quote from the last paragraph:

> I didn't cry at the wake, I was laughing at one point, and then I was mad at myself for it. I was scared but bent down at her casket. Grandma's cheeks were too puffy. She had too much make-up on. When no one was looking, I touched her arm. Her skin didn't slide on her arm anymore and she was cold. It wasn't my grandma, just her body. Before the funeral, our family sat in front of grandma's casket. I watched two strangers close my grandma's box. They dropped the lid; I started to cry. Grandma was dead. Tears rolled out of my eyes; I couldn't see. My cousin Richard held me as I shook and sobbed. I didn't stop crying until after the car ride, after the prayers, after we left the cemetery. As we drove down the street, all other cars followed the Canadian tradition of pulling over and stopping to pay respect. It was then I realized that no one had let me say goodbye. (176)

And this, of course, is why Tina's first writing effort produced a blank—because no one had let her say goodbye. She needed to remember how she felt about her grandmother's death before she could write about her life—and to do that she had to go back to the images and connect them with how she really felt. I asked Tina after she had completed her essay to write a bit about her writing process:

> When you asked me to close my eyes in class on Wednesday, I faced strong images of my grandmother and her apartment. Grandma died when I was in sixth grade, and I found it remarkable that I

remembered some of the items on this list . . . Upon closing my eyes, my grandmother's apartment was in front of me. Piece by piece the furniture in her apartment "appeared." I could remember the entire room. Once the settings of the rooms were established, I swear I could almost smell her apartment. The rest of the images were almost like a dream sequence. I remembered running my fingernail along the grooves in her couch. Playing with the doilies that covered each table-top. The fence outside her window. Bottles in her bathroom. Even the bottle of Canadian Club that was on the counter half-empty. (This image was spookiest to my mom because I told her that I remembered that bottle and grandma mixing it with coke, something that my mother never would have mentioned in conversation.) I don't know why this was so vivid to me. I surprised myself in how much I remembered! Writing my essay later that night was so easy because everything just spilled out. (176–77)

It all "appeared" because Tina was connecting the images deep in her mind to the emotions they generated, which enabled her to produce a narrative more connected to her emotions at the time.

This is what Lutgendorf and Ullrich mean when they write that integration can only occur when the negative mood is evoked and tied into the cognitive element. The authors set up a ratings system they use to locate individuals along a scale that measures integration and assimilation of difficult events:

Stage 1: Individual is remote from feelings. Reported experiences have an impersonal quality. Feelings are avoided and personal involvement is not present in communication.

Stage 2: Individual does not directly refer to feelings but a personal perspective emerges to some extent. References to the self indicate an intellectual interest but only a general and superficial involvement.

Stage 3: Individual refers to feelings with ownership but does not describe personal aspects or deeper ramifications of feelings.

Stage 4: Individual begins to draw directly from experiences to describe feelings and personal reactions.

Stage 5: Individual elaborates and explores own feelings, using an inner referent.

Stage 6: Individual explores feelings and finds a step of resolution. Feelings and personal meanings are immediately available as clear referents for action or self-awareness.

Stage 7: Individual has an emerging understanding and integration of present issues in a new way, and these have meaning for other areas in a person's life. (181)

This process is similar to what happens when writers attempt to gain access to their deepest stories and put words to them. First, they are often aware that a topic they've chosen has emotional weight but they aren't focused on what that is or why it is. As we saw with Lauren, she wanted to write about her subject (Matt) but had no idea why. The same was true of Tina and Jonathan. As the writing process begins, the writer becomes more attached to the material, once the images and the moments that have the most weight are discovered and experienced. The inner referent is both the core emotional and imagistic reality of the experience *and* the elements of the writing process that help to create a focus for this work. The writing process allows for, even often mandates, that the work be done in stages, with revision often being a true re-imagining of the material. This is what Tina had to do: She had written the beginnings of a first draft that did not connect her images with her emotions. Lauren, too, wrote a first draft that was placed at level three—she was drawing from experiences that seemed meaningful, but she did not yet know why because she had not yet connected them to her feelings. Jonathan needed nine drafts (five of which he turned in to me) to realize that the compulsiveness he really wanted to write about was his own. Only in the revising process do writers begin to create the cognitive distance and resultant awareness so crucial to the writing process.

For teachers it is important to remember that all we have to do is our jobs: We focus on the text. Is it clear? Can we see, hear, smell the details? Do we know what the essay is actually about? Does it have a coherent center? As we let the writer know where we were pulled in and where we were locked out of the text, the writer can see us responding as involved readers, which helps the writer to be more involved in his text. Since, as I have said, healing is an ambient effect of good writing, we are engaged in a therapeutic enterprise when we respond to such texts; however, all we need do is respond to what the text needs. When I read Lauren's first draft, I was drawn into the one sentence that included Lauren:"I sleep more soundly in that bedroom than I did in my own." And I told her that this sentence pulled me in, made me want to know why she slept more soundly in that room. In answering my question, Lauren had to move to stage five: She had to explore her feelings, and this is what moved her forward. In that moment both healing and effective writing can happen because the details of the essay are married to the emotional weight of the event and organized into a coherent narrative that provides focus and direction for both the writer and the reader. We create our texts; our texts create us. The recursive process of writing—that feedback loop—is what gives writing its therapeutic potential.

Dori Laub, a psychiatrist who works with Holocaust survivors and is himself a concentration camp survivor, wrote, "The survivors did not only need to survive so that they could tell their stories; they also needed to tell their stories in order to survive. There is, in each survivor, an imperative need to tell and thus to come to know one's story, unimpeded by ghosts from the past against which one has to protect oneself. One has to know one's buried truth in order to be able to live one's life" (63). Writing is an act of resistance, a way to push against the accepted worldview, our own as well as the view constructed by others. Kali Tal argues for the revolutionary quality of writing: "Bearing witness is an aggressive act. It is born out of a refusal to bow to outside pressure to revise or to repress experience, a decision to embrace conflict rather than conformity, to endure a lifetime of anger and pain rather than to submit to the seductive pull of revision and repression. Its goal is change" (7).

Once Lauren wrote her paper she realized how bound her life had been to the adjustments necessary to deal with her dysfunctional home life. Her need for stability and peace had pushed her into the arms of men she did not really want. She began to evaluate her relationships with men and with her parents. She then made a courageous decision to discuss her perceptions with her parents, telling them that divorce would be far preferable, that they could then find partners more suitable, and the tension would cease. This action brought Lauren a sense of relief and empowerment. She went from feeling like a pawn to believing she could generate change, even if that meant only in her. The seventies feminist dictum is just as true today as it was then: "The personal *is* political."

Five Cases

At this point I would like to investigate closely the work of five student writers, each one demonstrating in detail some of the pedagogical and theoretical principles we have been investigating.

JEAN

Lauren's and Melissa's experiences demonstrate that we create a worldview to organize the universe in predictable ways and that writing that investigates the emotions behind that worldview can produce cognitive change. But trauma can subvert those predictable patterns we rely on to provide security and a sense of grounding. Often, as in Melissa's case, we create a fiction to protect ourselves from a truth that we are not yet ready to confront. The following example is similar. The assignment again was to write about a person or place that had a helpful or a harmful effect on the writer. This student, Jean, chose to write an essay about her uncle, who had died recently. Although Jean provided some descriptive details, and her energy and passion peek through, the conventional phrases and generalized moments cannot help us to "see" this man or the bond he shared with his niece.

My Uncle

Reality didn't hit me until I stepped into the church on that sunny Sunday afternoon. I didn't think about how hard it would be for me to cope with the loss until I was standing over the coffin, taking one last look at the man that I considered as the most fantastic uncle that any kid could possibly ask for. The family didn't want the environment to be too somber and too depressing. Brightly colored flower arrangements and colored pictures of my uncle during his happiest and proudest moments decorated the church. I knew we were here not to mourn, but to *celebrate* the life of my Uncle Jim. But I couldn't stop the tears from coming. When I thought about the way his eyes twinkled when we laughed together, and the cigarette smell that he always carried with him that was just so comforting to me, I thought about how I would never see the twinkling and smell the smoke ever again. When the tears started coming, I couldn't hold it back. It was like someone turned on the faucet full blast, and the knob got stuck. There were just so many memories that I had with my uncle that I knew I would treasure forever. But I couldn't help but think about the times that I shared with Uncle Jim; those times I would never be able to experience again. It hurt me to try to accept that fact.

As far back as I can remember, my uncle was always there. According to my parents, he was the one who bought my diapers for me, and my baby formula and bottles, too. Since my uncle had access to shopping on any military base of the United States, it was easy for him to find necessary products like my diapers and bottles with a better price.

Uncle Jim taught me how to watch football and baseball. He always told me, "ESPN is the way to go!!!" I always watched the sports channel with him until I was about eight years old. Then I discovered that television had more than one channel, and it was the greatest discovery I made since I discovered how to *turn on* the television set. Ever since, almost every moment was spent on arguing about who gets to choose what programs to watch. Whether it be at my house in Cerritos, California, or at Uncle Jim's house in Riverside, I would always want to watch "I Love Lucy" or "Gilligan's Island" or "Rugrats." Uncle Jim, on the other hand, would be wanting to know what the score of the Dodger's game was, or he would be screaming at me because it was *Monday Night Football,* and he was missing the game. No matter how hard we argued though, he would always let me win. And being the naive little girl that I was, I would always gloat about my triumph.

My birthday was always the best too. We did almost the same thing each year. Yet I never seemed to get tired of it. Uncle Jim always took me to my favorite Italian restaurant: The Olive Garden. He never liked Italian food. In fact, he didn't seem to like anything except tacos and hamburgers. But he knew I loved Italian, and he would have a plate of potato skins or a bowl of chicken soup, while I had my *humongous* plate of spaghetti bolognaise. He didn't mind, though. We would eat our dinner, sometimes with a comfortable silence between us, and other times, with conversations that ran as if they were on a schedule.

I will skip over the next section, which describes the writer and her family relocating to Malaysia and her uncle's diagnosis of cancer, and move on to the announcement of her uncle's death:

It was the afternoon of March 19, 1999, when we received the phone call that would rip my heart into shreds. My mom's brother called and told us that Uncle Jim didn't make it. His body was just too weak to fight the cells that took over his body. He fought in Vietnam . . . and had malaria, so his liver just crumpled. And the fact that he had been smoking for the past 20 or 30 years didn't help matters. Because of this, what would have been a minor case of prostate cancer for any other man became a case that was beyond treatment. After trips and trips to the hospital, Uncle Jim finally said he didn't want to go through any more treatments; he wanted to make the most of the time that he had left. On March 19, 1999, my uncle died in front of the television set at home, while watching *Monday Night Football*. It didn't seem real. It was like a dream; Uncle Jim couldn't *possibly* be dead. My favorite uncle was gone.

Although we do not doubt the writer's sincerity, the lack of dialogue and the generic sense of the writing do not help us to engage very directly with the text. The use of the conditional "would" prevents specific scenes from being included, which contributes to that generic quality. This does not mean, of course, that the feelings are not real; it does mean that the emotions appear muted by the lack of imagistic moments, which makes it difficult for the reader to connect with them. When I asked Jean what she thought of her essay she said it felt "safe," easy. She said she was not happy with it, but that it might be the topic. I asked her what topics seemed to have weight to her, which come back to her when she isn't looking. She smiled and said she knew exactly what she needed to write about. The following is from her first draft, which just poured out of her:

Mickie
"I HATE YOU! I HATE YOU!" I kept screaming. It didn't matter that she was struggling against me, and it didn't matter that she was screaming just as loudly as I was—except her scream was one of pain. The smoke cleared, and I finally realized just what I was doing. I was hurting my sister! What the hell was I doing?! I let go of her arm, and stood there numb. I wasn't supposed to hurt her; I was supposed to take care of her; I was supposed to make sure that she was the happiest girl on earth who has everything that she asked for. I was evil! Suddenly, I felt the tears coming. I knew that if I let them come, I wouldn't be able to stop them, but I didn't care. The years of agony, frustration and pain finally caught up with me. I started crying, and I kept crying . . . and crying . . . and crying. I grabbed my sister, and hugged her and held her as though if I let go, she would disappear. "I'm so sorry, Mickie, I'm so sorry. I love you. I love you more than anything!" I cried into her shoulder. "It hurts, Jean, it hurts. I love you," she said back to me. I couldn't help it.

Even though I have a sister who is two years older than I, I feel as though *I* was the older one: *I* had to accompany Mickie when she wanted to go out for a walk, or to go out shopping, or whatever; *I* had to accompany Mickie when she needed help with her junior high homework, even though I was still in sixth grade; *I* had to make sure Mickie was warm enough with enough clothing on her back and enough blankets on her bed during the winters. Yes, my parents were there, too. They gave her a roof over her head, they gave her food on her plate, and they gave her someone to call "Mom" and "Dad." But still . . . it felt like it was always *me, me, me.* Mickie was born a premature baby by four months. No one knows what happened, but it did. At two pounds, my parents told me that she was hardly bigger than the palm of my father's hand. She was rushed to and from the hospital during her first six months, struggling to keep the life that she was just introduced to. She had intestinal problems, and her stomach had to be operated on; she had vision problems, and her right eye had to be operated on before she started wearing glasses at the age of two; she had hearing problems, and by the age of four, Mickie was wearing hearing aids, too.

We had just finished our shower routine one evening: My mom finished bathing me, then she bathed my sister, then she bathed herself. She was dressing my sister, and I was gathering the popcorn, soda, and the candy bars, getting ready to settle down for a movie that night. "Jean!!! Come here!" I suddenly heard my mom yell. I stood behind her, wondering what the excitement was all about. She was kneeled behind my sister, and she was tracing Mickie's spine with her finger so short and small that it was hardly bigger than mine at almost ten years old. She grabbed me and told me to stand next to her. She told me to take off my nightshirt and traced my spine too. Then she traced Mickie's again. Then mine. Then Mickie's . . . Mickie had an acute case of scoliosis, the curvature of the spine. Another problem to add on to the long list that we already had.

The house filled with the luscious smell of ginger beef, and I knew that dinner was almost ready. Good. After the long day at school, I was *starving.* "Jean!!!! Why didn't you set the table?! My mom screamed from the kitchen. "But it's Mickie's turn!" I yelled back. "Jean, I am getting so sick and tired of you trying to blame everything on Mickie!" my dad added, raising his balding head and small brown eyes from the

Los Angeles Times. Huh? Blame everything on Mickie? I've never done such a thing! And it's always been a routine with us. I set the table every other day, and Mickie every other day. It *was* her turn today. "Jean, you know there are just some things Mickie can't always do. She needs to stay off her feet whenever she can. You should *know* better!" I don't even know who said that one. I stopped listening because I *should* have known better. When Mickie neglected her duties, it was up to me to take over and make sure that it gets done.

It was a night in high school. I wanted to go out clubbing with some of my friends. Mickie was watching me get ready, her eyes appearing to be huge behind her special-made glasses. "How come I don't get to go out with my friends?" "I don't know Mickie," was my reply. "Your friends just do different things than mine." I got to the front door before my mom stopped me and said, "Why don't you take your sister out once in a while? You know she doesn't have any friends, and it wouldn't hurt you to stay with her once in a while." I tried to explain that taking Mickie to a club downtown just wasn't a good idea. She wouldn't be able to handle the creeps down there who think they can lay their hands anywhere on a lady if they're drunk enough. I didn't want to end up losing her in some way, and most of all, I didn't want what was supposed to be a fun night out to end up being a babysitting job instead. "But if *you* can handle it, what makes you think your sister can't?" My mom just wasn't getting it. I pictured my friends: the girls with their heavy makeup, their miniskirts and tight tank tops showing off their figures, and the guys with their baggy jeans and even baggier shirts as they walked into the club, adjusting to the booming dance music over the speakers, settled down at the bar, and chilled for the night. I picture myself with my heavy makeup, my form-fitting black pants and my white halter top, going out onto the dance floor, under the strobe lights and the colored lights, and dancing like there was no worry in the world for me but to have fun and to show off my dance moves. But I decided to do the right thing: I stayed in with my sister instead.

Yep . . . my routine was to always make sure I was there with my sister. It was a natural reaction for me to make sure that Mickie got to choose the movie that we were about to see; I had to make sure that Mickie got enough to eat before I started eating myself; if I wanted to go out with my friends, I had to make sure that my parents didn't have any plans, and that someone was gong to be home with Mickie if I wasn't there. Routine . . . I laid in bed that night, let myself analyze my life, and I started crying. Tears of anger, tears of frustration, tears of sadness, tears of longing, and tears of guilt. It occurred to me that I never got a chance to experience being a kid. What was it like not to have to always think about the consequences before you do something; what was it like to be able to live on the spur of the moment once in a while and not have to worry about how my actions would affect my family? . . .

I took my sister out for a Chinese lunch one day, just in the Sheraton Hotel next door to our apartment. Mickie had been unusually quiet for the past month or so. My parents and I would often find her sitting in her room in a catatonic state, with a blank look on her face. We thought that it was from the stress of final exams that month, so I thought I would cheer her up by taking her out for a "sister, sister" luncheon. Throughout lunch, she was quiet; she didn't say *a thing*. Then, during our walk on the way home, she started talking. "Wow! There are a lot of birds around!" she exclaimed to me. I turned to look at her. There were no birds. "There are birds flying everywhere above my head!" I walked into my house sobbing . . .

Two shrinks later, Mickie was diagnosed with schizophrenia, and was put on medication . . . When I talk to her on the phone now while I'm on the other side of the world, her voice is somewhat comforting—even with the hallucinations and the delusions.

"You know what, Jean? There's someone in my room, and they want to kill me, and you have to be careful too, because they will go into your room to kill you."

"Mickie, how is our little dog doing? Is Feline OK? Are you taking her out for walks?"

"Dad takes her out because I can't."

"And why can't you? You should go out for a little exercise."

"Because someone will try to kill me." She's still hallucinating. I sighed, and my voice started to crack. "Well, listen to me carefully, OK, Mickie? You need to make sure you take care of Mom and Dad, OK? I'm not there to do everything, so you have to help me and make sure that everyone is OK. Can you do that for me?"

"Yeeeeeees, I can."

"Thanks, Mickie. I love you. Remember that, OK? I love you. And I'll talk to you later. Bye!"

"Bye-bye."

I kept the phone against my ear a bit longer . . . I hit the talk button, held the phone against my heart, and let the tears fall.

This topic is much closer to Jean's emotions—because it is far more complex for her. Her uncle's death was sad, very sad, but her relationship with her sister continues to be a challenge, producing contradictory feelings: love, guilt, resentment, feelings of responsibility, among others. Jean wrote about her uncle as a kind of proving ground for herself: Can she, dare she, tackle her relationship with her sister. The essay begins inside a specific moment, which engages us immediately because *she* is present. Note that this first draft, fragmentary and eruptive as it is, still offers more detail, more dialogue, and clearer moments than the essay about her uncle. This is where the energy is for Jean, and her writing was only improved by that fact.

GREG

"Follow the energy" can be used in fiction and poetry as well as in the personal essay. Greg, a talented writing major in my Trauma and the 20th Century honors class, was stuck for a story for a fiction workshop. His psyche had been occupied by a recent near-death car accident, and after realizing that powerful images and emotions for that experience were intruding on his efforts to write fiction, he decided to follow where those feelings would take him. He ended up writing a story called "Headlights" that begins with the following:

Once when we were in the seventh grade Matt and I called each other at the exact same time—as simultaneous as parallel lines—so that there was no ringing, just a click followed by our own astonished hellos As eighteen wheels and three hundred horses barrel into us, Matt makes a similar call, the self-same astonished voice erupting in the air all around us, filling the van—"That guy is right on your ass!"—except that this time we're way beyond phone lines. He is in the car in front of us that we've just hit, spinning towards the future.

Regina is asleep in the back.

And then she's praying, spouting verse in tongues like a Seventh Day Adventist. I know this because I turn to look. Her eyes are closed and her fists are clenched before her, clutching the invisible rail that will keep us all anchored to earth. The tractor-trailer headlights are with her in the back seat, breaking through glass, reaching for us like angel hands.

Greg Tebbano is an award-winning fiction writer. Ideas for stories flow from him like pebbles down the Niagara River, but until he looked squarely at the images that crowded his mind, he was blocked. Greg wrote the following about his process:

Early on in the semester I found myself in a desperate situation for my Fiction II class. I needed 25 copies of a story for class the next day, and . . . I didn't have the goods. It was probably only the second or third week of classes, and my knowledge of trauma was still minimal, but we were talking about trauma narratives in class—something about how traumatic memories make for good sensory details, good writing—so I decided to try something new. I was fresh off my closest near-death experience to date: a three-car smash outside of Owego, New York, rear-ended by a tractor trailer whose driver had fallen asleep at the wheel. So I sat down with my laptop and for four hours I just wrote about it. It wasn't a story, just images: non-sequential and fragmented like bits of flash fiction sharing a page. As I started writing, I started remembering things, crazy impossible things but I wrote them down anyway; Regina in the back praying nonsense for the two seconds while we were being battering-rammed into the ditch, big truck headlights that were inside our car, the voice of Matt who wasn't even in our vehicle, trying to warn me what was happening. I was so into it that when my roommate came in to ask me about dinner, and I didn't hear her come in, the sudden shock of her presence was comparable to the moment of a nightmare that sends you awake. That's when I realized that I wasn't at my desk writing a short story; I was actually back in the crash.

The writing of "Headlights" was a tremendously enlightening experience, and the result I think was one of the most powerful pieces I've ever written. Sure, I had to fidget with the draft. Some things I exaggerated, others I made up intentionally, and still others I made up entirely by accident . . . If truth was my goal it wasn't a factual truth I was after; it was a feeling truth. I wanted the story to capture that night, its mood more than anything—my mood, I guess—how unbelievable it was that I survived and how surreal it was to interact with the world in the crash's immediate aftermath.

The writing process that Greg experienced is intense, automatic, even natural. The images of our most powerful moments are all there, full-blown in our minds. They are already affecting us. But when we go after them, find them, and write them, we use them, rather than allowing them to use us—and sometimes that results in writing that is not only healing but also work we are proud of.

KAITLIN

Another case involves a writer, Kaitlin, who found her topic but had no idea how to write about it. Her first draft used the common "talking head" technique that we see so often with beginning writers—reliance on a narrative to talk about the events rather than allowing the moments to emerge. Here is part of her first draft on the assigned topic "Write about a significant moment from your childhood that taught you something important about life":

> It is easy for me to think of a lot of moments in my life that felt significant, but it is hard to pick one that stands out for some reason. Learning how to ride my bike when I was twenty was significant because I finally did this simple thing which I was forbidden to do by my parents at an early age (I might get "hurt") and that I was afraid to fail at as I got older. But learning how to ride a bike did not sufficiently change the person I am today, and I want the moment I choose herein to be "important" to my persona. I am thinking of a lot of sad, scary moments that transformed who I am, inside, deeply. I know that successes have played that transformative role too: playing a clarinet solo on stage for the first time, getting that poem published, dancing under the lights in front of everyone. But it is the painful moments by their nature that seem to still be challenging me today.
>
> I was twenty-one when I finally hit my father back. Kicked him in the stomach, actually. Watching him fall to the floor was one of

the most scary, guilty, relieving, and empowering experiences I've ever had.

I was talking to my mother, debating over some silly issue, but not arguing; our voices were not raised and we weren't talking over each other yet. My father was trying to watch a *Seinfeld* episode he's probably seen before and would surely see again. He told me to "shut up," his usual refrain. What made this moment significant is that I finally decided that it should be the last time he would say that to me, at least without severe consequence. I don't remember what I said to him; it was a long way of saying, "No, I have a right to talk in this space too." His reply sounded like this to me, "This is my house, paid for by my money; it is not your space, and you may not be yourself here." We had had this discussion before. And to end it, he had taken me by the hair and had dragged me down the hall, before.

The hallway to my bedroom is very narrow and short, and it took only a few slams into walls and scuffles before I was almost in my room. Actually, it was not my room but rather my father's designated holding cell for me, reserved for moments when I tried to stand out more than the furniture. The peak of this significant moment was when something snapped, something clicked in my brain. Though I had dug my heels into the floor whenever I had been dragged for so many years of my life, I had never taken it a step further, and given the violence back. This time I did. I kicked my father in the stomach, hard. It felt good and strange, strange because he fell so easily. I marched back to where I had been standing in the living room before the "dragging," and said firmly, furiously, "Don't you ever touch me again! Just because I'm a woman and you're a man doesn't mean you have the right to touch me! Now, can we talk about this, can you listen to me?!" The words were much harder to utter than they are to type now; I was sputtering, flushed, dizzy, hysterical with sudden newfound "power."

The writer then tells us that her parents threw her out of the house, that she took a bus back to Ithaca and spent Christmas alone in her apartment. She ended the essay with the following: "My significant moment is not 'perfect'; it did not have a clean resolution full of apologies and hugs, or even any forgiveness that I can see. What makes it significant is that I did more than just digging in my heels; I fought back. I have not used violence against anyone since. I have, however, been sticking up for myself a lot more."

Kaitlin begins the essay with that expository "voice over" that demonstrates to the reader the mental processes she went through to find her topic. The moments that count are only touched on descriptively. The narrator's voice has taken control of the story, rather than being used to shape the moments that form the bedrock of the narrative and her reaction to it. In the words of the writing workshop, she is telling and not showing, probably because showing means she will have to relive those moments consciously to choose exactly what details to include. The ending is particularly significant. When I asked Kaitlin how she felt about her ending she said, "I want this to be true. I want to think that I got something out of it, but it didn't end that way. First, it's a lie that I didn't use violence ever again, and second, I'm not even sure I've been sticking up for myself since then." I suggested to her that she begin with the incident she wants to write about and not to worry about explaining too much to the reader. Let the story emerge from the details. If they are there, we'll follow them. I also suggested that she not worry about the ending—just write the story and see where that takes her. Here is the opening of the revised draft:

> It's a typical conversation between me and my mother. What we are saying I can't remember, but it's not like we're really listening to each other anyway; we just want to be heard. [We] haven't yet resorted to the yelling stage; the argument is young. Besides, I rationalize, this time I'm being reasonable, trying not to speak in "that tone." I hate that my parents refer to my own voice as "that tone." Is my emotion so annoying that if it creeps into my voice it has to be so termed?
>
> "Shut up." My father's voice is sharp and rude with a strong Worcester accent. He's sitting on "his chair," which he always pulls too close to the too-loud TV. He's watching a *Seinfeld* episode he's seen before and will see again . . . My throat tightens threefold, and I start to grind my teeth. I always say, "If he tells me to shut up one more time . . ." I always say it to myself.
>
> "NO!" It burst out of my throat, ripping it open. "I'm having a conversation! My conversation! Do I have to get a f-ing permit to have one around here? I'm sick of shutting up!!!
>
> As those thoughts fly fast, my father slowly gets up from "his chair," pushing up with his flabby arms hidden by another smelly plaid shirt. His stride gets quick, fast. He knows just how fast he has to walk the few feet from his chair to the fake-wood-paneled wall where I stand in

order to gain the momentum to push a 125-pound annoyance (me) down the hall into "my" room. But I'm making some momentum calculations in my own head this time.

The hallway to my room is too narrow for two people to be in at once. Its walls are inappropriately pink and they are scuffed with black marks from past scuffles—my head hit there ten years ago, his foot made that mark there last week. My father takes me by the hair in one hand, usually all he has to do. But his opponent is alive now; for the first time, a fair fight has been arranged. I push back against his bony chest with my hands, hurting my wrists, smelling his stale garlic breath, feeling the spit fly out of my mouth on my face. My bare heels are sliding on the dusty wood floor, but they provide enough balance for my right leg to kick hard and strong. I have a well-directed kick from all those years of dance, and it makes me feel powerful. I decide his stomach is his point of balance; I want to kick it open.

Somehow my father actually falls. It is too easy; just that one kick to his pushy stomach. He falls against the wall next to his bedroom door, where my mother is standing, yelling at me to stop with the voice of a woman who is about to go over the edge of hysteria. She never yelled at *him* to stop hitting *me,* not once over the years. I'm wishing he'd fallen onto her and knocked her over too, so that she wouldn't be standing over me with her accusing face full of horrified "O's," her mouth, her eyes . . . I realized from her eyes that if she had the balls, she'd be hitting me too. I hate her more than him right now. She's a fellow victim, but she acts like I'm the enemy.

"DON'T YOU EVER F-ING TOUCH ME AGAIN!!! JUST BECAUSE I'M A WOMAN AND YOU'RE A MAN DOESN'T GIVE YOU THE RIGHT TO TOUCH ME!!!" I hear myself sound like a gender studies textbook, and I feel very college-cliché for a moment, before I return to myself and feel the desperate anger, guilt, illusion of control, and irrational calmness. "I want to talk about this. I'm sick of this. We need to talk about this; it needs to stop."

I'm staring at my 59-year old father as he gets up from the end of the hall, aided by my mother. He thuds his black-socked feet back to his chair, and as he passes me, he points a long arm with a pointed finger at me, but not his eyes: "Get out of my house."

The Christmas tree in the living room is badly decorated, not how I would have done it. It's short, on my father's insistence that it not scrape the ceiling. My mom always chooses the "wrong" tree. "You can't even pick out a tree using just one number, the height of the goddamned ceiling. You're brain dead," Dad informs Mom every year. "Why don't you get the tree?" she'll ask. "Shut up," my father's favorite reply.

I look at the tree, and I think about my mother—first about how Christmas Eve is the next day, and how she loves the holiday, and then about how she helped my father up when I made him fall. I look down the hall at her; she looks at me like I'm the ugliest thing she's ever seen.

"Fine, I'll go back to Ithaca tomorrow." My father's slumped figure is already back in his chair. I look at his back, studying for signs of any reaction. None.

Kaitlin then recounts a conversation with her mother, who came into her room and said:

"You shouldn't have done that."
"I don't want to be helpless like you my whole life." . . .
She doesn't agree with me, so I'm not listening to her anymore. I stare at her feet as she talks and stutters; she's wearing pants that are too high again, and her knee-highs are rolled down to her ankles, leaving a gap of dry freckled flesh visible . . .
"Fuck you!" I feel a little spit fly out of my mouth as I say it, just like my father does.

Kaitlin then describes leaving and ends with the following two paragraphs:

I'm on a cramped Greyhound bus crying freely, aware that strangers are watching me. The bus smells like people and piss. I'm writing my mother a letter that I don't intend to send her. I'm explaining why I left, apologizing for leaving her on a holiday, but remaining clear that I need to do this for myself. I'm writing the letter because if we actually had the conversation, it wouldn't go like this. I try to read it over, but I can't see through my eyes, just sad pools that are too full to see out of.

When I was twenty-one, I hit my father back for the first time and

I spent my first Christmas alone. The next year I went home again. My father hasn't struck me or disagreed with me since. He hasn't touched me to hug me or talked to me nicely much either. The replacement for bad contact has been no contact, and I don't know which hollows my heart more.

In this draft the focus is on the images, the moments themselves, not on the voice over talking about them. The tense shift from past to present is a sign that this focus change has occurred. She dispenses with the expository first paragraph that discusses her mental process prior to producing the draft and begins with the moment itself. The descriptive details are sharp and clear: We see the black marks on the wall, hear her swearing at her father, smell his garlic breath, almost feel her foot kick into his stomach. Everyone is implicated in this draft—mother, father, and daughter are all clearly locked into a struggle from which no one emerges victorious. This is why Kaitlin allowed us to hear her words, witness the satisfaction she took in doing violence to her father, and feel her emptiness. This is also why she changed her ending. In her first draft she wanted to feel like the victim who overcame her abuser and in the process became a "better person for it." As she said, she wanted to show that she "got something out of it." But she realized that she could not see what she had or had not gotten out of it until she let herself tell the story fully, until she gave the images and emotions their due. Therefore, in the next draft she wanted to focus on the pain and loss, in which she was implicated as well, because this is where she is with this story now. She may be somewhere else after this is written, but this is what she needs to write now. This critical crafting of narrative can "contain and transform emotion," as Kamler says (167). In the process of this transformation, writers, "without exonerating their own responsibility, [can] learn they need not carry all the blame" (167).

As is obvious to Kaitlin as well as to us, this is a complicated story, one that pulls in guilt, familial dysfunctions, role expectations based on cultural, psychological, and emotional pressures, and other contextual factors that affect both her and her parents. Barbara Kamler and others may argue that narratives such as this provide opportunities for writers to locate themselves within a broader cultural context that allows for more analytical approaches. This is, of course, true. The personal essay, however, allows for a depth that is necessary for writers to understand their own subjectivity vis-à-vis a topic, and this is essential to any further academic investigations, whether these narratives are included in a formal way or not.

CONNOR

Earlier in this chapter I quoted from Patricia Foster, who wrote, "The truth is that often I don't know what I know until I see it revealed on the page" (B2). It is not that we have amnesia for events, because we usually remember what happened. What is more likely to elude us is what it meant to us. Connor was a high school football player—and he looked it. A massive yet gentle presence in the classroom, he engaged fully in the writing process but was taken unawares when he discovered how he really felt about the end of his high school football career. His team had been undefeated in the regular season and was now in the playoffs, pitted against a team they beat 66 to 0 in the regular season. Connor and his friends—all football players—threw a big party a few days before the playoff game, which was clearly against the rules. They were discovered and not allowed to participate in the game. With six of their best players unable to play, their team lost the game. Connor ended the paper with these words:

> I couldn't believe it, nor understand why I had to helplessly stand on the sidelines watching my team suffer our first loss of the year that would end our season. I heard a fan yell, "Was it worth it?" . . . In all my years I had never heard the many cheers of encouragement from the stands, but I heard this one. The field taught me about integrity, honesty, and joy, but this idiot only cared about winning. After losing the last game I'd ever play on that field, I came to the realization that the only difference between winning and losing doesn't take place in the field, but rather how the outside world treats you. I stood on the sidelines in my last game ever on that field. If I had been able to help, maybe I wouldn't feel so bad. Walking off the field and past the row of fans that had formed around the gate, I noticed they looked more upset than me. The truth was my community was morally blinded by the Friday night lights, turning football into a religion, and anointing high school kids as gods. The only life they knew was between those white lines that were painted onto a grass field by an underpaid janitor. As I walk up the path towards the locker room my shoes drag across the pavement as my mind wrestles with what will happen to me now.

Connor and I met in conference after I read his first draft, as I do with all my students at that point in the writing process. After outlining the parts of the paper that I liked, I told him that I wasn't sure of his theme. Because the ending and the earlier parts of the essay appeared in conflict, I couldn't tell if his theme was tied to the response of others and his concern for their shallowness, or if it was linked to his own sense of personal responsibility for this incident. I asked him how he feels about that experience now, and he said angry. I asked him who he was angry at, and his eyes brightened. "I am angry at that guy for his comments, but I am even more angry at myself." Connor turned in a second draft to his paper and a process piece that demonstrates how he made decisions about his second draft. My students keep journals throughout the class, which meant that Connor could mine that for information about his mind frame during this process. The following is an excerpt from his journal:

> I wrote this entry shortly after writing our second paper for the class. After writing this paper I was rushed with emotions towards a single incident that occurred in my senior year in high school . . .
>
> The nerves are raging, mainly in my stomach as the butterflies flutter to no end. Is everything going to be OK? Will everything go as planned? I couldn't stop thinking about what might happen. Images were racing wild as I thought about my teammates going to battle without me. I couldn't comprehend why I had to let them handle it on their own. I had played with them since we were in eighth grade, and when they needed me the most, all I could do was stand and cheer. I hated this feeling of helplessness and wanted to puke after watching them give their best effort only to lose because of my one bad decision. It's three years since this event, and I still have this feeling that everything is going to be OK in some strange way. I probably think about it everyday in some shape or form without knowing it. It was the single worst experience of my life, so far, and to this day I wish I could go back and change things.
>
> Looking back on this journal entry . . . I noticed I wrote down almost exactly what I wrote in my paper. I didn't write about how I felt about this situation now looking back on it, but rather how it made me feel at the time it was happening. This was both surprising and disturbing to me when I read it over. I was surprised because at the time I wrote this entry I wasn't conscious that what I was writing was exactly how I felt about the situation when it happened and not reflecting back on it and how I feel now . . . It was very disturbing to me

for the reason that I had made up in my mind how I felt about this event to make myself feel better. I avoided the simple facts that it was mainly my fault for what I had done.

Connor saw once he looked back at his writing that his emotions were still caught in the past because he had not yet understood what those emotions really were. He was angry at the fan for his lack of understanding, but he was even angrier with himself for letting his team down. But until he wrote the paper and the journal entry and read them over, his emotions were stuck in the past—and every day he reminded himself of the "worst experience of his life." Understanding can bring integration. Once Connor owns his own emotions he is more likely to let the past be the past.

ADELE

Another student presented an interesting challenge. She was already an accomplished writer; however, she was not happy with her work, which, she said, seemed remote to her, not fully present. Adele writes musical theater. She has won writing prizes since childhood, and indeed has already had her plays performed. Yet I understood her response to her work because I found her writing vague at times, disconnected from details. Although my class was an honors class, not a writing class, students wrote for the class, and I read and commented on their work, as I would for any class. I knew Adele has talent: Her mind is crisp and sharp, and she hears language the way a writer does. However, her work lacked the precision of descriptive detail and the thematic unity that comes from such detail. She had not yet found her voice. As she wrote in her journal, "I am ready to turn a corner. I am ready to go beyond." But Adele couldn't do it in this class. The press of the semester was too much upon her, so she decided to take an incomplete, finish the work after intercession, and then take an independent study with me to try to break through her writer's block. And she did:

The water's fresh and everything is blue. The sides of the pool look white and the sky and the trees and wall are all blurry from under the water. Don't breathe in. Aren't you too young to die? It's a hot day outside. The citrus trees are a deep brown and sometimes the bark peels. The leaves dark and light and yellowy green. Some leaves are burnt on the edges. The sun is so powerful. The sun lights up the water too. It lights up the inside of the pool and makes it shine blue. The plastic is soft because underneath in the ground is sand. All around the pool there are mauve stepping squares that burn your feet if you walk on them barefoot. Sometimes it's fun to run really fast and try not to burn your feet. There is sand in between the hot stones and under the pool liner. Dad and Uncle Greg dug the hole for the pool during the hottest day ever. It was 122 degrees. The pool is only partially in-ground. There is a white metal and plastic ladder that comes up from the ground— the big mauve squares, not the stepping-stones—and goes over the side of the pool into the water. The part of the ladder on the outside of the pool can be folded up so that kids don't get in the pool and drown when no one is watching them.

Mom and her friend sit under the trees in cushioned chairs and talk. They smile and laugh and enjoy the shade of the orange trees. I see the rim of the pool. It is white. It holds the pool liner in. Hair swirls around my face, blonde and fine and turning brown underneath but getting bleached blonder on top by the sun. My arms flail and punch up on the green turtle raft. Light green, hard plastic with two big eyes painted on the front. It had a little seat-thing that you stick your legs through kind of like how shopping carts are set up for kids to sit in the front. But this basket was made out of green cloth with yellow trim to match the hard hollow body of the turtle that floated around the pool. It was my brother's pool toy, his floaty. I was not supposed to be in it. I was too big for it. But I fit into the little turtle seat and could kick my legs and paddle all around the pool. I put my hands on the side of the plastic turtle to steer. Really my legs steered. My hands rested on the sides of the turtle. The turtle had big hands and feet that balanced it on the top of the water. I was in the water from my waist down with my arms on the fake turtle shell. Now I was backwards. I was upside down. I was in the water from my head to my waist and my legs were in the air. It's beautiful underwater, looking around, taking everything in. It's scary. I was swimming toward the edge of the pool with the back half of the turtle up in the air so my arms could paddle in front of me, and I flipped the turtle I was not supposed to be wearing. I thought I was going to die. How old was I? Too young to think that I was going to die. I shouldn't have thought that. I did think I was going to die. I was no longer invincible. I was five or six or maybe seven and I knew what dying was going to feel like.

I thought my mom was going to regret this—if I drowned while she was having such a good time with her friend. How come she wasn't watching me? Why couldn't she hear me splashing around and thrashing in the water? Kids always splash water. "Crying wolf" was the essence of swimming. I blamed her. I wasn't even dead and I blamed her for letting me drown. How old was I? I don't remember thinking. I remember thoughts, but no thinking. I should have gone to the ladder, maybe I did, and inched myself up by pulling my body hand over hand up the ladder backwards. Maybe I went to the side of the pool and walked my hands up the side until I pulled up on the edge of the rim. It took so long for me to get to air. Every time I tried to flip myself back over, every time I tried to wiggle my hips out of the turtle, every time I tried to arch my back enough to get my face out of the water even though my legs were stuck up in the air was time I could have been trying to just get air. Go to the ladder and pull myself up. Long drawn-out hours in between every action I made. Thoughts popped up. What should I do? What are my choices? Where is my mom and why doesn't she just save me? She hears me, I know. Maybe she can see me but wants to know if I can figure a way out of this myself. I could just hang here and let myself breathe in the water. I don't want to go to the hospital. Swim in two directions at once while the blood rushes to your head. I'm not supposed to be upside down like this. The blood rushes to my head and my heart pounds as I can feel the veins and blood vessels get heavier and heavier with pressure. I think everything will go dark, like when you stand up too fast or when you are blinded by the sun—that first moment. But I can still see the clear blue. My head gets so heavy I think I should fall out of the turtle from the weight. My legs kick as if swimming in the air will do any good. My fine hair falls across my face and takes away the blue for a moment. Hair is so smooth and graceful in the water. It always moves in slow motion, as one big flowing mass, all together. Paddle towards the sun. Doggie paddle until I reach air then breathe and call out to my mom. Fall back into the water. Try to muster the strength again. I hit the side of the pool. I swim up and grab onto the metal on the side of the pool. The white side edge of the pool that wobbles because it is wider that the rim of the pool and its only screwed in in two places. And I can feel the screws and the raised parts of the metal and it has no temperature. It should be hot. The sun shines down on metal and makes it hot. It makes the stepping-stone hot. The edge has no temperature. I arch my back and pull the top of my head, my forehead, my nose, my mouth, my chin, my neck, my chest out of the water.

Breathe and breathe and breathe and breathe and never take it for granted again. The hot air that smells like orange blossoms and dirt and sand and hot stone and chlorine water and swim suit material. And blink my eyes to get the water off my eyelids so I see when I cry to my mom. Didn't you hear me? No. I flipped over and I couldn't get up. I was kicking. I didn't hear you. I called you. I didn't hear you. I could have drowned. Are you okay now? I feel like crying now. Did I cry then? I got out of the turtle. I never played with the turtle again. Mom got me a towel and I sat wrapped up and shaken on top of the ladder. The ladder folds up so that kids won't get in the pool and drown when no one's watching. What about kids who drown when people are watching? No one held me. I'm sorry I didn't hear you. I just assumed you were playing. I wasn't playing. I got so angry. Did I yell or did I just think about screaming? I wasn't playing I could have died I was calling out for you and you never came. I could have died with you being right there and you would have never known you would have missed it. I am too young to die. I am too young to think about dying. I can't trust you to save me. I can only save myself. Or, God, maybe God saved me. You didn't save me. You weren't there.

I sit in a bright colored towel on a hot Arizona day. The sun shines off the water. The blue, blue water so still now. No little girl splashing in it, sounding like she's playing. Everything outside is just as peaceful as it had been all afternoon. The hot breeze blew through the two orange trees and the bushes that lined the side of the house. Some leaves from the bushes, the high plants, fell into the pool. The plants cast shade on the water but the sun still beat down. And the chairs were still there. One facing the pool, one facing away from it. When I pulled myself up from the water, I saw two women talking under the orange trees. I saw the face of the person facing the pool. Was it my mom or her friend? Who came to help me out of the turtle first? I think I saw my mom; she didn't look worried or concerned. I could have died and she was having a good conversation. I told her I had been stuck and she got up then. She pulled me up over the side of the pool and the edge of the pool, helped pull the turtle off. I kicked it away. Why didn't you swim to the ladder? I don't know. I sat there in the hot afternoon, in the peacefulness that had never left nature. No one was aware that I had seen the world from under the water. The trees were still burnt and the stones were still hot. Nothing had changed. Everything had changed.

I have included this complete piece to demonstrate the stream of consciousness quality to the writing. Adele let the editor/censor voice go quiet. Her narrator's voice is clearly that of the child she had left behind that day, as we can see in the sentence fragments and run-ons that Adele lets slip out in that voice, something we would not see in the writing focused on her adult narrator. I had asked her to write a process essay after she had completed the writing for her independent study, and this is an excerpt from that:

I didn't realize how stuck my writing was until I found myself holding back tears while reading Guy Allen's essay "Language, Power, and Consciousness," in *Writing and Healing*. I sat in my room reading the essay about a professor who encouraged his students to write about personal events—a professor who was genuinely concerned about developing his students as better writers—and I couldn't help thinking, "Why the hell have I never experienced this? I have been in school seventeen years and I can only remember once being asked to write about something that affected me personally." Whatever it was Mr. Allen gave to his students, I wanted that. But I didn't know how to get it. Luckily, I didn't have to search. When Marian suggested I do an independent study with her, I *did* cry (though those tears were mixed in with ones I was shedding over a previous assignment). "My senior year of college, and I am finally going to learn what I've needed to know all along: how to write about what matters to me."

I began the course wanting so badly to be able to automatically open up and let my soul spill out onto the pages I was writing. The process, however, proved incredibly trying. I began with a paper on my literary history. It was boring, to say the least, and sounded like any other academic paper mixed with a little personal short story to add flavor. I didn't like what I wrote. This was not what I was supposed to be getting out of the course. Maybe the next assignment will open me up. The second paper focused on boundaries. My paragraphs were like hills and valleys—just when I'd start to go deep, to the verge of letting go, I'd pull back and tread in the "this is an academic paper so don't bare your soul" mentality. I distanced myself from really feeling what I was writing. After all, I never had to do that before in a paper! I felt the need to write, the desire to write, but I couldn't. I was frustrated. I knew I was getting "there," but that I needed something to push me over the edge. Marian asked me to write about a moment from my childhood . . . When she suggested the topic, the subject immediately popped into my mind; I was going to write about my almost drowning when I was younger. So, a few days later, I sat at my laptop and had the weirdest regression experience of my life. I relived the panic, I saw the water, and I smelled the air. The memories and feeling flowed through my hands and onto the screen. There. That is how writing is supposed to be. It's not telling about the experience. It *is* the experience. This was the first time I wrote about almost drowning and I thought it was going to be about my coming to terms with death and how that made me grow up too fast. Instead, it turned out to be about how I blamed my mom for not saving me and how I realized I was really alone (needed to be independent) in the world. Despite the harsh reality of my paper, I was so excited to discover something about myself through this process! I was also proud, having finally figured out how to write.

After this I tried to write a piece about a place that held significance or was traumatic for me. I began to write about the after-school day care at my elementary school. But I couldn't concentrate. I could not get myself into the same mindset I had when writing about the drowning. I knew I was coming at it . . . not all wrong . . . but not at all right. I ended up writing about how my next-door neighbor was crying to her mom and how little kids cried too. I linked the ideas and that seemed right, but it wasn't what I needed to write . . . and then I hit bottom. After not being allowed (by my RD) to go home for Easter weekend with a friend, I found myself crying for hours and not knowing why I couldn't convince myself of a logical reason to stop. I got so mad at myself for wallowing in self-pity that I decided to do something productive. I sat down to write the Mary paper [a paper about a school friend] and as I was sitting there, hating being alone and hating my writing, I realized that the thing I couldn't describe in Mary was exactly what I was feeling right at that moment—extreme loneliness. Of course, it all makes sense in hindsight! I typed frantically, spilling out whatever came to mind. I typed eleven pages in a daze of ecstasy (from solving the Mary riddle) and sorrow (from still feeling lonely).

Once again, I experienced writing as it should be. If I hadn't been prompted to write, if I hadn't been encouraged to write about myself, and if I hadn't believed that Marian truly cared about what I felt and that I become a better writer through my personal experiences, I would never have been able to unleash that pent up frustration. I would never have discovered how to write so that the reader can live through an experience with me (the narrator). I began this course as a good writer and, I'll admit, I had been in that intense "writing mode" a few times before. But I never wrote about myself; I always wrote through characters I invented for plays. Now I know how to write about me. I know how to access things I have kept hidden, afraid to share, and unable to share if I had wanted to. I had to take steps. I had to start with the boring paper. I had to struggle and be frustrated. And I had to have that epiphany when everything miraculously made sense. I had to learn how to write from my soul, not just from my head. I needed that so much. Why? Because I am a writer, and I had forgotten how to write. I still have a long way to go in my journey as a writer, but I am leaps and bounds ahead of where I was a few months ago. I was at a place where I cried over other people's amazing writing experiences. Now I've had my own experiences, and I never want go back—I don't think it possible to go back to where I was before. I finally got unstuck.

All Adele needed was permission to allow herself to feel, to connect her emotions to her work. She had so clearly absorbed the archetype of the independent writer/observer that was set up from the time she nearly died at five that she left out the source of her creativity—her passion and whatever generated it. Once she had that permission she could take herself where she needed to go, and in the process transformed both her life and her art. She is now able to construct a voice that can both engage fully and create the proper distance: As the personal essayist Vivian Gornick describes in an article in the *Chronicle of Higher Education*, "What I didn't see, and that for a long while, was that this point of view could only emerge from a narrator who was me and at the same time not me" (B9). The key to this process is finding the subject—the story, as Gornick calls it. Gornick argues that the situation of an essay is the plot, the "what happens," but the story itself is the theme, what I call the "so what factor." As she describes it, "The situation is the context or circumstance, sometimes the plot; the story is the emotional experience that preoccupies the writer" (B7). This theme, the core of the piece, is virtually never immediately apparent to writers. Rarely does a personal essayist begin a piece saying, "I'm going to write an essay about youthful isolation, or appearance versus reality, or the finality of death." Indeed, if he did, the piece would probably lack the rootedness in life moments that is the hallmark of the personal essay. Writing is a recursive act: As we write, we change, and so changes our text. Gornick tells the story of J. R. Ackerley, author of *My Father and Myself*, a memoir. The book is only a little over two hundred pages, but it took Ackerley more than thirty years to tell it because he thought all he had to do was put together the sequence of events, and the book would fall into place: "But nothing fell into place. After a while he thought, I'm not describing a presence, I'm describing an absence. This is the tale of an unlived relationship. Who was he? Who was I? Why did we keep missing each other? After another while he realized, I always thought my father didn't want to know me. Now I see that I didn't want to know him. And then he realized, it's not him I haven't wanted to know, it's myself" (B8).

How to Proceed

It takes time and a commitment to the writing process to find our subject, story, theme, and create the voice to tell it. And the process is the product; that is, the revision process is what allows us to find the story. The award-winning fantasy and science fiction novelist Ursula K. Le Guin writes, "It doesn't seem right or wise to revise an old text severely, as if trying to obliterate it, hiding the evidence that one had to go there to get here. It is rather in the feminist mode to let one's changes of mind, and the processes of change, stand as evidence" (7). This seldom happens with one draft, as was apparent with Lauren's and Adele's work. What can we do as writers and as teachers to facilitate this process? Over the years most writing teachers have developed techniques that enable writers to engage more fully in the writing process. I organize all our formal essays around free-writing prompts, exercises that enable us to release what wants to be said. All of us in the profession are indebted to Peter Elbow for demonstrating the power of such free-writes in virtually any writing setting. For me as a teacher the following are the key elements that we look for.

Writers must locate the moments that speak to them. This is not always easy. Moments are made up of separate images layered together. Any one of those images might be a key but might also be hidden within other moments. So I teach my students a process for visualizing a scene. We begin with a usually innocuous task: In class we all close our eyes, get relaxed and I ask them to visualize their childhood bedroom. What do they see when they look at it in their mind's eye? Where is the light coming from? What is under their bare feet on the floor—wood, carpet, something else? Once they are fully present, I ask them to find an object they cared about when they were children and write about that object and how they used it. This assignment begins the process of finding images that matter and turning them into words. We used this image-finding technique to good effect when Tina, the young woman who wanted to write about her grandmother, couldn't remember anything. As she recorded later, everything just "appeared" in front of her. If we visualize and list images instead of trying to write narrative when we first begin this process, we are more likely to connect with our lived experience. I provide prompts for all the general topics students write about. For example, for the "place" topic, I give them general instructions and the following list of prompts, from which they choose one or more as brainstorming exercises:

1. Write about a place where you felt imprisoned. Why did you feel imprisoned? What did those feelings say about you then? How do you feel about the place now? What did you learn about yourself from the experience?

2. Write about a place that you escaped to, a place that you went to hide from or get away from life's pains and/or injustices. Let us see it, smell it, feel it as you did. You may begin with a moment when you needed to escape, a specific moment.

3. Write about a place that influenced you to be foolish, silly, or carefree. Why did you do what you did? What does your action say about you, about your life? What effect did your action have on another person, if someone else was involved? What did you learn about yourself?

4. Write about your place of work. This job could be paid or unpaid, present or past. How does/did the place affect your mood, your personality, your maturity?

5. Write about a place you loved as a child or thought was impressive or comforting or safe. How do you feel about that place now? If a difference exists, why does it exist? What has changed?

6. Write about a place you loved or hated as a child. Describe it clearly. Why did you love or hate it? How do you feel about that place now?

7. Write a list of pictures you see when I say the word "home."

8. Many students like to write about their grandparents or their grandparents' houses. yet find it hard to remember details. If you would like to remember more about this part of your life, close your eyes and try to recall a specific object that your grandparent used, or an object you associate with that person or that house—a rolling pin, a piece of jewelry, a tool, a chair. It can be a smell or an article of clothing—anything to get you back to the moments in that house. Try to imagine what one room in your grandparents' house looked like. Is there an overstuffed chair, a fireplace, wood floors, carpet, or linoleum? What room do you associate with your grandparent? What activities do you "see" him or her doing?

A general way to proceed: When recalling a place, close your eyes and try to see the place in front of you. Once you can be there in your mind's eye, pick ten objects you see and list them, providing details so that you help us to see them. too. And don't simply label them—"tree, flower, and brown house"—but shade them in: "the massive weeping willow with the swing rope that hung over our spring-fed pond." Create the following lists: what you saw, heard, touched, smelled, tasted there, including snippets of conversations you heard there, the textures you felt or saw (for example, the splintered wood railing, your mother's polished fingernails with garden dirt under them), and the smells and tastes you remember. Simply list the images first; then begin your description.

Exercises for a Person:

1. Write about a person who frightened you, hurt you, intimidated you, or forced or persuaded you to do something you didn't want to do. Describe the situation by showing a scene where the conflict took place.

2. Write about someone who taught you something important about life. It could be something you learned from a painful experience or a happy one.

3. Write about someone who helped you once when you needed

it. What did the person do? How did you react to it? How did this change you?

4. Write about the oddest person you ever met. What made this person so strange? Would you consider this person strange today? What does this say about you?

As you write about this person, take into consideration the following: specific behaviors and mannerisms, clothing, living arrangements, etc. You must also look at how this person interacts with you and others and what effect the person has had on you. Be sure to show this with specific moments that show behavior. You may want to begin by closing your eyes and remembering the person. List images of that person—for example, a flour-coated rolling pin in a wrinkled hand, thinning straight black hair lying limply on top of an egg-shaped head, a heavy-linked gold chain hanging from a fleshy neck, wrinkled crooked fingers with a wedding ring twirling around the finger.

These exercises are not the topics for their formal papers, but they help jumpstart the writing process, and we do them frequently in class. Students freely select what they want to write about, but I have found that 75 percent of my students write about painful rather than joyful topics. Given what we know about trauma and its aftermath, this is, of course no surprise. We illustrate this tendency with an exercise: I ask my students to close their eyes and imagine a happy time, some moment when they were very happy; they then write for ten minutes on that moment. Then I ask them to close their eyes and visualize a sad moment and to write for ten minutes on that. They can write whatever they want because I tell them they will not have to share their work with anyone. When they are done, I ask them how many found the happy moment easier to write about and how many found the sad moment easier to write about. Usually about two-thirds of the students find the sad moment easier to write about. This opens up a conversation about how we process painful memories versus happy ones.

While extreme joy can be remembered as clearly as extreme pain, our traumatic experiences are usually the ones we have not integrated into our lives, isolating them into the nonverbal parts of the brain. The images from those experiences pop in because they are the least connected to a narrative that fits with the rest of our lives. For example, one student, Meg, wrote her first formal essay on an argument her mother and aunt had. While the paper was well written and inventive, it lacked a core that makes personal essays speak to others. It offered no details that create immediacy and verisimilitude. I wasn't sure why Meg was connected to this topic, why she wrote the paper. As Meg and I talked about the paper, I told her that I felt she had told her mother's story, not her own. She thought for a moment, then said, "I know what I really want to write about. You gave us a class exercise to write about two moments in our lives, a happy one and a sad one. I'd like to write about the sad one. It's about my dad helping me with math, but I'm afraid to write about it because it will be depressing. He was awful when he helped me learn math." I suggested, "No, Meg, now this is depressing. After you write about it, it will just be sad." She smiled, nodded her head and turned in the following paper, a universe away from the first attempt:

> I take small steps out of my room of fish tank mural and Apple computer and clothes hamper and paint pens and green almanac and blue globe and *Little Women* and rainbow stationery and corduroys and turtlenecks and acrylic sweaters and size 10 Carter's and Pine Bros. cherry cough drops. I'm new to this school and this state and thirteen years old and school newspaper founder and editor, and too short hair, and thick glasses and school lunch and principal's favorite and bussers and walkers and morning announcements and gym and was there recess? and Space Shuttle memorial and *Romeo and Juliet* and David Bowie and writing short stories with heroines named Audrey and Kate Wing and Stephanie Lerner who were my only two friends and no bra and no breasts and no hips and no period and no boyfriend and needing to be out of Owen Brown Middle School before I had begun and Suzi Lobbin, Sun—In streaky hair and popular whose sole purpose on this earth was to torture, ridicule, and berate me, yet I was mature and well-adjusted and highest reading group and gifted and talented and high potential and intelligent and task commitment and works well with others and a pleasure to have in class.
>
> And failing Algebra One.
>
> There is acid swishing about in my stomach as I walk out of my bedroom onto the brassy orange carpet that lines the hall. Angry red algebra book open to the homework, notebook open too. My tall girl's body in a nightgown, flannel with puffy sleeves, lavender floral pattern that my mother can't touch because it tears at the dry skin of

her fingertips in winter. Book and notebook against chest, breathing strained, I keep swallowing and composing sentences in my head. I make my way through yellow linoleum kitchen and orange dining room . . .

I am headed to the den, where my father sits, with the *Wall Street Journal* and a TV sitcom blaring.

"Dad, kenyou help me with this?" indicating the book, I ask in a voice softer and higher than my own.

"Aaaheee," he replies exasperatedly. "Jesus Christ, Meg, you might want to think about this before the last minute." Acidic sarcasm raises the inflection and with it his dense, wiry eyebrows.

"It's not the last minute, Dad. I've been doing it in my room, there's just so much stuff I don't get. Couldja help me?"

"Yeah," he says, brows furrowed. He crumples the newspaper down on his lap. I walk to the couch to sit next to him. "What is it? Gimme," reaching for the red book. My handwriting is precise. My numbers are well formed and the problem headings lettered beautifully. "Meg, how many times do I have to tell you? You HAVE TO WRITE DOWN EVERY STEP."

And I wonder, is this a rhetorical question? If forced to answer I fear the number would be quite large.

"Dad, I don't know what that means, write down every step. What do you mean?"

"YOU'VE GOT TO WRITE EVERYTHING DOWN! YOU CAN'T LEAVE ANY STEPS OUT! YOU HAVE TO WRITE DOWN EVERY STEP, GODAMMIT."

This is spoken fortissimo. Dad and I have an understanding that the more decibels he employs, the more clear these mathematical concepts will become. This system, thus far, has been somewhat unsuccessful, but neither of us has given up yet.

The lesson continues with Dad doing an example problem, muttering about "new math" and procrastination, then instructing me to do the next problem while he turns back to the regularly scheduled programming. I start to work the equation, hunched over my flannel lap, stingy tears forming in my eyes, heat crawling up my back, my breath caught. I get stuck, don't understand, how did he get from here to there? Why do I have to be in smart math? Why do I always leave the den crying, nose running, my algebra understanding still minuscule?"

My father is a chemical engineer for a steel manufacturer. He earned two degrees in college, one in chemical engineering, the other in metallurgy. He's a member of MENSA. He reads a lot of science fiction books, the kind that feature scantily clad, buxom women on the covers. He knows the scientific name of nearly every growing thing. He hybridizes daylilies and fashions ornate walking sticks from branches of trees in the neighborhood. He has a neon-colored Super-Soaker water gun which he purchased at KIDS "R" US so he can terrorize the neighborhood kids. Monsters, as he calls them. He snacks on uncooked spaghetti. He drinks a lot of wine and would smoke cigars in the house if my mother would let him. I don't know much else about him except that he yells, he's impatient, he says the wrong things, he's got an explosive temper, he makes broad judgments and character assassinations not based in truth, he's got a fairly closed mind, he's a horrible algebra tutor, he's cynical, thinks everything's a fraud, and he gets a lot of speeding tickets.

I did indeed fail algebra one that year. It was probably the best thing. I took it again my freshman year with the "average" kids and did fine. Suzi Lobbin was in my class. I think it was the next year that she got pregnant and stopped attending school.

I never asked my dad for help with math again. I never much asked for anything from him after my thirteenth year. (Qtd. in Anderson and MacCurdy 186–87)

Art cannot change the past. It does not obliterate the pain of deeply flawed parenting or make us forget our most difficult moments. But it can help create distance and clarity, and these two enable us to move beyond our traumas into the larger world. "Only the very greatest art," wrote the novelist Iris Murdoch, "invigorates without consoling" (qtd. in Raab 13). The invigoration comes from the knowledge that we are more than our traumas; art helps us join the rest of humanity in all its wounded glory. When Robert Frost was asked by an interviewer why he believed in education he replied, "You know, it lifts sorrow and trouble to a higher plane of regard. I don't say it gets over it, or makes any difference in it. It lifts it to a higher plane of regard" (qtd. in Raab 13). Laurence Raab wrote in an article in the *Writer's Chronicle,* "Art changes the way we look at the world. It doesn't tell us what to think so much as it gives us the means to think more clearly" (13). In the process of writing and reading again what we have written, and revising again, we revise our language and our lives.

Artists know that pain can be transmuted through their art. Picasso's *Guernica*, Maya Angelou's *I Know Why the Caged Bird Sings*, and much of Emily Dickinson's poetry remind us that grief is inevitable but can lead to a deeper understanding of what it means to be human. In a section of *I Know Why the Caged Bird Sings* Maya Angelou writes of a moment in her graduation from public school when the students' accomplishments meant nothing, when the white monolith appeared too heavy to move. The valedictorian of her high school began singing what in 1940 was called the Negro National Anthem:

> Lift every voice and sing,
> Till earth and heaven ring
> Ring with the harmonies of Liberty . . .
> We have come over a way that with tears has been watered,
> We have come, treading our path through the blood of the
>   slaughtered.

After the entire audience spontaneously sang this song, Angelou records, "We were on top again. As always, again. We survived. The depths had been icy and dark, but now a bright sun spoke to our souls . . . Oh, Black known and un-known poets, how often have your auctioned pains sustained us? Who will compute the lonely nights made less lonely by your songs or the empty pots made less tragic by your tales? . . . We survive in exact relationship to the dedication of our poets (include preachers, musicians, and blues singers)" (900).

Adele survived, climbed up through the dark water to reach the sun; Lau-ren discovered her own feelings and in the process created a more honest re-lationship with herself and her family; Melissa's re-visioning of her experience enabled her to fall asleep at night; Connor discovered that his anger and shame made his past his present. Writing was the vehicle for these young people to find their own voices as writers and in the process make these dis-coveries—and this work occurred within the context of the academic com-munity. Telling our stories links us to ourselves and to each other. As Dorothy

Allison wrote in *Two or Three Things I Know for Sure* (72): "Two or three things I know, two or three things I know for sure, and one of them is that to go on living I have to tell stories, that stories are the one sure way I know to touch the heart and change the world"—and if we are fortunate, to change ourselves in the process.

CHAPTER 3

Savior or Shadow

Transformation in Sexual Abuse Narratives

The disobedient writer is no longer a shadow on the text, but rather makes the text a shadow of her own.

NANCY WALKER

THOSE OF US whose professional lives are defined by the classroom need to be aware that every student we address has probably borne witness to some difficult moments that can affect learning. The more violent and threatening our culture becomes, the more we need to acknowledge the effects of trauma on our students. In their book *Testimony* Shoshana Felman and Dori Laub argue that personal and cultural recovery from trauma requires a conversation between the victim and a witness, that indeed the witness is an utter necessity to complete the cycle of truth-telling. Providing opportunities for writers to bring to the surface difficult experiences can result in teachers and fellow students becoming witnesses to the telling of those experiences, which presents challenges and opportunities, particularly with sexual abuse narratives.

For many of us in the writing classroom a decision to allow or not allow personal material is moot. In a class such as Personal Essay, students will include traumatic material whether or not I ask them to describe difficult experiences. Sexual abuse narratives, in particular, are often offered in the writing class no matter what the assignment, given the unfortunate frequency of such abuse. However, the tone and style of these essays is often initially driven by the affect the writer brings to the topic. Often that tone is flat, without emotion, given the many years the writer has had to bury her topic. This presents challenges for peer readers and teachers: How should we respond when a writer presents horrific stories of abuse with no apparent awareness of their enormity? If we ignore the flat tone, are we being responsible to the writer, since that tone often cuts out the reader from the essay? If we comment on the tone, a key element in the personal essay, are we stepping into difficult territory? What is the role of peer editors in this process? What happens when they offer their honest responses to a text? What tools do we have to enable the student to come to this material in his own time, in his own way, without being driven by any external expectations? How can this be accomplished safely, allowing the writer to control the process?

For some writers, particularly victims of incest or on-going abuse, the methods we have discussed in the previous chapters—focusing on the traumatic images and describing them, then constructing a narrative using them—can be too difficult, perhaps even too overwhelming to approach initially. In such cases writers may choose to approach their stories obliquely rather than directly. One method is to incorporate archetypal images into those narratives, sometimes unconsciously. When personal images are too threatening to be easily assimilated into consciousness, archetypal images can be used to locate and address personal traumatic images and connect them to childhood literary images. Archetypes provide a language code with which to translate the most intimate, frightening images into narratives that can exist outside the psyche of the writer. If these narratives are shared with others, the presence of a witness shifts the picture, and the archetype with it.

Some genres lend themselves quite easily to archetypal material—science fiction and fantasy writing, for example. The personal essay provides opportunities for a more unconscious but no less powerful use of archetypal images. Personal essay writers must learn to create a narrator's voice that can provide both verisimilitude and identification for the reader, yet allow the author to take a journey into imagistic, archetypal territory deep within.

Sexual abuse survivors have additional challenges: Addressing their inner worlds means confronting a perpetrator who in their minds may still have power over them—a fearsome shadow that can cause everything from writer's block to personality changes. Marie-Louise von Franz in her classic study *Shadow and Evil in Fairy Tales* defines the shadow as simply a "mythological name for all that within me I cannot directly know" (5). Von Franz cites Carl Jung, who argued that the worst sin is not becoming conscious when one has the possibility of doing so (177). When one does not live up to this inner possibility, then this inner psychic energy can turn destructive—"Those to whom evil is done do evil in return," in the now oft-quoted lines of W. H. Auden. Ursula LeGuin argued that "a man who will not confront and accept his shadow is a lost soul . . . If the artist tries to ignore evil, he will never enter into the House of Light (52). While we tend to think of the shadow as an evil force, it actually is a collection of unconscious personal and collective elements. Allowing these elements into the conscious mind requires great courage because we cannot know how our consciousness will accept what it has historically hidden. We must assimilate the shadow into our consciousness, not our consciousness into the shadow. The shadow is a consistent aid but a dangerous master. The method of expressing one's shadow is extremely important, as simple projection can continue to hide the truth. Writers of sexual abuse narratives are often drawn to the transformative power of archetypes in fairy tales and myths, particularly when those images connect with autobiographical ones.

One young woman writer, Kirsten, took Women and Writing with me, a creative writing class in which writers can produce personal essays, poetry, and/or fiction. Kirsten, wrote several stories about a goddess figure who was blonde, beautiful, and omnipotent—utterly impervious to threats of any kind—but the character had no humanity, and the stories lacked depth. The goddess was a kind of composite of Hera, Diana, and Madonna: a sexy, maternal huntress. When I asked what drew her to this archetype and pointed out to her that the stories seemed removed from her, she stared at me, nodded her head, and said she would rethink the assignment. She came back the next day with a powerful poem about a rape, her own rape, and said, "This is what this goddess was protecting me from."

Kirsten decided to read this piece to the class, whereupon her entire demeanor changed. She looked up and out to the other students, not down to her feet as she had been doing. This archetype of protection was necessary for Kirsten to contain her trauma. The goddess in her text was blonde and powerful; Kirsten was blonde and rather frail. The goddess was fearless and omnipotent; Kirsten was vulnerable and afraid. But once Kirsten took charge of her past and addressed it directly, she brought that archetype into her consciousness and got in touch with her own anger and strength. In order to do this she had to connect the images that she had been avoiding to the emotions they called up. Once she did this, she could look out at the class and read her poem, which was a clear, focused, and detail-driven description of her experience. In addition, sharing her piece openly seemed to strengthen her by validating her experience. She had seventeen witnesses to what had previously been locked inside a darkened past. Her earlier writing had been vague, full of clichés, and without the details that draw the reader into a story. Once she consciously connected her own experience to her creative life, her writing evidenced a power, economy, and descriptive focus previously lacking—a clear demonstration of the efficacy of writing our lives rather than having our lives write us.

A crucial part of this process is the reaction of the teacher and the other students. We must listen carefully and respond honestly to the text, both emotionally and intellectually. As I have said before, the first necessity is to honor the fact that the writer chose to produce this text. This class of seventeen found this easy to do, partly because we were all women and had developed into a close community, but also because we discovered from this one student's bravery that nine of the seventeen women had been victims of sexual abuse at some point in their lives. The writer could see immediately from the level of the conversation that she was not alone, both in the compassion presented to her and in the identification of those nine women. The presence of men in a class, by the way, does not render this kind of response impossible, since this has happened in mixed classes as well. (And although it is less frequent, I have also received essays from men on the subject of their sexual abuse.) The key is the kind of modeling the teacher presents to the class. This is particularly important during one-on-one peer editing. Once the humanity of the writers is acknowledged, we can go on to the critique of the text.

Kirsten, in choosing the Amazon for her persona, projected her shadow into her story. In so doing she could not make conscious the figure of power in her own psyche. This became particularly clear from the character of that Amazon. She was not particularized, had no clear character details, was not a personality with archetypal elements, but was simply a force, a concept. She functioned as a shield to protect the writer from her own truth. Kirsten could not incorporate the archetype's strength into herself until she could put that archetype down and look at what it protected her from. She had begun to make the unconscious conscious, and her writing as well as her psyche grew in strength and power. When teachers encourage students to gain access to the energy that comes from their lived experience, the resultant truth-telling can take a piece of writing from cliché to authenticity, from projection to inner ownership.

Telling the truth, however, is difficult in our culture, particularly for marginalized people, as most survivors at times feel they are. Jill Johnston describes autobiography as a deliberate creation of a self: "Of course when we write the life, we are making it up (not the facts but the ways of seeing and organizing them), and this is a political act of self-recognition" (29). The emergence of autobiographical stories constitutes an antidote to the culturally prescribed concepts of the lives of marginalized people. As such, it can be seen as a rebellious act. Adrienne Rich has said that writing is re-imagining our lives. To her it is an act of re-visioning, "of looking back, of seeing with fresh eyes, of entering an old text from a new critical direction . . ." And for women it is "more than a chapter in cultural history: It is an act of survival" (1137). Janet Todd discusses women writing in the late seventeenth century, when it would have been a subversive act: "The writing lady could be equated with the Amazon, the whore, or the witch, indulging in improper verbal freedom as well as or in place of a sexual one" (33). My student used the archetype of the Amazon to protect her precisely because the Amazon could fight back when Kirsten felt she could not. But she had to tell her story before she could become the Amazon, that is, incorporate the Amazon into her conscious mind. For her, silence equaled powerlessness; story telling equaled power. Nancy A. Walker, in *The Disobedient Writer: Women and Narrative Tradition*, argues that for women writing has been an act of disobedience against a culture that prescribes sex roles, against a literary history that continues to devalue women's part in the formation of that history: "Women's relation to language, literature, education, and cultural traditions has been made problematic and complex by centuries of unequal access to power and agency within these systems. For women who are members of ethnic and racial minorities the distance from the center of these cultural systems has been exponentially greater" (2). Writing can be an act of power, a way to break the destructive silence that perpetuates oppression.

It takes great courage to violate the culturally pervasive rule for silence, but this courage is necessary for both creative and personal growth. When a writer chooses to break a silence, it is crucial for others to be ready to hear the story. The responses of peers and the teacher are critical in helping the writer to move forward. As mentioned earlier, when chosen with conscious intent, archetypes that connect a literary image with a traumatic one can give writers the framework to speak the unspeakable. I would like here to tell the story of one student I will call Sarah, the child of a Japanese mother and a Haitian father, who created such a framework in her personal essays. Sarah's family dynamic discouraged strong action on the part of women and allowed for the abusive behavior of men. In the beginning of the course, Sarah's writing showed little emotional response to her lived experiences. Indeed, one could say that she demonstrated quite clearly the kind of emotional dissociation that can occur as a result of trauma. Sarah wrote five papers in this course. Her first paper, titled "I Could Have Screamed but I Was Thinking," detailed instances of sexual abuse perpetrated by her father's friend when Sarah was thirteen. Yet the essay demonstrated no anger in tone, no connection with the young girl who is experiencing these horrors. Instead, it showed, in the second draft, such a puzzlement that Ange, Sarah's class editor and reader of the first draft of her paper, could become angry at hearing this story while Sarah herself could not—and Ange's anger was the beginning of change for Sarah:

> Ange was yelling. I knew she was not mad at the girl I was in my tale but at the woman I am now, the woman who will not feel anger, the woman who accepts his actions, the woman who makes excuses for him. Mr. ___ she does not pretend to like. Though she has never met him or talked to him, she hates him. I never would have guessed that the incident would affect her like it did because it never was that big a deal to me, then or now.
>
> As I watch him across the dinner table, I notice that he is getting redder with every glass of scotch that he consumes. It is probably because of his pale white skin . . . Is he talking about her again? The poor man. "My wife hates me, and except for the occasional blow-job, I get nothing from her." I turn my head quickly toward my food. My father's ulcers will reappear if he thinks I understand . . . I do not think my mother likes the table conversation . . . "Why don't we all go to bed now, it's getting late." Ma must be pretty mad because she usually does not tell anyone to go to bed. I guess we are all being punished.
>
> Mr. ___ is now in front of me as he makes his way toward the bedroom. He is unbelievably skinny, so skinny his legs look stiff and inflexible as he walks . . . His big nose dominates his face, his rabbit teeth move together and then apart as he talks to Ma . . . His greasy hair is dirty blond and he is wearing the same blue pants he always wears. Either he is a dirty man or an unimaginative shopper . . . Poor, poor man.
>
> All the lights are out. If I am really quiet, I can creep past my parents' room and watch television in the living room. It is not difficult. I

have a lot of practice. I can barely see the TV at the other end of the room. All the cushions spread around the room look the same color in the dark . . . Shit, there's someone else in the room. It's probably Daddy, and I guess I'm in for a beating. He is coming towards me and . . . Oh, it's only Mr. ___, and he can't even hit me. He is whispering something to me: "Are you looking for me?" I wonder why he's asking. If I was looking for him I would have looked in the bedroom he is sleeping in. He comes towards me and pulls me down onto the carpet with him. He takes my left hand and lays it on his tummy. "If my wife knew you were touching me, she would leave me and my two children would grow up without me. Imagine life without your father." I wish I could just watch television. "Feel what you do to me." His hand is so big, it engulfs mine. Where his hand goes, mine goes . . .

After she describes his hand taking over hers and touching him sexually, Sarah writes:

Life is so harsh; Ma says so all the time. But the incident is not over yet. Maybe if I ask, he'll let me watch television. Maybe he'll just get mad if I interrupt him. My hand is being moved slowly up and down his hairy legs . . . Maybe I can watch television while he moves my hand. But he sets my hand free. I guess he is done. No, I guessed wrong. He is touching *me* now.

Then the narrative breaks off with the unspeakable. The last paragraph reads:

There is no end to this tale. Until Ange, there was no tale. No trauma, no pain, no hurt. It is hard to control the things that people do to us, but we can control the way we react and the way we let it affect us. Physically, it does not matter what they do to me. They can beat me, touch me, and call me names, but they can't break me. I think Mr. ___ he never once pretended to care for me. He never confused me emotionally and so he never broke me (something I can't say about my daddy). That's all that really matters. I take care of me. It does feel good to have someone on my side though. Yell, Ange, YELL. Feel. I can't.

When I asked Sarah how she felt about writing this, she said fine. No problem. The incident was "no big deal." She said she felt little about it. Her affective stance throughout the course was curious. She often liked to speak of being beaten and abused by her father but always spoke of it nonchalantly, as if it meant nothing, had no impact on her. It appeared that she had shut herself down in order to cope, had dissociated her body and psyche to survive. As she wrote, "Without Ange there was no tale." Sarah's pain was so invisible, even to herself, that she could not recognize that she had a story until she could begin to see this through Ange's eyes. The reader/witness is indispensable to the writing/healing process. Through the essay, the writer is allowing the peer reader to bear witness to the event, and this may be the first time this has been permitted. Ange needed to react honestly, to allow herself to get angry, in order to demonstrate to Sarah another way to respond to this horrific story. The witness provides a safe mirror in which the survivor can see herself and her responses. "The testimony to the trauma thus includes its hearer . . . the listener to the trauma comes to be a participant and co-owner of the traumatic event: Through his listening, he comes to partially experience trauma in himself" (57), as Laub points out in *Testimony*. It is therefore important when running writing workshops to model workshop techniques with our students, to enable them to respond honestly but without judgments, as was discussed in chapter 2.

Sarah's emotional blankness, the numbing of feelings, is characteristic of child sexual abuse. Indeed, dissociation is common among child sexual abuse survivors. According to Jennifer Freyd in *Betrayal Trauma*, the closer the relationship between the child and the abuser, the more disconnected the child will likely be from her emotions. The child has difficulty resisting one with authority over her, especially if the abuser is a caregiver or linked in some important way to the caregiver. Jennifer Freyd offers the words of Lana Lawrence, who was sexually, emotionally, and physically abused by her father: "On an intellectual level, I knew that I had been a victim of incest, along with physical and emotional abuse . . . On an emotional level, I felt numb. When talking about my experiences, it was as though I were speaking about someone totally separate from myself" (Freyd 128). This was the affect I found in Sarah's first paper. She demonstrated a conscious awareness of her abuse but no overt emotional response to it. Her unconscious was crowded with conflicting responses, and I wondered how long it would take her to release some of its contents and what form she would choose for that release. She continued to work only with Ange as her peer editor, and in the process she developed a bond that enabled her to see herself through another's eyes.

She went on to write a couple of essays describing her attachment to her child self. One, "There Is A Child Inside, There Always Was," demonstrates from its title that this is a girl who had to grow up too soon and in the process froze parts of her child self, the parts described as loving lollipops and stuffed animals, monkey bars and chewing gum. As Sarah wrote in her essay, "This is a story about a young woman who cannot grow up. It is not time for her to be an adult. She has never had time to be a child. No one read stories to her or hugged her at night when she was scared of monsters in the room. She can never be a child again, but she can read her own fairy tales, watch cartoons and giggle uncontrollably." Sarah's text suggests that she has begun the process of circling back into her unconscious and gently asking it what it needs to come out. But she was not yet ready to "dive into the wreck," as Adrienne Rich puts it. Sarah wrote concerning this piece, "This essay is too safe . . . There was a lot more I didn't write." Sarah's experience is not unusual. Many times students circle around important topics for a while before encountering them fully. If writing teachers provide opportunities to re-write assignments or to return to topics that seem significant, both aesthetic and therapeutic benefits can result.

The fourth essay assignment for my students is to write on some aspect of their own bodies that they like or do not like, or some time their bodies let them down or enabled them to do something wonderful, or a time when their bodies were challenged, or ill, or injured. Sarah's paper called "My Body and I" offered a quotation from Jean Morgan as an epigraph: "In the story I have a protective feeling for my father, which is, of course, screwy as hell . . . I have great fear of the story . . . My relationship with my parents is very fine these days, and I fear that someday, sometime, they will come across it. I still want to protect them." Sarah wrote in the first paragraph of her essay:

> When I glanced at this paragraph I thought it had been written by me. Someone had taken my thoughts and put them down on paper when I could not . . . Finally, I know of at least one person who knows my feelings of confusion. My body. I always think of me and my body as two separate beings. My body went though experiences that I . . . do not think my mind was strong enough to handle. I admire my body. The events that my body has endured over the years would have killed

me. The body has no memory. It heals and gets stronger. My mind once tried to dominate my body. I would not allow food into my mouth. I starved myself and finally made it to the hospital . . . Eventually my body won. It had to eat. I think that my body just had a greater will to live than I did then. The beatings were often and some made more of an impact in my life than others.

Sarah then described a severe beating given her by her father and a second incident when she fought back. The essay ends with this: "It is not a story with a great happy ending. We all have our ghosts to deal with . . . I keep anger in check and my whole family pretends it was all a bad dream." Sarah wrote about this paper, "This was difficult for me to write about, though I do not know why. I considered it to be one of the less disturbing incidents, but it proved to be difficult. I did not want to recall the events. I did not want to remember details. Most of all it just kind of reminds me that I wasn't a total loser and once in a while I did stand up for myself. I guess that's a good thing. I do not think that the time has come for me to think of the events as having happened to me, the person I am today, maybe sometime in the future. This paper disturbs me."

Sarah freely chose this topic, as she did all of them, which indicates that she was beginning to allow her emotional responses to her life to gain sway over her desire to protect her family—and herself—from the truth. In order to keep silence she needed to bury the past, something that she could no longer manage. By recognizing that the paper disturbs her, that she was not yet ready to tackle the full brunt of her feelings, she was allowing for the possibility of doing exactly that in the future.

Sarah was becoming more aware of her own writing process. I knew her last essays would be close to the bone and looked forward to them with a certain amount of trepidation yet anticipated relief for her. What I had not anticipated was the archetypal vehicle Sarah would use to offer her story a context that made it bearable for her to tell: the fairy tale archetype of the imprisoned girl:

My World In Here
Did you ever hear of the girl who was in jail, but had no jailer?

I am Rapunzel. I live in a tower with Daddy. The blue-green walls keep me in and everyone out. This Rapunzel has no prince. She has no hair. If a prince tries to climb into this tower, he'll lose a lot more than his sight. I will lose a lot more than my heart. I am not a fairy tale Rapunzel. I am a real one. This Rapunzel does not want to escape, escape from the one who loves me? But I am ready to face the world. I need no money. I have something between my legs that men want—young ones, middle-aged ones, and old ones. This Rapunzel knows about oral sex, anal sex, kinky sex, birth control, the hard penis, the hungry penis, the angry penis and positions unthinkable.

Blue-green walls. All around me the world is a mess. My mess. There is no one here but me . . . It is my first week in hibernation, and I look forward to the next few weeks. I know that I will not be allowed to leave my room. The grills on the windows make it impossible for me to leave that way, if I even wanted to . . . I am a very desirable fourteen year old. Most of the men that pass through want me. Most seem to take what they want. But I hate my father the most . . . I know I should not hate. It makes my face all ugly, and I could get kicked for that. I think that it is hard to love and easy to be loved. Everyone says they love me; that is why they beat me, touch me, and play with my mind until I can do nothing but gaze out of the window rocking myself from side to side . . . I think I should tell all the wives, including my mother, what is going on. If they cannot control their husbands they should at least provide them with entertainment at home. If that cannot be arranged, I think I should be getting paid for my services. Maybe I'll demand that next time. The worst that can happen is that I will be kicked, punched, and thrown against the walls . . .

I'm in my third week of hibernation now, and I am glad I had the time off to put things into perspective. Sometimes I am so unappreciative and uncaring. To think that I was actually thinking of telling the wives. What about their children? They would be left without a father . . . They are all good people inside; I just bring out the worst in them with my eyes and clothes. When Mr. Smith cried in my arms after a "session" I saw a caring and human side of him . . . I'm sure my hibernation is almost over and my father will come and get me soon. I have learned a good lesson while in here. The hard part is to remember it when I am out there again . . . I'm glad that the anger has left me. Hate is unhealthy. It pollutes my mind and gets me into trouble. Life is just the way it is. Harsh. If you can find love and comfort like I do with my father, you should cherish it. One thought lingers—I really do think I should be getting paid. It is only fair. I will be back soon. I never learn my lessons as well as I should.

"Get ready. I'm taking you to lunch." Well, I knew it. Daddy has come for me.

Sarah wrote that she liked this paper because it captured the "swinging of emotions" well. She hates her father for imprisoning her, but being trapped physically also can be a mental trap when the perpetrator is someone who is supposed to love the victim and vice versa: "If you can find love and comfort like I do with my father, you should cherish it." However, Sarah holds onto a piece of her truth: "I never learn my lessons as well as I should." This essay was the beginning of Sarah's actively pushing back at her father. She had voiced her anger in an oblique way by demonstrating at the end the irony of the perpetrator becoming her "savior." The anger and hate she expresses at this irony is apparent to both herself and the reader, and her recognition of that begins to free her from the cycle. Author and fourteen-year-old narrator have some distance from each other. This essay is the fulcrum, the turning point for Sarah. The use of the imprisoned-girl image of Rapunzel helped to provide a context for her experience and enough distance from it to make the remembering bearable. She became Rapunzel, a character from her childhood fairy-tale world, a world she still occupied because she had become frozen in a childhood she had never been able to experience. Yet Sarah has inverted this fairy tale. In the original story an enchantress locked Rapunzel into the tower when she reached the age of twelve, the age of puberty. This tale, like Snow White, demonstrates the fear and jealousy of the older woman/witch figure whose fading beauty is juxtaposed against the budding sexuality of the child/woman. In the original tale Rapunzel finds her solution in her own body by allowing the prince to use her long tresses to climb up into her room in the tower. As with the original, the very cause of Sarah's entrapment, her sexual body, is the source of her escape. In the traditional story, however, Rapunzel was escaping from something *to* something. Sarah's narrator is escaping back to her original captor. Her body is not being offered but bartered. It is clear from tone and context that the author understands this irony and is angry at its existence:

I look at other girls and wonder if they live like I do. If they do not I wonder why. I cannot stand the beating. The other stuff is all right once you get used to it (the smell . . . the alcohol breath, the repulsion, the humiliation, the desire to run, and the hate) but the love has to be stopped. The talk of love and caring is confusing. I wish I knew a better love . . . One thought lingers, though. I really do think I should be getting paid. It is only fair. I will be back soon . . . My mouth always starts to shoot off, asking for trouble.

Rapunzel survived and so, therefore, would she, regardless of the price, yet she recognizes that other girls do not have this history, and the angry response from Ange helped to demonstrate that. In this essay Sarah is beginning to recognize and acknowledge in her own heroic journey into writing that her treatment was unfair, even monstrous, that she did not cause it, and that anger is an appropriate response. As yet, however, she can only indicate this anger with tone and innuendo: "My thoughts are always so confused. I know I should not hate. It makes my face all ugly and I could get kicked for that . . . I think I should tell the wives, including my mother, what is going on. If they cannot control their husbands they should at least provide them with entertainment at home. If that cannot be arranged, I think I should be paid for my services."

In this essay the archetypal image begins to function as a savior for the writer, a way to encounter her emotions relatively safely and with someone else, since her peer reader becomes a collaborator/witness. Sarah's anger gives her the emotional distance that can lead to salvation, even if she defines salvation as getting paid for her services—although, of course, that statement is part of the ironic anger of the narrator. Walker argues that women writers often invert the fairy tales they have been raised with as a way of subverting the tales' underlying ideologies. For all the elements of transformation in fairy tales, the possibilities for female exercise of autonomy are quite limited in the versions that have been in print since the seventeenth century: "The qualities associated with the best-known of the fairy-tale heroines—qualities such as innocence, passivity, helplessness, and vulnerability—make them dubious and even pernicious as models for female self-concept and behavior" (Walker 46–47). For this reason, many women writers subvert the standard values by re-writing the tales, as Sarah has clearly done. Yet the very fact of writing this indicates that the author is conscious of her actions. While Kirsten used her Amazon image to protect her from the truth, Sarah used hers to tell it.

Sarah's last paper, titled "A Moment in Time," includes two photographs of herself and her father—one taken when she was twelve, the other at four-teen. The difference is striking. In the earlier one, she is an innocent child lovingly touching her father's face. In the second she looks seductive with long hair left untied and dark glasses. The paper ends with this paragraph: "I have cut my hair and no longer try to flaunt my sexuality . . . I look at the photographs and feel a certain compassion for the girl who made such an ef-fort to be loved by the one man who could. If I took a picture with my father today, I would not smile if I was not in the mood. I would stare at the lens and let all my hatred pour out of my eyes and mouth . . . I said it! I am ANGRY."

This admission of anger is a major breakthrough for Sarah. She has finally acknowledged to herself and to the reader that she counts, that her percep-tions of her experiences are real, that her body and her emotions occupy the same space. Sarah's use of the image of Rapunzel, the imprisoned girl, was her doorway out of her own emotional prison. The archetypal image allowed her the safety to connect her own life images with the emotions she had hidden from herself to survive. She is no longer Rapunzel with the long flowing hair, representative of her female sexuality—the only weapon she felt she had. She now has other weapons: her emotional truth and the language to describe it, among others. She had spent many years of her life denying her anger because to admit it was to implicate her father and mother, people she still loves and attempts to protect, in an existential play of staggering personal proportions. In her culture simply telling her story is being monumentally disobedient, with all the repercussions that implies. This has been a serious problem for many women writers in particular. As Walker argues, "Because the concepts of individual selfhood and subjectivity have been problematic for women, merely to present publicly one's life is a disobedient act" (9). Sarah did not feel significant enough to tell her story. Her father's feelings were al-ways more important. Walker quotes from Claudine Herrmann in *The Tongue Snatchers:* " 'In the immense totality of culture, woman appears to have been placed between parentheses, emerging unexpectedly in connection with other things, when she can't be stopped, traversing texts like a shadow, to be elimi-nated as quickly as possible so that one may go on, without wasting time, to more important matters.' The disobedient . . . writer is no longer a shadow on the text, but rather makes the text a shadow of her own" (11).

This is what Sarah has accomplished. In connecting with her emotions, wedding them to the traumatic images she has buried, constructing a narra-tive that moves the locus of control back to her, and sharing this narrative with another, she has become her own hero and source of her own salvation.

As Charles Anderson demonstrates in his essay "Suture, Stigma, and the Pages That Heal," writing can free us from the limiting discourses of others: "To discourse with the other, when the other is the fluid text out of which one's story emerges, is not to be trapped and wounded by the worlds of the other nor to trade being for meaning, but to be released by those words, to experience a convergence of meaning and being, and to name a self not broken by discourse, but, immersed in it, in charge of it, empowered by it" (62).

Cathartic Writing and Art

Our culture tends to define the hero's journey as an outward one—to conquer lands, people, and nature, to plant a United States flag on the moon, to "tame" the western frontier or pull down the statue of Saddam Hussein. We have few public models for the hero's journey as an interior one—to delve within ourselves and discover what components of our shadows, what hidden, emotionally laden images, drive or limit our actions. Certainly we are a culture much given to psychological theories and the therapies that follow; at the same time therapy is a highly private matter, usually discussed only among closest family and friends, and many in this culture still see it as a mark of weakness. Nothing should affect us, which is why all the students but one in my senior seminar on twentieth-century trauma did not believe that they had had any experiences that they would call traumatic—until they examined their assumptions. It is no surprise that writing that produces a therapeutic effect has been denigrated as "confessional" in our culture. Richard Hoffman, author of a beautifully written memoir of family trauma and sexual abuse titled *Half the House* tells a story which illustrates this well:

> Soon after *Half the House* was published . . . I was in a radio station, about to be interviewed. As we prepared to begin, the interviewer told me that my book "must have been cathartic" for me. When I suggested that the term "catharsis," before it was commandeered by psychology, was a literary term and that it stood for what the Greek dramatists tried to effect in their audience, not in themselves, I was told that I was full of it.
>
> "Nonsense. Why else would you write such a book?" the interviewer said.
>
> Flustered, I said that I wrote it because I am a writer, and I had to. "Oh, give me a break," she said . . . I told her that Camus once

said . . . that we make art "to save from death a living image of our passions and our suffering." She was looking through a glass window at a technician using his fingers to count down from ten.

"So you think it's art?"

"Yes, or I would not have published it."

"Well, I look forward to reading it." We were on the air. "My guest is Richard Hoffman, who has just published a book about his life called *Half the House*. So tell us, Richard Hoffman, what's so special about your life that we should care enough about it to want to buy your book?"

"My book is not about my life," I said. It was one of those rare moments when panic produces clarity. "My book is about our life." (188–89)

Hoffman's book—about the effects of disease on a family, about the sexual abuse of a small boy, about families laid low by poverty and lack of good heath care, about the efforts of families to love and treasure each other in the midst of trauma and death—is archetypal. It is a story many struggle with, a story many experience and keep silent. And even if we are lucky enough to have escaped these particular traumas, the effects are still felt on our society, especially if they are kept quiet. The interviewer's tone clearly indicates our cultural distaste for vulnerability. The sound bite can distance, can allow us all to feel superior as we voyeuristically listen, but telling secrets without the desire for self-pity—a truly disobedient act, as Walker states—allows others to identify with us and possibly do the same. Judith Harris argues, "When testimony enters public consciousness, seeking to modify the moral order to which it appeals, it has implicit value. Confessional poets such as Lowell and Plath felt the urgency to record their personal anguish, not to perpetuate self-pity, but to bring pity into human consciousness, eliciting in the reader deep and comprehensive emotions that could be brought about only through human identifications" (34). As Hoffman said, "My book is about our life."

However, writing that is perceived to provide a therapeutic effect has been denigrated in our culture, particularly as it has often been associated with women's writing. Poets and essayists of "ideas," as opposed to personal experiences, have been so valued that when Adrienne Rich was a young poet she was not able to find literary guides that could speak to her experiences as a woman. As she put it, the girl or woman who tries to write "goes to poetry or fiction looking for her way of being in the world . . . and she comes up against something that negates everything she is about . . . So what does she do? What did I do? I read the older women poets . . . but even in reading these women I was looking in them for the same things I had found in the poetry of men, because I wanted women poets to be the equal of men, and to be equal was still confused with sounding the same" (1140). It took many years before Rich was able "to write, for the first time, directly about experiencing myself as a woman" (1144).

During the 1950s the confessional school of poetry surfaced, associated with the work of poet Robert Lowell, who based his psychoanalytic thrust on Freud's theories. His models were available for young women poets; however, negative judgments were still applied to women writers but not to Lowell, as Judith Harris says: "Lowell wrote a great deal about his conflicts and anxieties surrounding his relationships to loved ones. But what is most interesting about Lowell's confessionalism is that the term is almost never applied pejoratively to him, but only to women poets who use poetry as a therapeutic outlet" (27).

Harris argues that these judgments maintained regardless of the quality of the writing: "If a woman, such as Plath or Sexton, or later Olds or McCarriston, had written this poem [Lowell's "To Speak of Woe That is in Marriage," a "confessional" poem], the term 'confessional' would most likely connote vulnerability, even weakness, or confusion" (27). Lowell has adopted as his narrator in the poem the voice of a bitter, angry, yet fearful wife, which governs his stance toward the poem: "Lowell, like Browning before him, is most interested in his own cruelty and is willing to explore it. Plath or Olds is interested in the cruelty done *to* her, and therefore Plath's or Old's tone is more conflated with feelings of deep deprivations, disappointments, and the need for justice to help her break out of the molded cast society has put her in" (Harris 28).

Harris is saying here that a narrator that can be understood as arising from the author's voice is suspect when the text speaks of trauma or the need for justice. The labels "cathartic," "confessional," or "therapeutic" can be applied, which can prohibit the work from being seen as art, regardless of its aesthetic value. Obviously, not every verbalized wail uttered in a journal entry *is* art, nor is every memoir about trauma aesthetically pleasing. However, the confessional nature of a piece of writing should not disqualify it from being considered as art.

Alice Sebold addresses this concern in an interview with Terry Gross, a transcript of which is printed at the end of the 2002 Little Brown edition of her book *Lucky*. Sebold had earlier written an essay for the *New York Times Magazine* on the consequences of rape, which Judith Herman quoted in *Trauma and Recovery*: "When I was raped I lost my virginity and almost lost my life. I also discarded certain assumptions I had held about how the world worked and about how safe I was" (51). That comment was quoted by Herman to illustrate the loss of security experienced by trauma survivors. Sebold bought Herman's book for a very telling reason, as she explained in the interview with Terry Gross:

> I'd been such a miserable failure as a writer in my twenties that it was one of the few places I had appeared in print. And on the subway home with the book I realized that I was quoted in the first half, which was called "Trauma," instead of the second half, which is called "Recovery." By the time I got to the end of the book, I realized that I had post-traumatic stress disorder and went from there. So only after, I'd say, a full ten years away from the rape I was able to face the rape and deal with the clear memories of it. Luckily, one of the things I did right after the rape, because I was a kind of morbid, poetic kid, was write verbatim accounts of exactly what had happened to me physically and what the light had been like and things like that in a journal of mine. (6)

This quotation is interesting for several reasons. First, note that Sebold did not realize she had PTSD until she saw her writing in the "before" section of Herman's book, and this was many years after the rape. Second, she had not yet had success as a writer. Third, she had written the details of her rape in a journal but had hidden the journal away in her parents' basement. Gross asked her what it was like to read it many years later. Sebold replied:

> I would say it was mind-blowing for a couple of reasons, and not the least of which was to realize what I had actually experienced. Because I think while you're going through it, you just—especially if you have the chance of going through a trial, which I did—you need to keep your eye on the ball, you need to be focused. You can't really drift off into maximum pain. So to go back and look at the accounts of what was actually happening, you know, I have to say I just thought, "Hey, kid, you did OK." (7)

Sebold exemplifies what we saw in chapter 1: Survivors cannot both cope and process feelings at the same time. That means they need a time and a place to do the hard work of recovery. Since she did not do that work until after she read Herman, this may be a factor in why her published writing was not particularly successful until after she began that work. Sebold had written extensively in a journal right after the rape occurred but put the journal away and did not refer to it again until after she began her recovery in earnest ten years later. As she put it, the journal writing was "pretty horrible . . . It was extremely staccato, very direct . . . all very factual, flat, uninflected writing that just told the facts of what was happening" (9). Referring back to the second chapter that discusses what kind of writing appears to be the most therapeutic, we find that it is writing that combines imagistic details with affect, which she had apparently not done in her journal. Indeed, writing that is flat, that has no emotional content, is both therapeutically and aesthetically ineffective, as Sebold herself testifies. However, her journal did provide for her the facts of the events, so she could begin the process in therapy of externalizing the emotions those facts generated.

Sebold herself understands that her journal was not publishable, but it was instrumental in helping her to remember: "I never used that as a draft of anything. Basically, I went back and read it, and it brought me back to the time. And what I would say is that it was a way of waking up my memory" (9). This step of re-engaging with the traumatic images and constructing a narrative that puts them in the past is the process we have been looking at. It is not so much the product, a text, but the process of writing it that is therapeutic. The initial writing helped jumpstart her memory, and the process of using it to construct a self that is no longer caught by those memories is the hard work of therapy, as Herman and others have demonstrated. Sebold creates a clear distinction between therapeutic writing and art as a response to Gross's question, "Is writing therapeutic?" Sebold answered, "Writing can be therapeutic, but therapeutic writing should not be published. My job as a writer is to go through the therapy myself and, if I manage to get through it and I feel I have something to share from that, to share it with my audience or my readers" (8).

Sebold has sidestepped the issue of the artistry of therapeutic writing by her disclaimer that while her journals might have been helped her begin the therapeutic process, her published work is not therapeutic. She is emphasizing the fact that to be successful writing must be aesthetically good and must speak to others, and the writing she did in her journal was neither of these things. If we accept her definition, it can speak to the writing process: Our early utterances can lead us to our formal finished work. The process itself can be therapeutic but our finished drafts emphasize our relationship to our readers and the craft of writing that permits that relationship. This is what is appropriate for published prose. Although professional writers must be invested in the artistry of their work, writers' themes often reflect lived experience. Sebold's first novel, titled *The Lovely Bones,* is about the rape, murder, and mutilation of a fourteen-year-old girl, a novel she began before writing *Lucky.* When Gross asked Sebold why she wrote about something so horrible Sebold answered very much as Hoffman did: "Because it's part of life. You know, that's the simplest answer, I think, for me. It's very much a part of the experience of what it is to live in this culture. It happens all the time" (3). One of the characters in the book says that every time she tells her story, a drop of the pain goes away, which demonstrates that Sebold understands the power of narrative.

Text as Testimony

Professional writers know that the label "therapeutic" can be the kiss of death for a book, as Hoffman discovered from his radio interview. However, as Harris has pointed out, text as testimony can modify the social order and therefore has implicit value. Hoffman's abuser was a coach who had also molested others. When Hoffman's book was published, the story was picked up by the Associated Press. Police began receiving calls from all over the country from men in their twenties, thirties, and forties, even some very young boys who had recently been violated by this man. The coach was arrested. Hoffman began receiving phone calls from men across the country who were attempting to come to terms with their own abuse. By writing his story, Hoffman had given these men permission to tell their stories, resulting in both an arrest and the validation of the experiences of countless victims.

Survivors, especially those attempting to seek redress for or even simple acknowledgement of the abuse are often asked why does this matter now? The past is the past. We can't change it, so just let it go. Ross Cheit offers the following in discussing the betrayal he felt as a result of the denial of his experiences:

> Why does this matter now? I've been asked that all too many times in the last year. Why are you pursuing this old matter? There are several

reasons. The first is, pain endures. And this is not ancient history for me. I can barely look at my eleven-year-old [relative] right now without crying over his vulnerability. And I feel the stigma that's attached to this, to being a survivor of this crime . . . this is not ancient history. This is my life. Second, I just think healing helps restore social order and promotes healing, and that to me, denial is a continuing injury. And as long as they continue to deny it, they're still hurting me. Third . . . pedophiles rarely, if ever, stop. This man said to me on the telephone, "I know I shouldn't work with children." And he is working with children. (Qtd. in Freyd 163)

Ross Cheit, Richard Hoffman, and Sarah all had to resist the power structures that surrounded them in order to tell their stories. But their stories do not affect only them. A culture that permits abuse is a culture in need of redress. Only when survivors crack through our cultural denial will healing occur for all of us. This is seen no more dramatically than in the PBS documentary *What I Want My Words to Do to You,* an intimate portrait of fifteen female inmates at Bedford Hills Correctional Facility. Through a series of writing exercises and peer workshops/discussions led by playwright Eve Ensler *(The Vagina Monologues),* these inmates delve into the causes of their life choices, the nature of their crimes, and their own responsibility for where they are now. The film ends with a prison performance of the women's writing by Glenn Close, Mary Alice, Hazelle Goodman, Rosie Perez, and Marisa Tomei.

First, it is important to note that according to Bessel van der Kolk in a keynote address at a conference on trauma presented by Harvard University in 1996, 92 percent of the women at Bedford Hills are victims of drug abuse. Often women use drugs as a way to self-medicate because of their histories of sexual abuse, rape, depression, and/or parental abandonment or neglect, and this group is no exception. Many of the women in this film were victims of sexual violence or lacked mothers at home. One, for example, was raped by an acquaintance when she was twenty-one. Afterward, she was so confused and appalled by what he had done, and so upset that a friend would do this that she grabbed a gun for protection and went to find him to ask why. He pulled a knife and she shot him. When this young woman talked about it, she showed no emotion, just a kind of blankness. However, when Rosie Perez read her story, the writer's eyes glistened.

Another young woman was molested by her uncle when she was a child.

She became a prostitute and snapped one day, killing a seventy-one-year-old john whose wife had just died and whose loneliness and grief drove him to a prostitute. She had buried her rage from her past, and it exploded onto this old man, an act that has brought her intense guilt. As she said, "I'm guilty of my refusal not to face myself. I didn't allow myself to have feelings. Now I can, so now I can feel for others," and that includes this crippling guilt. Another woman serving fifty years to life for murder did not know who she was. She didn't know if she was a victim or a perpetrator or some combination of the two. As she said, "I don't know what my truth is." In the documentary Eve Ensler said to the women, "Start with one part, write that, then write another part . . . When you get to own full responsibility, you get to be free . . . Part of the writing process is to find what's under there." Many of these women have committed crimes so heinous that it is easy for us to distance ourselves from them and justify their incarceration, maybe even their execution. This film crashes through these assumptions. Joan Gelman in O magazine wrote in a review excerpted on the film's jacket, "Watch it and see the monsters you imagine turn into the mothers, daughters, wives, and friends they once were." Writing became for these women a way for them to learn about themselves, to create a supportive community, and most importantly to be seen by others. As one inmate wrote, "I want my words to disrupt your day, thirsty in the deep discomfort of ambiguity . . . I want you to ask 'why.' " And another, "Let my words congeal in your bowels . . . whatever you partake of, be it sumptuous or rancid, that you pass the plate and let others partake."

Writing becomes a source of inspiration to the deadened and power to the powerless. The act of communicating brings with it entry to a community: "The communicative act of bearing witness to traumatic events not only transforms traumatic memories into narratives that can then be integrated into the survivor's sense of self and view of the world, but it also reintegrates the survivor into a community, re-establishing bonds of trust and faith in others" (Brison xi). In the case of these inmates, it can establish faith and trust in themselves as well. I have seen this same process work in the writing classroom: When peers and the teacher can bear witness the to the traumatic stories of others, the community established can help the writer to gain truth and faith in herself both as writer and human being.

Daniel Goleman argues in *Emotional Intelligence* that without a passing acquaintance with our emotional lives, our behaviors can be suspect, even dangerous to ourselves and to others, as these inmates have discovered. But it takes courage to tell the truth, and it also takes witnesses to hear that truth, which requires its own kind of courage. We are all implicated in each other's survival. Sarah needed to hear Ange yell because she could not yet do so for herself. But once she became part of a larger community, Sarah discovered that being a disobedient writer could start her on the hero's journey. Facing her lived experiences and the fear and anger she had hidden from herself for so long brought her integration of feelings and images, insight, and an inner softness that her brittle exterior belied. She had also become a writer, and in doing so was poised to discover herself.

CHAPTER 4

A Crisis of Listening

Trauma in the Classroom

If anyone else could have written my stories, I would not have written them. I have written them in order to testify.

ELIE WIESEL

IN FALL OF 2002 I taught a senior capstone honors course called "Trauma and the Twentieth Century" to eighteen of the brightest and best at Ithaca College. Given the events of September 11, the Honors Program thought a course such as this would be appropriate and instructive for this group of seniors. Not surprisingly students were apprehensive to take a course with "trauma" in the title, especially a required honors course in which they feared their performance might be even more stiffly evaluated. In addition, these students had known each other since freshman year and had had three years to discover each other's strengths, foibles, limitations, and defenses, all of which were rapidly present on that first day. They eyed each other and me for intelligence on the possible dangers of this provocative but potentially threatening class topic. The following is the course description from the syllabus:

> *Course Description*
>
> > I and the public know
> > What all schoolchildren learn
> > Those to whom evil is done
> > Do evil in return.
>
> > W. H. AUDEN

Human trauma inflicted on a grand scale is a defining feature of the twentieth century. Two world wars, one fought with nuclear weapons; two major genocides involving world powers; countless other genocides around the world; localized wars that devastate entire populations; these are only a few of the sources for trauma in the twentieth century. Unfortunately, it also appears to be a defining feature of the twenty-first century as well, as the tragedy of September 11, 2001 demonstrates. We now have a nation that has been touched deeply by trauma. When we add to these horrors the dangers of living—and going to school—in America with its high rate of violent crime and its racism and sexism, we have the environment that most American young people face every day. This seminar will explore trauma, its causes and effects, on cultures and on individuals within those cultures. We will first define trauma and investigate within the history of psychology how trauma has been identified and treated. Then we will study the neurobiology of trauma, that is, what happens in the brains of traumatized individuals, and investigate some treatment models. We will read examples of trauma narratives and watch films that illustrate artistic responses to trauma. For most of the remainder of the class we will study two manifestations of wholesale genocide—the Armenian Genocide and the Holocaust—to investigate cultural manifestations of trauma and the responsibility of others to such horrors. In the last two weeks we will investigate what is necessary for individuals and cultures to begin to heal from massive traumas.

1. Definition and conceptual history of trauma (two weeks).

Pre-Platonic conceptions of illness and healing—technê (informed practice). Platonic and Aristotelian notions of emotions and art. The Christian canon as a response to trauma. Conceptions of trauma—Janet, Charcot, Freud, and Herman. Freud's abandonment of his seduction theory and his ambiguities about trauma. The PTSD diagnosis.

2. Neurobiology and Treatment of Trauma (two weeks).

What happens inside the brain when trauma occurs. How do treatment models try to modify that process? What do we mean when we talk about "healing" from trauma? Is there any such thing as "recovery"?

3. Trauma Narratives (one week).

What makes a trauma narrative? What is the purpose of reading such a work? What is the purpose of writing it? Selections from trauma narratives such as *Beloved, Every Secret Thing, In the Lake of the Woods*, and examples from students and survivors of 9/11.

4. Trauma and War (one week).

How does a society get its citizens to commit what in peacetime would be murder? What happens to soldiers upon committing such "crimes"? Where is the line in the tension between obedience to cultural/military authority to preserve a group and destructive peer pressure?

5. Genocides (four weeks)—Armenian Genocide and the Holocaust.

What causes genocide? What factors do different genocides have in common? How does genocide affect individuals and their descendants within a culture and the culture itself? What part does denial of genocide have to play in re-traumatizing the survivors? What part do bystanders play in the perpetration of genocide? Can one "recover" from being a survivor of genocide? Can a culture recover? If so, what promotes such recovery? How do we prevent genocide? What is the relationship between the Armenian Genocide and the Holocaust?

6. Are We Our Brothers' and Sisters' Keepers? Toward a Morality of Justice and a Context for Healing (two weeks).

What is the role of the secondary witness to trauma? What is secondary trauma and how should it be addressed? What is the role of writing in healing from trauma? Can we heal from trauma? What would healing look like?

7. Research Presentations (two weeks).

Students will offer a brief talk on the subject of their final projects and the methodologies they have chosen to execute them. While these projects are primarily research based, personal experience, artwork, music, etc. may also be included if desired.

The primary texts for the class included Judith Herman *Trauma and Recovery;* Anderson and MacCurdy, *Writing and Healing: Toward an Informed Practice;* Cathy Caruth, *Trauma: Explorations in Memory;* Richard Hovannisian, *The Armenian Genocide in Perspective;* and Art Spiegelman, *Maus, A Survivor's Tale: And Here My Troubles Begin.* A packet of supplemental materials also was assigned—academic and personal essays, memoirs, fiction, poetry, and so on, from Aristotle, Freud, and Jeffrey Masson to Toni Morrison, James Pennebaker, and Gillian Slovo.

Class was run as a seminar with students taking responsibility each day for one text. Although everyone was to do all the assigned reading, each day one student's job was to provide a brief summary of the salient issues in the day's text and ask the class questions on that text. This was to take approximately fifteen minutes. The rest of the class was devoted to general discussion of the material and other class activities. For the first two months students dutifully prepared summaries, offered questions, and sat waiting for responses. We learned about the iconic nature of trauma images, how they emerge not as narrative but as separate bits disconnected from the rest of memory. We learned how talking or writing about a trauma can help link those images into a narrative, then provide a feeling of control over the uncontrollable: the past. We read trauma narratives and responses to them. We studied the value and price of listening to trauma survivors. The students dutifully did their work, but still few spoke, and when they did, few responded. The class was silent and suspicious, eyes down or scanning their peers, depending on level of aggression and extroversion.

Defining the Class Problem

At the start of class, I made it clear to the students that speaking of personal issues was neither a spoken nor an unspoken requirement in this class. What was required was engagement—doing the work, speaking of the work they did, and actively relating to each other as members of the class community. I've been in the classroom virtually all my working life. I've taught inner-city teenagers, community-college students, and the entitled rich whose cars cost more than I made in a year. Never had I faced a more intimidating environment than that presented in this class. I did not know until a few weeks into class that this particular cohort within the Honors Program had become competitive, even combative, as first-year honors students, and time had only exacerbated the problem. That historical stance toward each other plus the nature of the topic set us up for difficulties. None of my pedagogical tricks made a dent in the hostility level and the silence that greeted us in each class.

One requirement of the class was to keep a journal in which students were to respond to the readings and the class. As the syllabus stated: "You may offer feelings, thoughts, personal experiences, anything that informs your responses to the readings and the class. You should expect to have several entries per week. Information from these journals will be shared with no one but me, and I will not read every entry if you wish to keep some private." I suggested that they use a loose-leaf notebook so they could remove pages that they wished to keep to themselves. Oddly enough, although students did not wish to share anything with each other, it was soon evident from the journals that virtually everyone in the class had had a brush with trauma. The effects of divorce, parental alcoholism and physical abuse, mental and physical handicaps, suicide, mental illness, accidents—a cross-section of the ills and life traumas of American culture—could be found in this class. I thought of Lucille Clifton's observation quoted earlier: "Every day . . . children are bearing something you could not bear . . . Every day something has tried to kill [them] and has failed." Having taught Personal Essay for so many years, this was not a surprise. A writing class offers methodologies to deal with these problems: Focusing on text, relying on peer workshops, and sharing rewrites allows participants to offer their stories in a venue in which the essay becomes the focus, not the life.

This was not a personal essay class, however, but an honors course, which meant I was limited in my tools for approaching this issue. But I needed to come up with some because the tension produced by these unsaid traumas was palpable. As one student wrote in her journal: "I am often frustrated with the level of tension I feel in this class, specifically during class discussions. I am beginning to think that this is due to the nature of the material of the course rather than how it is structured . . . Now that we have begun to study more specific traumatic events, there seems to be a tension between discussing the events and the trauma of individuals or keeping the discussion at a theoretical level. Many times, we seem to resist letting our discussions become personal, whether personal means our personal reactions to what we are reading or our personal situations that can be compared to those we are reading about."

A few students named the problem right from the start. One young woman, Sharon, who is quoted in the introduction, set up the issues with utter clarity:

> Writing in a journal . . . this is a task that I haven't done in quite some time. Most of my writing in the last few years has been dedicated to analyzing or deconstructing famous texts, or detailing the procedures and results of my latest genetics research. I have to say that writing in a journal like this one is quite refreshing, mostly because I feel the freedom to speak . . . what I truly believe rather than critiquing works as I believe a professor requires me to. But as I think of the word "journal,"

the word "journey" resonates in my mind. I hope that this journal actually takes me on a journey, as I have similar hopes for our class in general. In my young life . . . I have experienced quite a few traumatic events—suicides of family members, deaths of friends, personal eating disorders, family relationship disintegration . . . and to be honest, I have done little to actually confront these experiences. Instead, I immerse myself in my life at school to compensate for it . . . by working extremely (overly) hard . . . and trying to be involved in way too many responsibilities. As I began to read Herman's text, so many of her words were like mini-alarms going off in my head . . . In our last class you spoke that it may be very difficult to digest some of the material if you are going through a traumatic period in your current life. With alarm, I choked back my fear because right now I am having trouble in my family life, as my parents are most likely going to get divorced when my sister enters college in the fall. I hope to detail some of the events in this journal while also tackling the questions and issues of this class . . . I truly hope that the writing I do in this journal begins some sort of healing process for me . . . Sometimes I think I should speak to a therapist about some of the issues have tried to deal with by myself . . . I think that this journal may spark something in myself . . . On a similar note, I truly hope that my peers open up in this class. As I am sure you have seen, the senior class is quite competitive and at times, downright rude . . . There are so many intelligent individuals in the senior class . . . but I pray that the cynical attitudes of many do not spoil the experience for those who truly want to personally and emotionally grow.

This student demonstrated one of the key problems for the class: As we might expect, some students were already aware that they faced difficult issues, and they hoped the teacher and the class would be a place where they could combine theory and life in a positive way. Sharon asked to see me and in a conference tearfully told me about her childhood sexual abuse, as described in the introduction to the book. I listened for more than an hour, then told her she was very brave and very smart to be looking at how this issue has affected her life. I told her I would read anything in her journal she wanted to write but that I would not share any of it with the class without her written permission (these are the rules of the road in my class, but I wanted to restate them for her), and I suggested that she make an appointment with the college counseling office to help her sort through this problem, which she did. This began an intense journey in which she combined the class reading material, our class discussions, her writing for the class, her talks with me, and her therapy sessions to create a context for her childhood trauma, one that by the end of the semester finally placed it in the past.

Why They Wouldn't Talk

Most of the students were not as ready as was Sharon to "dive into the wreck," as Adrienne Rich described the process of self-discovery, nor was this a requirement for the class. As it turned out, however, most wanted to link personal and public, cognitive and emotional, life and theory but had no model to do this.

Within three weeks it was clear that most of the students were willing to be engaged intellectually in the class. We had productive discussions about the neurobiology of trauma—for example, does an imbalance in neurotransmitters or an immature brain absolve a perpetrator from responsibility? This becomes particularly important in dealing with teenage criminals, a significant question for all the budding teachers in the class. Other students were fascinated by the causes of genocide; others focused on the nature of healing from trauma. Discussions were limited, safe, and slightly hostile. Many students said they were not affected by the trauma of others because "it is so far away from me." This, of course, antagonized those whose empathy cannot permit such distance. I began to suspect that the distance was a safety device, and this was confirmed by reading journal entries. The students would write about their experiences and their relationship to the class material in their journals for me to read but did not trust their peers enough to share any of this with the class.

It was clear that no one in the class was willing to speak in depth for fear of judgment. They had never before been part of a listening community. This was a class of high achievers who had learned the rules of the academic road and followed them utterly. They knew how to memorize, synthesize, argue, persuade, experiment, lecture, even declaim. They saw each other as competitors for scarce resources—the sought-after A, and they knew how to succeed. Higher education rewards these characteristic behaviors, so they got very good at them. What it does not reward is exactly what the students needed to be able to engage well with each other: These students did not know how to listen. They had never had such skills modeled for them in their classes, never had any teacher expect listening skills of them. And even more difficult, the students wanted to share their own traumas in the class, but were convinced that this was not only inappropriate but dangerous because it would reveal private information to competitors. I knew from their journals that they had a great deal in common, but of course the requirements of confidentiality prohibited my discussing any of this with the class. The hostility in class was borne of frustration, fear, the sense of potential disaster, and, paradoxically, relief that might erupt if anyone violated the code and began to relate the topic of the class—trauma—to his or her own life.

What to Do

By the end of October it was clear to me that something proactive had to be done to salvage the semester. I had to figure out how to create community in this class, and soon, or it would only serve to solidify the conventional dichotomies so intrinsic to higher education: personal versus professional, spirit versus mind, public versus private. I had invited two Holocaust survivors to visit the class, a husband and wife who had both been imprisoned in the camps and met and married after their liberation at the end of the war. The students and I talked a bit about what they might experience with this visit. Both Jerry and Jean had remained silent for many years. Jerry broke his silence in 1985 after hearing a Holocaust denier speak on the radio. His anger drove him to write an article for a local newspaper, and he began speaking in area high schools and colleges. He noticed an immediate change: His frequent nightmares ceased. Jean remained silent until after Jerry's first visit to a class I was teaching two years before. Upon his second visit, she decided to come.

   This couple is an archetypal example of the wages of silent trauma and the results of finding a voice. Jerry spoke first, describing how he was captured and sent to the camps; lost his mother, then his father; futilely attempted to save a fellow prisoner who was dying of typhus. Jerry's stories were clear narratives that he commanded. Given his seventeen-year experience speaking of these horrors, Jerry had constructed a narrative that had helped him organize the chaos and trauma of the camps. Jean remained silent until Jerry had spoken for close to a half hour. He turned to her and asked if she was ready. Jean began: "You can't know. You can't know. It is impossible. I cannot describe. You cannot know. I saw my mother, my mother . . ."

   Her voice trailed off and she began again. "My mother and I were separated. I was young and blonde, looked German. I never saw her again. I asked a woman, 'Where's my mother? Where's my mother?' The woman pointed to the tall chimney and said, 'You stupid, there's your mother.' "

Jean's face was red, and tears were pooling in her gray eyes. I looked around the room. Every face was riveted, some in tears, some just staring. You could hear a feather fall to the floor. Then she pulled up her sleeve revealing her tattooed number and said, "This is who I am."

The following are from student writings after this visit:

> "I think the most memorable moment for me was when the woman showed us her number . . . I was forced to hold back tears"
>
> "I think it was quite evident [that the husband and wife were at different stages in the healing process] . . . in the way the stories were told. He took us on a very detailed and structured journey . . . Her story, however, was much more broken. She kept repeating how impossible to describe everything was. . . . . The funny thing was that she was able, to some extent, to relay some of her experiences . . . The most surprising thing for me was that he was able to remember the days of the week when each event occurred. I can't even remember what day of the week I had spaghetti for dinner. After class and even now as I write this I am amazing myself with all of the details that I can remember from both of their tales . . . I am honored to listen to their story."

Another student, a biology major, began her final project titled "These Things You Just Cannot Describe; It Is Impossible: The Neurobiology of Speaking about Trauma and Emotional Experience" with these words:

> One of my most moving experiences in the class "Trauma and the Twentieth Century" and in my college experience as a whole was listening to Mr. And Mrs. Jerry G. narrate their experiences as prisoners in German concentration camps during World War II. The experience moved me to the point that I was almost in tears and was left with an entirely new appreciation for the horror of the Holocaust. Though I have encountered Holocaust narratives and stories many times in the past . . . I had never before met a survivor of the Holocaust in person . . . When I arrived home the evening of the day I met the Gs, I was eager to share my experience with my roommates. However, I only managed to get out the statement "I had a really amazing experi-

ence today. A husband and wife who survived the Holocaust came in and talked to us today. " After muttering this simple phrase which did absolutely nothing to convey the power of this experience, I could not come up with the words to explain what made the experience so emotional or even what [they] talked about. I almost felt there were no words to describe my emotions or the emotions of the Gs. So I gave up. I took the experience for what it was worth to me personally, told myself that I would do all I could to prevent allowing evils such as the Holocaust from occurring in the future, and went on with my life, sharing my experience with no one.

My students were discovering that witnessing to trauma is itself a kind of trauma. Symonds' concept of the secondary witness has been expanded by Dori Laub in his and Shoshana Felman's book *Testimony:* "By extension, the listener to trauma comes to be a participant and a co-owner of the traumatic event; through his very listening, he comes to partially experience the trauma in himself" (Felman 57). We see this in the following student's journal entry:

One particularly striking aspect of listening to the Gs was the difference between the way Mr. G and Mrs. G spoke about their experiences. Mr. G had spoken about his experiences many times in the past and was able to tell a logical, sequential story of his final days in the concentration camps and after he was liberated. He was even able to incorporate some humor into the narrative . . . Mrs. G, in contrast, had not talked about her experiences very much and had a very difficult time speaking. She jumped from story to story rather than telling a sequential narrative . . . She also presented individual images such as her frozen nipples and toes, piles of dead bodies, and ashes from the crematorium that she could not bend down to pick up out of fear of being shot. These images were not incorporated into any form of story or narrative. Nearly all of her statements were qualified with the phrase, "These things you just cannot describe; it is impossible."

The students found witnessing to this trauma confusing and difficult, if compelling. First, they felt tearful as they listened to such horrific stories, but they did not want to appropriate the moment by demonstrating their emotions when the speakers were able to manage theirs. Second, they found themselves experiencing in miniature some of the emotions the speakers were implying—fear, anger, pain, sadness—and had to address this to proceed. Empathy was happening, and they had to learn to feel yet go on. As Dori Laub explains: "[The listener] comes to feel the bewilderment, injury, confusion, dread, and conflicts that the trauma victim feels. He has to address all these, if he is to carry out his function as a listener . . . The listener has to feel the victim's victories, defeats, and silences, know them from within, so that they can assume the form of testimony" (Felman 58). However, the students needed to learn how to manage this empathy: "The listener . . . has to be at the same time a witness to the trauma witness and a witness to himself. It is only in this way . . . that he can become the enabler of the testimony . . . as well as the guardian of its process" (Felman 58). After the speakers' visit, we discussed the students' emotional responses so they had the opportunity to express themselves and recognize that many of their peers felt the same, which helped to establish community in the class. Only after that emotional validation did we move on to talk about the stories themselves. Since we had already studied the effects of trauma, the students could respond both cognitively and emotionally to the speakers' narratives, which helped them to maintain appropriate balance.

The Effects of Language on the Iconic Nature of Trauma

The students understood from both the differences in the Gs' narratives and from Mrs. G's own verbal limitations what Bessel van der Kolk and others had argued about trauma: Its iconic nature is hard to capture; yet it is precisely the connections between emotion and image that make trauma so compelling, so difficult to integrate into the rest of life. The only way to mitigate the emotional hold of these powerful iconic images is to repeatedly verbalize them, construct a narrative, and share this narrative with another person. Jean had chosen to keep silent for more than sixty years. She did not even discuss the Holocaust with her children. Jerry, too, attempted to keep silent, but his anger at a warping of history propelled him to speak, and once he did he reaped immediate benefits in the cessation of his nightmares. Jerry's use of humor, transitions, narrative structure, and other devices made it obvious to the students that Jerry was further along in the process of creating a narrative that gave him a measure of control. Jean kept repeating over and over, "It's impossible, it's impossible," when speaking of her experiences at Auschwitz. She was able to create excruciating moments of crystalline purity, but they were all separate moments with no narrative thread. It was clear to us that she had not had Jerry's practice in sharing her story with others. She was still in it herself.

Felman and Laub, Testimony Archives

The Gs' experiences with testimony reflect those of other Holocaust survivors. As Felman and Laub discuss in their book *Testimony*, breaking silence is a significant step for survivors. They repeat the story of one man, a child survivor of the camps, who was haunted by his past with nightmares, sleeplessness, and anxieties. Once he offered his testimony to the Video Archive for Holocaust Testimonies, his nightmares disappeared, he felt free of the past's stranglehold on him, and he was able "to experience feelings both of mourning and of hope—and as a transfiguring illumination, a transforming insight into the extent to which this burden—and this silence—has in fact affected, and reshaped, his whole life." (46). The survivor is quoted as saying, "The thing that troubles me right now is the following: If we don't deal with our feelings, if we don't understand our experience, what are we doing to our children?" (46). The students heard Jerry and Jean say that they kept silent about their past even with their own children until 1985, when Jerry spoke to counteract a Holocaust denier. At that moment he spoke up not only for his truth but for the truth that affects his children and those of other survivors as well. He validated their experiences as well as his own. It soon became clear to my students that healing is possible, but only through breaking silences. Another student, Maxim, also referred to the Gs' visit in his journal:

> Listening to both these Holocaust survivors speak reminded me of the readings we did. The way they recollected their trauma is the same way the books said they would. Their recollection lacks a sense of order. It just comes out—different flashes and glimpses. I wonder if they ever had a moment in life when they wish they had died during the H. How has the H changed them? ... Listening to them speak was just very difficult ... Laub stresses the importance of the listener to the healing process. I must say I am compelled to agree ... It was as if I was a co-owner—I felt their pain and defeat. But at the same time, I felt their triumph. And them speaking to me and being given a venue to do this contributed to their recovery—the guy no longer has nightmares.

As Felman and Laub argue, personal and cultural recovery from trauma requires a conversation between the survivor and a witness; indeed, the witness is essential to complete the cycle of truth-telling. The Gs' visit modeled for the students the benefits of actively listening to a survivor, being present, fully present, when a survivor offers his greatest gift: his story. The visit by these two elderly Holocaust survivors provided the impetus for the turning point of the class. Suddenly the students saw the actual utility of learning about trauma, what produces it, what mitigates it, what heals it. If breaking his silence could end Jerry's nightmares, then finding a voice—that risky, scary, most disobedient act, as Nancy Walker argues in *The Disobedient Writer*—has efficacy. Perhaps this conclusion can be generalized. Perhaps speaking can benefit others as well. But for this kind of speaking to work we must have listeners, and effective listening has not been a valued skill in higher education.

Eliza

At this point in the class the students read a personal essay I wrote about my maternal grandmother, Eliza DerMelkonian Sachaklian, a survivor of the Armenian Massacres of 1896 and 1909, the forerunners to the Armenian Genocide of 1915. Both sets of grandparents in my family were survivors of the Armenian Massacres. As a child of four, my maternal grandmother hid on a roof to escape the Turks in 1896, and I was told that my paternal grandmother's hair turned white overnight as she ran to the American mission in Turkey to escape the slaughter. I offered my essay for two reasons. First, for historical value. My grandmother's experiences demonstrate the outlines of the first major genocide of the twentieth century, the precursor to the Holocaust, and one that is still not officially recognized by either the U.S. or the Turkish governments, although it is by many European governments. If the Armenian Genocide had been recognized, it is possible the Holocaust would not have occurred. When Hitler first voiced his plan to invade Poland and exterminate the Jews, his advisers protested, saying he would be stopped. Hitler replied in the now famous document in which he outlined his plans for invading Poland. He had issued the command "to send to death mercilessly and without compassion, men, women, and children of Polish derivation and language. Only thus shall we gain living space which we need. Who after all, speaks today of the annihilation of the Armenians?" (qtd. in Bardarkjian's *Hitler and the Armenian Genocide*).

Second, in reading my personal essay I, the teacher, was demonstrating that some personal stories are appropriate to be told in an academic venue, that they can, in fact, add a great deal to our understanding of our chosen topics. This did not mean that I expected the students to follow suit. But it did mean that I wanted them to choose what to write and talk about and not feel constrained by any expectations in either direction. Here is a response to my essay in Maxim's journal: "I admire the fact that the professor wrote something and gave it to the class to read. I think that sets the tone. She has shared something with us . . . Given the class and the dynamic, I think we should all begin to share with each other, and we will eventually get closer to and have more respect for each other. Perhaps these revelations will help us see each other in a different light."

This entry was written at the end of October. The student who wrote it was one of the most combative in class. Indeed, I soon learned that he and several of the other young men had once been friends, but their egos clashed so deeply that they no longer tolerated each other. This young man's comments in class were virtually all negative and all political. He was quick to tell us what was wrong with the world, but he could not or would not respond more holistically to the texts, only as a budding politician. It set other students' teeth on edge. But now clearly something was beginning to change for him.

It became clear to me that the students wanted to respond in different ways to each other, to me, and to the texts, but they had no models for such a process. They had been successful honors students all their lives, learning well that objective voice so prized by higher education, so indicative of subject "mastery." (That term says it all: We conquer our subjects. We don't engage in a process of inquiry with them.) Since the Gs' visit had such an impact on the class, and since we had been reading Laub's comments on witnessing, I thought we might benefit from learning a technique called active listening. In this technique a listener's role is not to offer advice, to judge, or even to comment on what a partner is saying, but only to hear the speaker's words and understand why they are important. It is content-driven listening, not action-oriented. It is not the listener's role to help fix the problem or even help sort out its parameters. Her only role is to listen and listen well, not only to hear every word but also to ask questions that help the speaker probe the content further until it is clear to both speaker and listener exactly what the salient issues are.

Active Listening

We set up a workshop with Ellen Schmidt, the Education Director of Suicide Prevention and Crisis Service of Tompkins County in Ithaca, New York. Ellen's job includes offering training workshops for phone crisis volunteers, so she has extensive experience helping novices learn active listening. The workshop is conducted in both large and small groups, so students practiced listening techniques in the presence of the entire class and also worked in groups of three: one speaker, one listener, and one observer. At the end of the four-hour workshop we asked students for anonymous evaluations. They were virtually all positive, with most students commenting on the value of this technique in their lives with partners, future students (for those going into education), friends, and family members. The following are a few responses from journals regarding the active listening workshop:

> Although the active listening seminar was a bit longer than I had expected, I think that the experience had great value. I never realized how difficult the reflective listening was. When she (Ellen) would come up with examples, it would seem so easy, but when we went around the room I realized how difficult it really is . . . I definitely see how it could make a big difference if you even just try a little. In my day to day interactions I have been thinking about it, and even attempting to use the techniques on a small scale, and it is interesting how different your responses become. I think that I was very much caught up in giving advice and trying to find the solutions myself, so it's a very different animal to try and just let them figure it out, to just listen really. I think it is great that we are actually learning something that is applicable to our daily lives.
>
> I thought that listening and observing were almost the same roles. Both roles taught me more about the person and gave me a better understanding of the person . . . I never knew that Lisa lost both her parents . . . She seems to have come a long way since freshman year. This year she is very nice, cheerful, upbeat. She intimidated me when I met her in Spanish class freshman year. She seemed quiet, angry . . . Knowing her background explains her behavior to me. I view her as a completely different person . . . I enjoy listening to people in class and learning more about them. I feel that it makes me have a greater

respect for my peers. They are no longer just faces in the classroom but people as well.

And Adele, who wrote the essay about her near-drowning in chapter 2, offered this:

> I am ready to turn a corner. I am ready to go beyond. I am ready to do something different. Today I hit a point where I was ready to say, "Enough reading and discussion." . . . Before this class I never would have written about some of the situations I've been in as "traumatic." From what I have learned and read, I would have to say that it is important to write about these experiences no matter how insignificant they seem to me (nobody died or was raped).

Class Results

But the real test was to see how the possibilities presented in this workshop might affect the class dynamic. The next week I received the following from Maxim, the student who spoke aggressively about the state of the world but never anything about himself:

> I was sitting at home on the patio as I usually do when I get home from school in the evenings. I heard her car horn honk. This time her honk was different. It was not the usual two beep-beep. It was more like six or seven long and uninterrupted beeeeps. I quickly ran through the door to open the garage and then the gate. She drove in fast. She did not smile while she was coming in and she did not greet me either. I ran up to her, "Mommy is everything all right?" "Did you get suspended from school again?" she replied. OOPS, the cat's out of the bag, I murmured to myself. Her eyes were . . . red. She started to swear at the top of her voice. "What the f__k am I going to do with you? You are just like your f__king father! I am gonna f__king kill you." As soon as she finished swearing, she then headed for her bedroom. I knew that it would take 156 steps to get there and back. And I also knew she would return with an electric cord that she was gonna use to beat me. Why did I not run this time? All it would take is 23 steps through one room and I am out of her reach. But instead I waited, as usual. I

pleaded, I begged, I started crying . . . "Mommy please don't . . . I will never do it again . . . I am sorry." She beat me straight for at least twenty or thirty minutes. However long it was . . . I may not remember . . . But all I know is I could no longer stand. I remember her blue dress being crushed from the grip of my hand . . . And my shirt being torn from the hits of the cord.

For me, there was a time in my life when more bad things happened to me than good. They were almost like a way of life, regular as clockwork. Happy events and moments then to me seemed like fantasies you would see on an American TV show. It is these horrible memories that still to this day haunt me . . . They force me to question certain things . . . Did my mother love me? . . . Was everything my fault ? . . . Could my mother have chosen a better way of disciplining me? . . . And most importantly, was I abused? By American standards, I was abused horribly . . . But by Jamaican standards, I was not—that's how you raise a kid there. This course has provided a framework within which I can analyze my past experiences. It has given me the tools to assess, name, and claim what happened to me. Reading about and listening to various traumatic narratives have helped me to shed light on what would have been an otherwise murky issue. Now I can say with absolute confidence and certainty that I was abused. I have moved beyond this whole idea of cultural relativity. To that end, I condemn the way Jamaicans raise their children. This portion of the class has taught me that human and children's rights are universal; there are no geographic exceptions. The process by which I have come to name and claim my own trauma was not all peaches and cream—It had a negative effect. You see, for me to say that I was abused means that I must indict my mother as my abuser. This is something I do not want to do. I love my mother. I respect my mother. I don't want to make her out to be someone bad. I know she loves me. I know she would do anything for me. But acknowledging this has placed me between the proverbial rock and a hard place. How do I reconcile between these two things? I was indeed abused, but I don't think my mother is an abusive person. I do not know how to resolve this dilemma. The thing is, I have never written or spoken about my trauma before now. Now that I have, I feel better. It's as if 100 pounds has been lifted from my shoulders. Seen in this light, I wonder, would my life have turned out differently if it had involved some sort of active or reflective listening?

Because of my past experiences I find it hard to trust people. Along those same lines I am also very defensive and impatient. I live my life in such a way that I make it hard for anyone to even think, much less try to abuse me. All these defensive mechanisms have made me bitter and unforgiving towards people more times than I wanted to be.

Judging from our class activities, Active and Reflective listening has its benefits. What if I had had someone to talk to, someone who listened and understood? Would I have still internalized my abuse? Also related to the issue, would I have had some sort of closure? I want to have close friends, but it seems like the costs are too much. Sometimes I think that if my own mother abused me, then who wouldn't? She was my flesh and blood; if she did it to me I think anyone can. This realization has given me a very negative and suspicious outlook towards the world. As a result, I am always wary of people. I expect the worst—that way I will always be prepared.

Since Maxim is from another culture, one that sanctions what we would term physical abuse, Maxim never questioned his mother's behavior until this year when he was a senior in the United States about to graduate. It never occurred to him that his experiences were not the norm. And when he did question his mother's behavior, it caused him to indict his mother and his culture, a most threatening enterprise given his love for both. His chosen field, politics, provided myriad opportunities for projecting his anger and mistrust into the world. With the writing of Maxim's essay, which occurred after he opened the door in the active listening workshop, his combative demeanor changed. Students could sense the difference, and the entire class responded. They began to speak in new ways in class; their voices were quieter, more tentative. They listened. Alice Miller points out that "learning is a result of listening, which in turn leads to even better listening and attentiveness to the other person" (101). As the students began to feel heard, one by one, they began to take risks. They asked questions rather than proclaiming answers. They began to allow me to read to the class from their journals, which enabled them to see each other as if with new eyes. We learned that Joshua's parents suffered from mental illness, Tim's father was alcoholic, Carol's family was torn apart by greed, Mary's grandmother committed suicide, Carrie has a Down syndrome brother whom she adores but who also sapped the resources of her mother. Here is an excerpt from Carrie's journal:

> Listening and observing have always been easy tasks for me. Maybe this started when I was a little girl. My father and elder brother were seldom home. When my mother was having a stressful day, she would release her troubles on me. I quickly learned how to read body language, tone of voice, and how to respond in a way that would be beneficial. However, I also learned to reply in a way that would not be helpful, resulting in the end of conversation. This I utilized to avoid confrontation . . . Talking is not something that I am overly fond of. Later in the semester, in the writing and healing unit of the class, we all read an essay written by Jean, a former student, about her mentally disabled sister. The essay began: "YOU THINK YOU CAN GET AWAY WITH ANYTHING IN THIS HOUSE JUST BECAUSE YOU ALWAYS GET THE ATTENTION? ! I knew the neighbors probably heard me screaming with the window open, but I didn't care."

Carrie's final project for the trauma class was precipitated by this essay, which triggered her own memories of growing up with a brother with Down syndrome:

> These two sentences did not bring me into Jean's house. Instead, I was placed into my dining room . . . It was around 7:30 on a June evening. Billy was sitting on the floor next to the coffee table. He had just done something wrong, and I was furious. Maybe he broke another dish, stole food out of the refrigerator, or was hurting himself. I really could not remember. I do remember that I yelled as loud as I could, exactly the words that were in capital print, down to the last syllable. I was aware that the front door was open. I knew that the neighbors walking past might hear. I just didn't care. I had had enough.
>
> At this point I put down the paper. That was . . . an event buried in the past. I was shocked that a school reading brought such memories back. Nothing ever relates to my childhood situations. Continuing with the rest of the essay, I repeatedly found more phrases that sent me back home, and not to Jean's house in California. If Jean and I have similar responses to growing up with a disabled sibling, what

other effects do we share? Are these effects common to all siblings of disabled children? For this I began looking.

And this began the study that formed the core of her final project for the class, a research paper that included her own experiences as part of the evidence. Other students also began to think about family issues that they began to realize had deeply affected them.

The young woman identified as Sharon in the introduction to this book had asked to speak with me in conference to talk about how the class was helping her to examine her sexual abuse and the effects of that abuse on her psyche. The combination of professional counseling and writing in her class journal, which she used for both class reflection and personal study, produced immediate change: Not only did she begin to be more aware of her feelings, but also the relief she felt in voicing her long-kept secrets was so immediate that she wrote in her journal, "I can already feel a genuine life in my spirit lately. I actually smile for random reasons . . . I am beginning to feel the excitement of my future." Then after a few weeks in therapy, when she could apply the techniques she had been reading about in class, she wrote in her journal:

> I think that an emotional telling of the story is more important than a factual one. If I did not have the option to melt-down and cry during my therapy sessions, I wouldn't be as honest as I am. The emotions that come with the words cannot ever be separated. As the images become normalized, the quality and type of emotion may change, but the emotion or image never goes away. If I were constantly being pressed for "the truth" of what happened, I would probably try to find things that weren't there so that my story could "make sense," but instead, I am thankful to let the fragmented pieces trickle out and then worry about putting them together later, if they even can be put together. I don't plan on trying to make my narrative neat and tidy . . . but rather let it fill the space around me and eventually cradle me. Each survivor's narrative is their life story; without it, s/he would be wandering helpless . . . fragmented, and alone. It is the emotional narrative that ties everything together . . . to allow the healing and "moving on" process to begin.

By graduation she had internalized a process to heal herself—ironically by letting others in. The following is from her journal:

As much as I understand that there is a hazard to listening to another's trauma—is it not our duty to free our own people from such emotional burdens? I feel that in our narcissistic society, we perpetuate the silence that sickens and degrades its victims, which prevents the transition from victim to survivor. Is not this perpetuation of silence as horrific as the crimes that are committed?

These personal changes began to be felt in the class itself, as reflected in this journal entry:

Could it be true????? Yesterday's class was amazing—I was never so happy to hear all the new voices yesterday! I actually felt some of the tension dissipate . . . The whole class was just amazing in general because I felt that the dialogue was opened up, more people were "present," and Maxim even made some comments that weren't totally ridiculous! I have so much hope for the rest of the semester.

Maintaining professional distance is the front-line defense against teachers being drawn into a student's emotional difficulties. But most of us also know that the line between therapist and teacher is not always clear and distinct. Just asking the right question about a text, as we have seen, can plunge the writer into therapeutic self-examination, as so often happens in writing classes. M. Garrett Bauman, professor of English at Monroe Community College, discusses this exact question in his *Chronicle of Higher Education* article titled "Crossing the Fine Line Between Teacher and Therapist." He tells of a wheelchair-bound student, a Vietnam War veteran, whose anger and bitterness were evident:

"You don't know what all I took, Teach. You lay flat on your back for a year. Being crippled ain't just a thing that happens to you once. I got a son. Yeah. He was born while I was in Nam. I saw him twice since I been back. The last time he was nine."

"Why don't you visit him?"

"Like this?" He slapped the chrome wheelchair. "He's better off without Daddy to shame him. I ain't dragging him down with me"

"He might see past the wheelchair," I said.

I was a teacher, not a therapist. Yet to treat Jimmy as a purely educational issue would be not only heartless but truly stupid. While it may seem best to keep academic and personal issues separate, it's hypocritical. Personal heartaches, neuroses, and rage account for part of the vitality of great books *and* their best teachers. Surely it is the same for our students and their studies. Jimmy's crippled body and psyche was an unhealed wound in our collective spirit, and part of his intellectual contribution in our class.

Bauman continues with a description of a conversation he had with Jimmy in which Jimmy worries that his son would be better off without him:

"Your son's in his twenties. How can you be bad for him? You love him." I had intruded where professors are not supposed to go, but didn't care.

"I'm trash. Pin a degree on me, an' I'll still be trash."

"You don't have to be a rotten father because yours was."

He pounded his armrest. "I already am, dammit!" . . . He pushed violently on his wheels and rammed the door, escaping.

I collapsed into my chair. How little I knew of what it was to be him. Could I really teach him unless I did? I lifted my feet and shoved my hands against the desk so I rolled in my desk chair across the office. I stranded myself in the center where I could reach nothing. I told myself to remember that feeling.

Jimmy's writing sometimes transformed his pain into insight; sometimes it enraged him. I didn't have a plan, didn't know if I pushed him to deliverance or disaster. But we slogged together through the tangled places he's inhabited for twenty-four years. He was eager just to move somewhere. No matter what else he did, he wrote, and I hoped we both might stagger into one of education's ordinary miracles, when learning ought to be impossible but happens anyway.

I told myself that shortly after the middle of the term, when Jimmy punched a police officer who had arrested him for selling pot. He railed in my office.

"Who cared if I smoke dope? Am I going to be a doctor? Fly an airplane? Play shortstop?"

He was hunkering down in his miserable foxhole and I prodded him. "You didn't hit the cop because he arrested you."

He took off his purple mirrored sunglasses, and I saw his old, exhausted eyes for the first time. The skin around them was sickly white from lack of sunlight. "That's right."

I rolled my chair closer and said what had been brewing in me. "Daddy's gone. The cops are not the army. You can't get even with anonymous bullets. Let go of what you were—that boy's dead. Live what's left!"

He laughed and rolled back a few inches. "This is life? See, my big problem is, what's a hardbody do with a diploma? Jerk off a computer all day? Wear a suit?

"See your son. Write your papers. It's not what it could have been, but it's better than rotting in Vietnam for the rest of your life." He sighed and nodded.

Jimmy's GPA turned ugly despite the C+ he was earning in my class. By December he looked exhausted. During finals week, I heard the familiar whizzing, and Jimmy rolled into my office. "I got to tell you something."

"You're dropping out?" I hate students' choosing failure, but I knew Jimmy was not surrendering. He was pricking the bubble of hypocrisy that said we could help, could atone for the loss he had suffered on behalf of all of us. And I knew he had fought harder in college and learned more than most A students.

He shrugged. "Sure. But I finished your last paper. Here." He swallowed. "I also . . . uh . . . wanted to tell you . . . I ain't been honest with you. I got some leg movement. I can crab around with crutches; I just don't practice. Watch."

He slowly straightened one leg parallel to the floor, then the other . . . "I don't have to be in this chair."

"Show me," I said. Jimmy shook his head. My hand hung in the air between us.

"I walk like an epileptic duck," Jimmy said. I extended my hand closer and he took it. I felt the full weight of him as I pulled.

This teacher could not turn his back on his student regardless of the discomfort it caused him both personally and professionally. Watching one of our students make destructive life choices is painful, and it would be easy to hide behind the wall of professionalism that decrees, "This is not my problem." But if we are in the business of education, how can we ignore these students without feeling that we have failed them in some way? The teacher/student dyad is a relationship, one that can be among the most important in a student's life. Many of us have been lucky enough to encounter one teacher who believed in us when we needed it most. In an article in the *Chronicle of Higher Education* titled "Opening Ourselves to Unconditional Love in Our Relationships with Students," Sara Hopkins-Powell, vice president for academic affairs and provost at Southern Oregon University, argues that unconditional love, while an "unlikely topic for college faculty members to consider in this time of sexual harassment and consensual relations policies, is one of the greatest gifts we have as teachers, mentors, and co-creators of learning." She defines unconditional love as "the ability to care so deeply for individual students that we hold them in our hearts regardless of whether we agree with their life choices" (B5).

Although loving teaching is seen as laudatory, it is not fashionable to speak of loving our students. I argue, however, that we cannot truly love teaching without loving our students; otherwise we face the risk of our work being driven by our egos rather than our ethics. Love is the great leveler, and students know this. I once had a famous religion professor in graduate school, a massive European with a booming voice and an even larger persona who had spent much of his life living as a Buddhist monk in India. Such a cult had been created around this man that I was shocked and honored when one evening he happened to have dinner with my late husband and me. My husband was an eager student of world religions, finding in them a spiritual outlet sorely lacking in his stern Presbyterian upbringing. He attempted to initiate a conversation about this professor's area of expertise, but the professor turned his steely eyes toward my husband and said, "I find your enthusiasm boring." He may have been right. Perhaps this man was pummeled with hopeful penitents grasping at his saffron robes; however, each penitent was attempting to learn. This is what Lauren was doing when she wrote her rambling first draft about her friend. It was her enthusiasm, her passion that took her beyond that first draft into the topic that freed her. The same is true with Melissa, and Maxim, Adele, and Meg. Love also means establishing and preserving appropriate boundaries. Students need their privacy and must be able to choose what and when to speak and write, but sometimes establishing human contact through listening and responding empathically is what loving teachers must do.

Susan Brison writes in *Aftermath* that after her assault she experienced terrifying, isolating flashbacks that only abated when she was speaking of her experience to the police, doctors, a lawyer, and a prosecutor: "Although others apologized for putting me through what seemed to them a re-traumatizing ordeal, I responded that it was, even at that early stage, therapeutic to bear witness in the presence of others who heard and believed what I told them" (54). Even though we may feel helpless and useless simply bearing silent witness, listening can be a powerful tool for healing. Dori Laub explains how articulating trauma is important to the therapeutic process: "To undo this entrapment is a fate that cannot be known, cannot be told, but can only be repeated, a therapeutic process—a process of constructing a narrative, of reconstructing a history, and, essentially, of *re-externalizing the event*—has to be set in motion. This re-externalization of the event can occur and take effect only when one can articulate and *transmit* the story, literally transfer it to another outside oneself and then take it back again, inside. Telling thus entails a reassertion of the hegemony of reality and a re-externalization of the evil that affected and contaminated the trauma victim" (69).

In 1991 Jane Tompkins published an essay, "Me and My Shadow," in which she asserts that the depersonalization of academic prose is confining, frustrating, and ultimately a lie, because it forces scholars to pretend that they do not have personal contexts that color their scholarship. Her position on this issue is similar to that of Judith Harris, who argues, "In light of postmodernism's inevitable diminishment of the autobiographical center as generative of any text, I begin this book by arguing that all writing emerges from a person, and a person's unique and often painful inscription within what may be an otherwise culturally, socially, or even biologically determined language" (7). The concept of objectivity is limited by the subjectivity of being in a particular place, time, and psychic state. This post-postmodernist view acknowledges that a self is a constructed entity, formed by an amalgam of genetic material so pressed upon by our social constructs that we cannot even identify all that influences us. For Tompkins, the denial of personal contexts became so limiting that she could no longer maintain the false dichotomy between public and private, scholarly and personal:

> There are two voices inside me . . . One is the voice of a critic who wants to correct a mistake . . . The other is the voice of a person who wants to write about her feelings (I have wanted to do this for a long time but have felt too embarrassed.) This person feels it is wrong to criticize . . . because [it] only insulates academic discourse further from the issues that make feminism matter. That make *her* matter. The

critic, meanwhile, believes such feelings, and the attitudes that inform them, are soft-minded, self-indulgent, and unprofessional.

These beings exist separately but not apart. One writes for professional journals, the other in diaries, late at night. One uses words like "context" and "intelligibility," likes to win arguments, see her name in print, and give graduate students hardheaded advice. The other has hardly ever been heard from. She had a short story published once in a university literary magazine, but her works exist chiefly in notebook and manila folders labeled "Journal" and "Private." This person talks on the telephone a lot to her friends, has seen psychiatrists, likes cappuccino, worries about the state of her soul . . . Her father is ill right now, and one of her friends recently committed suicide.

The dichotomy drawn here is false—and not false. I mean in reality there's no split. It's the same person who feels and who discourses about epistemology. The problem is that you can't talk about your private life in the course of doing your professional work. You have to pretend that epistemology, or whatever you're writing about, has nothing to do with your life, that it's more exalted, more important, because it (supposedly) *transcends* the merely personal. Well, I'm tired of the conventions that keep discussions of epistemology, or James Joyce, segregated from meditations on what is happening outside my window or inside my heart. The public-private dichotomy, which is to say the public-private *hierarchy,* is a founding condition of female oppression. I say to hell with it. The reason I feel embarrassed at my own attempts to speak personally in a professional context is that I have been conditioned to feel that way. That's all there is to it. (1080)

It is important to acknowledge here that patriarchy's public/private dichotomy affects all of us—men as well as women. My point in raising the issue of this split, however, is its effects on education. We are taught very early that cognition and emotion are split, that emotions are to be controlled, hidden, often not even acknowledged in a public venue. (Yet we make public policy, go to war, and design educational systems often based on emotional responses that may or may not have any objective reality.) This educational straitjacket limits creativity, affects the career choices young people make, and contributes to the frustration and anger many young people feel toward education. Wilson High School in Long Beach, California, was one of the most violent high schools in the United States, but after a young teacher named

Erin Gruwell asked her students to contribute their feelings and experiences to their classes changes occurred: All 150 of her students graduated from high school and are attending college. As Carl Jung argued, we can move naturally toward integration if offered the opportunity.

One of the students in my capstone honors course is an example of this process. Maura was an English major who wanted to go on to graduate school with the ultimate career goal of becoming a college literature professor. She had been studying the life and work of Mary Shelley and wanted to continue this effort in my Twentieth-Century Trauma class, but she was confused and nervous because she had no models for the structure of such a project. Scholars had certainly written about Mary Shelley's patriarchal relationships with her father and husband and the influence those relationships had on her work. But Maura wanted to go further: She was clearly drawn to Mary Shelley, caught by Mary's anguish upon the deaths of her children, stung by her father's coldness and lack of sympathy, outraged when Percy Shelley abandoned her when she needed him most. Maura wanted to investigate these areas of Shelley's life, but she also wanted to delve into what connected her own life to Mary Shelley's, what made Mary's life and work speak to a young woman today. She wanted to unmask her personal context to demonstrate how it affects her professional life. In other words, she wanted to pick up where Tompkins left off and allow into the public conversation the elements from her personal life that affect her reading of Mary Shelley. Within the field of literature and writing, we have seen scholars locate themselves in critical discussions of text; however, as Kirsch and Ritchie argue, it is not enough to "make the facile statements that often appear at the beginning of research articles" (9). A "politics of location" also requires a self-examination of what is problematic and difficult, perhaps even including areas that demonstrate our own limitations.

Maura begins her essay with the conventional biographical details, but note how the discussion moves quickly into her thesis—that *Frankenstein* is a trauma narrative that reflects Mary Shelley's own anguished life:

> On August 30, 1797, the liberal feminist political writer and author of *A Vindication of the Rights of Women*, Mary Wollstonecraft— considered by much of England's population to be infamous for her views and actions—gave birth to a daughter who bore her name. The newborn's father was William Godwin, the atheist political philosopher and author of the highly influential book *Political Justice*.

Wollstonecraft and Godwin had married only five months earlier, despite their mutual belief in free love and distaste for the outdated and oppressive institution of marriage. Neither, however, wished their child to be stigmatized by society for being born out of wedlock, as Wollstonecraft's first daughter to another man had been, and so the two middle-aged political activists set up housekeeping—in separate, although close, homes—and settled down to raise Wollstonecraft's daughter Fanny and the expected baby . . . Wollstonecraft died ten days after her daughter's birth from an infection introduced into her uterus by a doctor, who like any other doctor who might have attended her, did not realize the danger of using unsanitized hands to retrieve pieces of broken placenta from the womb. Ironically, the woman who fought so passionately and wrote so boldly in support of women taking their place as men's equals and putting an end to the artifice and vapid pursuits which weakened the female intellect and subjugated their bodies to men's, was put to death by an ignorant man as she experienced one of the most defining and confining moments of womanhood: becoming a mother. Her small daughter's inheritance was a daunting name to grow into: Mary Wollstonecraft Godwin.

Nineteen years later, small Mary would add Shelley to her name—significantly dropping Godwin—and the weight of literary expectation placed on her would be complete. During her time she would be considered somewhat of a disappointment to her name by her liberal circle of literati, but more tragically by herself. In her journal, she rarely reflected on the importance of her writing or on herself as an author, yet she left behind one entry that reveals the loneliness and self-doubt that her profession brought to her: "What folly is it in me to write trash nobody will read . . ." Never mind that her first novel, *Frankenstein*, outlasted and outsold the works of Byron and Shelley, the poets who had engaged with her in the ghost-story writing contest that gave birth to *Frankenstein*. Never mind that she lived by her pen, buried four children, a husband, and a father, raised her surviving son, Percy Florence, alone, and salvaged his inheritance . . . On top of the emotional distress these two men put her through . . . both writers directed and edited her written work. They shaped the products of her imagination in the ways they saw fit, giving her a voice that was a hybrid not completely her own. All of these traumas, and subsequent ones to come, would find their way into the "ghost story" she began writing at the age of eighteen, published at twenty, and revised at thirty-four when her husband was dead and her father a diminished old man.

In *Frankenstein* Shelley articulates her isolation through the words of three male first-person narrators, pulling the strings of these male characters and manipulating what they say. Yet despite the dominance of masculine dialogue in her novel, it is the female characters buried in the story, and their words, or lack of them, who speak the most eloquently—even more so than the "eloquence and persuasion" of the creature whose first-person tale so many critics believe to be the "center" of the novel. These women "speak" through their socially conditioned language, enforced roles, and especially through their very absence. Mary Shelley could not (maybe did not even want to) write a novel outwardly criticizing the men she loved most as well as her responses to them, but she could work within the oppressive structure of a male-dominated literary world. She took the familiar genres of gothic and epistolary novels, which, if they weren't written by women, were written expressly for women, and bent and sutured them as Victor Frankenstein does the pieces of his creature, creating a vital offspring which transcends his origins. Her story is a tale of imposition, rejection, and trespass, in which isolated people search for "sympathy." . . . Her first novel, a tale of loneliness, fear of failed motherhood, rejection by those closest to her, and the anger and pain of being constructed and written upon, is a trauma narrative. It is an examination of an argument against repressive structures and action which becomes an impassioned plea for understanding spoken by the creature—a rejected, outcast, and misinterpreted "child" like Shelley—who, finally, leaves the readers to decide the "truth of my tale" that all the narrators claim.

At this point Maura makes her rebellious turn: She directly addresses the reader, using italics to define her own voice:

> *I, Maura the critic, a woman, the voice who will guide You through this novel, take you on a quest for sympathy, cannot begin without expressing why I wish to do so. It would be dishonest of me to interpret Mary, to explain her and her book by rewriting her the way so many other people have done, if I didn't expose myself as a medium of interpre-*

tation with her own flaws, agendas, and beliefs. Who are You to believe me? And who am I to be believed? These are the questions every reader should ask the first-person narrators of Frankenstein. It's a tangled story, you see, with much of Freud's (bless his misogynistically closed ears) double speak. So be suspicious Reader of me. Of words. Of yourself. Of the parts I stitch together and the offspring I produce. "But Soft! By and by I come." And if my shadow does offend, I will not make amends.

Maura's study of Mary Shelley's life and work, combined with her understanding of feminist theory, do not allow her to write on Shelley's text without exposing to scrutiny her personal context and its relationship to her reading of *Frankenstein*. This is a bold turn but an honest one, reflecting her intellectual integrity and emotional connectedness to the material, as is clear in this next excerpt:

Despite claiming to know little of his daughter's character, Godwin realized her potential as a writer, telling her Scottish host father, William Baxter, "I believe she has nothing of what is commonly called vice and that she has considerable talent . . . I wish, too, that she should be excited to industry. She has occasionally great perseverance, but occasionally, too, she shows great need to be roused." A scene from my childhood displaces the picture of Godwin scrawling this letter at his study desk to be sent to the rolling hills of Scotland. *I am nine or ten, swinging my legs beneath the bench of our ancient and sturdy black barroom piano, and my father is giving me a violin lesson. I have a violin teacher, a talkative woman who sells insurance and owns a fat orange cat, but dad thinks it's his job to instruct me. Over and over I practice a song which has grown teeth as my father stops and corrects me, disbelieving that I could make the same mistake so many times and that I can't count six/eight meter. Aching lines dig into my forehead from holding back my tears of frustration, but I lose control of them when my fingers dance the wrong direction. I run to my room weeping for my imperfections and crying because I've let my father see them. This is the day he tells my mother, "There are two things every musician has to be able to do—get the right rhythm and play the right pitches—and she can't do either." I vow that I will prove him wrong some day, and do, with a ten-thousand-dollar music scholarship, but not at that moment. My fingers and shoulders and soul hurt too much.*

We see now that Maura identifies with Shelley's isolation and anger toward her father. But rather than allow that to be a palimpsest in her writing, she invites us into her intellectual and emotional world. We see now that descriptions of Mary's life with her father and Percy Shelley take Maura immediately to her own traumatic images. Here she takes us a little further. Mary's child has just died and she is overcome with grief, feelings for which Godwin has no sympathy:

> In simplest terms, Mary is acting like a woman and not the "something great and good" her father had planned for her . . . there is no record of Mary defending herself or cutting off communication with her father because of his cruelty. *Every time when I was little—a small grown up—and my father said something terrible to me, I would vow to write it down in a notebook, which would grow as I recorded his hatred. I intended it as a present to give to him the day I moved out of his house . . . I never started that notebook, though. Some of it was laziness. The other part was the horror of seeing his bared-fang words outlined in my pencil strokes. His words wouldn't hang in the air above me then, but would move down through my head, my chest, into my arm, hand, fingers, and the pen they wanted to control . . . Once, London (a former* boyfriend) *called me a mouse for squealing when he picked me up, the same name Mary was given by Percy and Hogg and Byron for her timidity. She was not timid in her love or her writing. Neither am I. But I know what it is to accommodate and respect their beliefs even when cold theory comes between you. I know what it is to bend, because I've done it all my life. I copied my mother, who lowers her voice and her head when my father shouts, "Kathy! Just let me do it! You're doing it all wrong!" I keep my radio at a whisper, refrain from running up the stairs, don't talk about vulgar topics at the dinner table, use my "indoor" voice, don't tread in puddles of oil in parking lots, run the fan in the bathroom, and double check the locks to keep him from yelling.*
>
> *I too would like Mary to rise up and protest. But I rarely protest either. I hear the counterargument too strongly . . . Is being a mirror to the desires of others a lack of self?*

Maura ends her essay with a discussion of Mary Shelley's acceptance of the multiple interpretations offered of *Frankenstein* and her final discourse to the reader, in which she, too, embraces ambiguity:

Shelley knew the power of writing—shaping words and speech—lay in its ability to create "meaning." But she also realized that meaning is changeable and performative and has no point of origin or truth. She was "proof against man and woman, " because she allowed herself to be both and to feel for and listen to both. That is why there are no villains or heroes or moral to be found in *Frankenstein,* just loud counter-arguments.

Reader! I've been a naughty girl. I've showed my seams. Disregarded the advice of Mother. Flouted the words of Father. I've given birth to a premature me, a form stitched from pages not from flesh. I've created a Mary and presented her to you as someone who knew the pain of creating and being created and who turned this imposition into an offspring novel which stitched together life and fiction and science and literature. I think Mary appreciated the slipperiness of creation and interpretation, but I could be wrong. And I have no mirror to see if I'm a creature or a monster.

And Reader, I don't know if all this writing I'm doing is healthy or good. For the past few months I've "deprived myself of rest and health" as Victor Frankenstein did to create his creature, in order to create my own literary offspring. I've become moody, distant, forgetful, and callous, all in an attempt to offer a dead woman and her novel sympathy. Is it "sympathy" I wish to offer or literary and critical greatness I wish to "pursue to its hiding place" and steal? Rain has tapped at my windows as at Victor's, and I have become distracted with the idea that it's pointing out my error as well. It's time for me to call my mother.

The ambiguity Maura locates in Shelley's text is replayed in the ambiguity of her own: Just as Shelley could not find a clear center between her own feelings, thoughts, ideas and those of her husband and father, Maura could not determine if her approach to her project was a product of "sympathy"—that is, identification,—or of a desire to match Shelley in inventiveness. Maura could not decide if her reading of Shelley is appropriate or if it appropriates Shelley's text, if it is a focused look into the relationship between the life and work of two people or a self-absorbed brooding. Her commitment to constructed honesty in this essay allows even this level of transparency: the questioning of her own motives. Clearly this essay is a work in progress, but so also is the process Maura used to produce it. Writing is a recursive act, a verb as well as a noun. It produces whatever level of understanding we can discover at that moment, but in the process of writing we change, altering both text and writer. In a talk at Syracuse University, Salman Rushdie told students in the Creative Writing Program about his motivation to write: "I do it because it's the way my mind works. It is my way of understanding the world."

This level of academic transparency, this merging of public and private is not the Oprah-like confessional Tompkins has in mind. Confessionals serve to distance us from the speaker. When we watch talk shows and hear about the unfortunate events that can happen to families, the medium can serve to make us feel better about ourselves. Our lives are not as out of control as those of the guests. This kind of confessional panders to the public's voyeuristic tendencies; it does not necessarily create new methodologies for inquiry. But as the responses to Richard Hoffman's *Half the House* demonstrate, trauma narratives can still be seen as confessional prose and therefore dismissed as art. Maura knew that an academic essay that blended the personal and the public was likely to be seen as even more problematic. However, she was also aware that as women, minorities, and the historically disenfranchised move into positions of greater power in the academy, the scholarship model can change. And indeed, today many scholars and writers as varied as Henry Louis Gates, Adrienne Rich, Claude Steele, Carol Gilligan demonstrate through their work the power of the personal within the academic. As Judith Harris said, "Personal writing, which is often dismissed as too self-referential, is not just about language or even the manipulation of language in an aesthetic container; it is about how we find our way to utterance" (11). Our stories count. They help make us who we are, yet our academic lives often render these stories irrelevant, so much so that they can become buried, but when we bury our stories, we have difficulty having true sympathy for those of others.

Only when we have acknowledged our own feelings and honored them by integrating them into who we are can we begin to grow the kind of empathy we will need as productive citizens. Empathy is not some effete psychological term: It means being able to recognize others even when their problems crash into ours. It means understanding how pain and trauma can lead to more pain and trauma: "Those to whom evil is done, do evil in return." Witnessing to the traumas of others is an antidote to this cycle of pain begetting more pain because it spares the survivor from being trapped in that cycle alone: "The listener to trauma needs to [be] a guide and an explorer, a companion in a journey on to an uncharted land, a journey the survivor cannot traverse or return from alone" (59), as Dori Laub states. "What ultimately matters in all processes of witnessing, spasmodic and continuous, conscious and unconscious, is not simply the information, the establishment of the facts, but the experience itself of *living through* testimony, of giving testimony" (85). As discussed in previous chapters, the act of speaking or writing the trauma can have a beneficial effect for both the survivor and the witness. It can establish our common humanity, which is the primary antidote to trauma.

In an article in the *Chronicle of Higher Education* titled "It's Not What You Know, but How You Use It: Teaching for Wisdom," Robert Sternberg, professor of psychology and education at Yale University, writes, "Our goal is not to teach values but to help children develop positive values of their own that promote social welfare. We try to give students a framework in which to develop those values—seeing things from others' perspectives as well as one's own, and thinking not just about one's interests but also about a common good" (B20). Learning to honor our own life stories and learning the skills to listen to those of others are essential to the development of a worldview and the values that help manifest it. But unacknowledged trauma can thwart our best intentions.

At the beginning of our class virtually no students identified any of their experiences as traumatic except the young woman whose parents had died. At the end of the class virtually all of them stated that some aspects of trauma had been visited upon them and had affected their behavior. This was not the product of group mind revising reality. These students had not recognized the effects of their experiences, regardless of the labels used to describe them. After studying the effects of trauma and hearing from each other, they understood that stress responses are common, and no one is immune. That awareness enabled them to function more productively as members of an academic community and as individuals. While the point of this class was not expressly to provide therapeutic moments for the students, they instinctively compared their experiences to those they read about. While they often felt guilty doing this—since genocide and sexual violence, for example, are in a different league from most of the students' experiences—they also realized that trauma, like beauty, is in the eye of the beholder, and it comes in many forms, depths, and intensities. Listening to others allows us to listen to ourselves—and vice versa. Perhaps nothing is more important in education than that. Sharon expressed this eloquently in her journal: "How do we honor survivors? Maybe we should just listen to them, and close our own mouths for a moment. Maybe we should just keep our ears ready for that moment when another image is translated into words and needs listening to. Without the listener the story gets reabsorbed and lost. So I think that may be a start."

This process can develop understanding at many levels. Dori Laub recognizes "three separate, distinct levels of witnessing in relation to the Holocaust experience: the level of being a witness to oneself within the experience, the level of being a witness to the testimonies of others, and the level of being a witness to the process of witnessing itself" (61). Students in my class encountered all three of those levels: They became conscious witnesses to their own traumas, they chose to witness to the traumas of others, and they were able to step back and in a meta-cognitive way witness the process of witnessing that we were all engaged in. They learned a process for encountering themselves and others that enabled them to fully engage while developing the appropriate cognitive distance to prevent them from being trapped inside their own experiences or those of their peers. This is essential to protect the students, the teacher, and the class enterprise from being overwhelmed.

Felman's Class Crisis

In the first chapter of *Testimony*, Shoshana Felman implies a relation between trauma and pedagogy. Indeed, she raises the question whether "trauma can *instruct* pedagogy"(1). As outlined in chapter 1, our era did not invent trauma, which is unfortunately an abiding feature of history, but given the contemporary magnitude and frequency of genocides, wars, and violence and our current awareness of the powerful effects of trauma, it is all too characteristic of our age. We are all survivors in one way or another. This fact has created a significant role for testimony. As Elie Wiesel stated: "If the Greeks invented tragedy, the Romans the epistle, and the Renaissance the sonnet, our generation invented a new literature, that of testimony" (qtd. in Felman and Laub 6). Testimony is essential to trauma recovery, on both a personal and cultural level.

Felman recounts the experience of a course she taught in which Holocaust testimonies were a central part of the class. The emotional impact of these testimonies put the class in crisis: The students were overwhelmed with the content and isolated from their peers who were not a part of this experience: "They were obsessed. They felt apart, and yet not quite together. They sought out each other and yet felt they could not reach into each other . . . They felt alone, suddenly deprived of their bonding to the world and to one another. As I listened to their outpour, I realized the class was entirely at a loss, disoriented and uprooted" (48). Felman turned to Laub for counsel, and together they decided that Felman needed to reassume her authority as the teacher of the class and address the class in a way that would summarize the "importance and significance of their reactions" and present an *"integrated view* of the literary texts and of the videotapes." Felman then assigned the following topic: "Write a paper on your experience of the testimony and on your experience of the class . . . What has this experience taught you in the end? . . . What *difference* did it make in your global perception of the class? What I am suggesting is that you view this paper as your *testimony to this course* (51–52). Felman goes on to argue that "if teaching does not hit upon some sort of crisis, if it does not encounter either the vulnerability or the explosiveness of a . . . critical and unpredictable dimension, it has perhaps not *truly taught"* (53).

What Must Be Remembered

Although I agree with some of Felman's assumptions about teaching— that vulnerability is essential to learning and that it makes the classroom unpredictable—we need to be aware of another crucial element in education: our students' own life experiences and the triggers that teachers innocently— or not so innocently—present that call them up. Once we ask our students to investigate the testimonies of others, it is essential that we allow the space for them to investigate their own, if they so choose. This is the key: choice. Mandating such an investigation is performing therapy without a license. But we can cleanse ourselves of life traumas if given the time, the opportunity, and the appropriate community. Without that chance the enterprise of education is hampered. As James Moffett said, "If education is supposed to help people get better, that's not only in the sense of 'get better *at* something,' like writing, but in a sense of 'get well' and in a third sense of 'becoming a better person,' People want to *get better* in all senses at once. We don't just want our *writing* to come out right, *we* want to come out right" (29). Language is one of the tools available to help us to "come out right," but only if language provides a sense of mastery and control. Jeffrey Berman in his book *Empathic Teaching* argues that Felman's approach to her class crisis "suggests that language has a life and death of its own, and rather than believing, as I do, that people gain or lose control of their words, she implies that language gains or loses control of people" (129). In this way, Berman argues, Felman "reflects the linguistic theory of her mentor, Paul de Man, who viewed language as a reenactment of traumatic loss, dispossession, and mourning" (129). Our students all too often see language as an enemy to be conquered rather than as a tool that can help them offer themselves to the world. It controls them rather than their controlling it. Therefore, when they saw these two Holocaust survivors use language in very different ways to testify to the horrors of their experience, they learned the power of words to effect change in our interpretation of experience. Language offers power.

It was clear that my students found the testimony of Jerry and Jean painful and challenging to their assumptions about the world and themselves. It was also clear that studying trauma for a semester, watching films, reading trauma narratives, gathering information on trauma—what causes it, what alleviates it, what heals it—can activate memories of past unresolved pain and especially can exacerbate current difficulties. The students' journal entries became a lifeline for them and for me. Through their writing, my responses to their writing, the sharing of their entries with each other that began after mid-semester, and the culture of listening we established, the class was able to create the one element that mediates the isolation of trauma—community. In learning to listen to each other we discovered that trauma is ubiquitous: No one gets out of life alive; we had better learn how to deal with our own difficult moments and those of others. Trauma is not an event but a response to an event, and a supportive community can temper that response. In this class we modeled for each other how to manifest such support. The students found themselves at times frustrated, angry, overwhelmed, confused, and nervous about their grades in a class where grades seemed almost irrelevant. But as one student put it in an anonymous evaluation of the class at the end of the semester: "I'm still not quite sure who I am, but in the past few months, I have completely turned upside down in the ways in which I evaluate myself and my life. In short, this has been an incredible experience—informative, humorous, painful, humiliating, embarrassing, completely eye-opening. I have never approached the people I spend most of my days with the way I do those that I have come to know well through this course."

And another commented, "I am a better listener after this class and therefore a better person. I can handle my traumas as well as other people's much better now."

And another: "I feel more confident about who I am because the course allowed me to look deeper into some of my past experiences and to evaluate how they have shaped the person I am today . . . There's nothing more helpful for each of us seniors than coming out of college with the knowledge to get us the jobs we need and being able to face who we are and what has happened to us with comfort and ease."

And another: "I handle situations differently than I did before I took this class. I also realize that sometimes my petty issues are just that: petty."

And perhaps the most important comment: "Is it only me or should I say that for a semester I have been privileged to share this class with everyone in it?" To my great delight, one student even wrote that the class was "fun," this about a class on trauma that I feared would self-destruct before Thanksgiving break.

Listening and writing are two primary methodologies that permit a recursive look at ourselves. As we speak, as we write, as we listen, we examine our assumptions about ourselves and our world and recreate ourselves in that world. That is the ultimate goal of education: to teach tools for living and learning.

CHAPTER 5

Truth, Trauma, and Justice in Gillian Slovo's *Every Secret Thing*

A little white house
lingers in my memory
Of that little white house
Each night I dream.

POLISH FOLK SONG

CONTEMPORARY CULTURE appears to have a fascination for traumatic memory, even perhaps a love/hate relationship with it. Confessional discussions and texts focusing on traumatic experiences are both popular and vilified. This should come as no great surprise, given that psychological, symbolic, and physical trauma has become so pervasive a part of the day-to-day human experience. While trauma has ever been a part of life, perhaps one of the over-arching lessons of the twentieth century is the recognition that civilization is no buffer against trauma and indeed can offer ever-more-heinous methods for producing it. In some cases, the best efforts of social institutions to alleviate the effects of trauma, to mitigate its consequences, and to promote justice, serve only to deepen psychic wounds.

Gillian Slovo's memoir, *Every Secret Thing: My Family, My Country*, presents a detailed rendering of one specific instance of this deepening of psychic wounds, since her memoir—about her mother Ruth's murder, a result of Ruth's resistance to South African apartheid—will never lead, as Richard Hoffman's did, to the arrest of the murderers. Hoffman and Cheit were empowered when their abusers were arrested. Lauren, too, felt vindicated when her parents acknowledged her perception of their family. What, however, is the role of writing when no justice is possible, when perpetrators go free, when all we have is our narrative? What is the role of the reader and the culture within which the narrative resides? As Elie Wiesel demonstrates, the survivor is compelled to write, to give voice to those who have none, to give shape and structure to the chaotic and insane: "Why do I write? Perhaps in order not to go mad. Or, on the contrary, to touch the bottom of madness . . . I write to understand as much as to be understood . . . To wrench those victims from oblivion. To help the dead vanquish death" (94–97).

This need to wrench understanding from the seat of chaos can be seen in the work of both student and professional writers, and the benefits of the process are also available to both groups:

- Writing helps to form a bridge connecting the traumatic image and the emotions it generates with the more cognitive centers of the brain.
- The solitary experience of writing can enable the survivor to reach out to the larger community, mitigating the effects of traumatic isolation.
- The reader can become an integral part of the healing process because the communication between writer and reader may provide the only justice possible.

In earlier chapters we focused on the trauma narrative and its effects on the writer and on his/her text. This chapter investigates these issues in the context of a professional writer's memoir—to look further at the reader's role and the larger culture's role in the healing process. How a culture responds is the measure of its humanity. All too often the world responds with indifference to traumas as catastrophic as genocide. As Lt. General Dallaire asked in a speech at Colgate University: "Are all humans human, or do some count more than others?" Gillian Slovo's narrative provides us with a useful demonstration of the complexities presented by this situation for both reader and writer. It also can help us understand our own role in this drama, particularly since the reader/writer dyad is an essential component in the therapeutic process when no justice is possible.

Slovo is the daughter of South Africa's prominent anti-apartheid leaders, Ruth First, a journalist and political activist who was assassinated in exile in 1982, and Joe Slovo, who led the South Africa Communist Party and who became minister of housing in Nelson Mandela's government. After the end of apartheid Gillian Slovo, who had lived in England since the age of twelve, returned to South Africa in search of the story of her childhood. Her memoir recounts her journey, in which she discovered much about her parents' lives she did not know. She attempts to come to terms with their shortcomings, the violence and resulting trauma their lives engendered, the murder of her mother, and the final assault: the lack of justice for that crime, an unintended result of the work of the South African Truth and Reconciliation Commission.

The Traumatic Image

As the first chapter indicated, most clinicians believe that recovery from trauma depends on the ability to verbalize or narrate the traumatic image, to connect the iconic to the cognitive processes of the brain and provide a context for an experience that appears to have none. A trauma narrative will typically contain an organized set of sights, sounds, and images that captures the traumatic event, conveys the horror of the experience to others, and conducts the emotion from teller to reader. Ideally, as the narrative unfolds, the events that produced the traumatic response become more clearly known and can begin to be integrated into the on-going life of the survivor. This is the beginning of healing and where we can turn to Slovo's text.

The book opens with a very human detail, one that places her mother, Ruth, squarely in front of us as an ordinary woman: "An hour before she died my mother went shopping" (5). This image sets up for us not a hero or an assassinated icon, but a woman, a mother—Slovo's mother. A second key scene occurs as Ruth, Slovo's mother, is being taken off to jail for her resistance work. The police allow Ruth to pack a bag to take to prison. In the following description, Slovo's attention to detail reflects the importance of the images that have remained with her all these years:

> Ruth was in her bedroom, packing. A man leaning nonchalantly against a wall was watching her every move. She greeted us, her face immobile: almost everything she did showed her iron control.
>
> I remember her tapered fingers painstakingly folding each piece of clothing and laying it carefully on top of the one that went before. Half-way through, she fetched a book from the dressing table— Stendhal's *The Charterhouse of Parme*—and put it in the suitcase. As I watched it going in, I heard the policeman snort. My mother heard

him too. She turned to look at him, her eyes blazing. He couldn't hold her gaze. He pretended to relax, folded one arm into the other and leaned heavily against the wall.

The suitcase closed with a final click. My mother picked it up and started walking. Men went with her to the door. I followed them. They put her in the car, in the front seat, one on either side of her . . . My mother looked at me, almost as if she didn't know who I was. I stood waiting for her to say something. Finally her eyes seemed to focus on me, and, leaning closer, she tossed a few loving, reassuring words my way, topping them up with one last injunction, "Look after Robyn," she said. (67)

The details that speak here are the immobile face, the tapered fingers folding clothes, the book with its exact title, the click of the suitcase, the position of her mother and the men in the car, and most importantly, her mother's last words before being taken to prison. Of course, the "loving, reassuring words tossed" to her are not remembered or offered; they are not what Slovo took from this moment. Slovo herself had no security, no one to look to. Most significant for her was the injunction to take care of her younger sister, an injunction she tries to fulfill but much later realizes that she cannot. Both of these scenes amply illustrate one hallmark of the trauma narrative: its reliance on iconic image to convey both the experiences described and the emotional weight of those experiences.

One of the most compelling iconic memories in the book is, ironically, not Slovo's own but her father's. Joe's mother had died when he was twelve. In the same year his dog died. He wrote in his autobiography:

I was not told of her death. I suddenly woke up in the middle of the night to find the mirror covered with a white sheet. The walk around the coffin, the hysterical wailing of women and, above all, the yellow, yellow face haunted me for years. But the shaft of horror and the shock which struck me on our return from the funeral still evokes a shudder within me. As we entered the dining room, staring at me from the mantelpiece was a large doll (a present for my sister Reina) completely wrapped in bright yellow cellophane paper. It was particularly horrifying since my mother had died in childbirth and I expected to see the stillborn child in the coffin. (Qtd. in Slovo 149)

Slovo herself then writes, "It was a tragedy almost too traumatic for memory. Although Joe could continue to commemorate Spotty's death, he could not later recall either the day or the month . . . his mother had died" (149). The images that appear here—especially the yellow face—are the subject of a traumatic haunting.

But it is not only the original loss that produced Joe's traumatic response. It is also the way his family dealt with it, by breaking apart, as is often the case with trauma. Slovo captures the effects on her father as she describes Joe's attachment to a particularly important dwelling:

> I watched the intensity with which he stared at the Rocky Street building. I saw the pleasure with which he shared a few memories, and I realized that to Joe, born as he was in Lithuania, separated from his father between the ages of two and nine, Rocky Street was the one remaining vestige of his early life. But it was more than that as well. In Rocky Street, for what must have seemed like a fleeting moment, the young Joe had experienced family life, sleeping under the same roof as his mother, his father, his two sisters, and his dog.
>
> His mother's death shattered all that. Unable to cope, Joe's father, Wulfus, disappeared, leaving Joe in the charge of his eldest sister, Sonya, and the toddler Reina, in an orphanage. Wulfus did eventually return but it wasn't long before he remarried a stepmother that the resentful, and now financially independent, Joe never got to know. (150)

Joe lost his father, his sister, and his mother all at once, and his remaining family members did not help him to integrate his loss into his ongoing life. This secondary wounding was quite probably as crucial to his long-term response to his mother's death as her death itself, and is a poignant example of M. Symond's "second injury" (van der Kolk et al. 27).

Joe Slovo, whether he intended to or not, perpetuated his secondary trauma by imposing it on his own children through the fragmented way in which his political activities forced his family to live, sometimes with him in exile and sometimes with them living in foreign countries, together or separately. Even more important were the psychic effects of the fear engendered by that way of life. The second chapter of the book, for example, describes a moment when Tilly, Slovo's grandmother and a person who offers love and stability to the children, set off to deliver supper to Ruth, who is in prison. Tilly is very late coming home, and panic hits the children. Gillian could not acknowledge her fear: "There it was: Somehow we had absorbed the lesson that if we expressed our fears together we would be lost . . . We had learned not to share experience but to hold it to ourselves" (16). This is often one of the most unfortunate and damaging results of trauma: secrecy, silence, and the resulting isolation.

Psychic numbing, a generalized flattening of affective responses to a wide range of emotional moments in life, is another common response to trauma. It affected Slovo, in fact, for many years. The description of Ruth's murder by a letter bomb occurs late in the first chapter. Joe decides that the coffin should be sealed. Gillian had listened to bereavement experts who said that family members who view the bodies of their loved ones have an easier time accepting the death:

> Now I know better. I had clung to Joe's account of Ruth's perfectly formed feet lying on her office floor and I had used this image to discount what I was also told: the hole in a brick wall; her four-pronged ring fused into one; the look on the friend's face who talked about identifying the body. I should have known that what lay inside that coffin was not my mother. Not my mother in one piece.
>
> It was years later before I read in a series of descriptions of life in exile, an article by one of Ruth's colleagues when he described the act of scraping what was left of her off the wall.
>
> And there was still more to come. Fourteen years on, I sat in Maputo's dingy Cinema Institute, staring at a screen of an antique Steenbeck editing machine on which was threaded footage on those days . . . There was a short section that had been excised from the news broadcast that was shown all over Mozambique: a slow pan across the room after the bomb had exploded. I saw the desks, covered in what looked like cinders, the gaping window and then I saw the walls. Was it blood that streaked the corner of two sides of the room: Was it blood, or was it also Ruth's flesh?
>
> I understood then, finally what Joe had been trying to tell us when he talked of the closed coffin. And I thought: Perhaps the mind does everything the experts say it can—including waiting until even the unbearable can be endured. (24)

In this case, Gillian Slovo concentrated on an image her mind would accept—the perfectly formed feet—in order to protect her from the reality of the crime's brutality. Only when time provided enough distance for the traumatic images to become integrated into her conscious sense of this event did she allow herself to take those images in. This allowed her a measure of control, one that may not generally be available to survivors and witnesses of traumatic events. A PTSD sufferer's ability to recover the central images of traumatic experience is what makes healing narratives possible. In the same way, Slovo's ability to face the actual images of her mother's murder signify her ability to tell the story that she hopes will open her past to examination and allow her to accept it.

Narrative and Truth

Like many healing narratives, *Every Secret Thing* provides a host of complexities, paradoxes, contradictions and ambiguities—all issues that surround writing about trauma. First, it is not a straightforward rendering of a traumatic experience. The primary trauma, the death of Ruth, is compounded by Gillian Slovo's childhood, with its history of fear and neglect. At any point, both Ruth and Joe could have been imprisoned or killed. At any point, Gillian herself could have betrayed her parents or others in the movement. No less important, Gillian grew up feeling neglected, since she believed that her parents were more committed to ending apartheid than to raising her: "All my life I had battled to get something from my father, some spoken recognition that would place me near the center of his existence. All my life I had wanted him to value me as much as he valued South Africa" (210). She tells the story of a visit with Nelson Mandela shortly after her father's death from bone cancer, when Mandela states that his child had a similar reaction: "He told us how one day when he had gone to hug his grown-up daughter she had flinched away from him, and burst out, 'You are the father to all our people, but you never had the time to be a father to me.'. . . They all knew it, somewhere, all their generation: As the state had poured out its wrath, they had watched their children suffer. And yet, and yet—what else could they have done?" (214)

The harshness of her realization is immediately followed by an empty space on the page and an image of her and her sister, Andy, walking together, "along the deserted streets" (214), an image that perfectly captures the unresolved emotional impact of the moment.

As Slovo attempted to discover the truth of her parents' lives, her search took her ever further into ambiguity and her subsequent exploration of the problem of subjectivity: "My father had tried to stop me delving in the past and I had defied him. I sat wondering whether I'd made the right decision. Already my search had delivered more than I'd expected. When I'd started out, I told myself I was looking for the truth. Now I was no longer so sure that this was possible. It happened all the time: a cousin would tell me one thing, an aunt would contradict him entirely, and neither of them would be lying. Their memories were not the clean-cut, crystal versions of the past I'd once assumed they'd be. Each version had a subtle twist to it, each person reinterpreting what had happened through their experience of what came next" (195).

She repeats this theme later in the book: "There was one thing I had learned. People always put themselves into the starring role when they talked about their pasts. That's why none of their stories fitted together; what they had seen, they'd seen through their own eyes" (278). Slovo herself follows this same pattern as she recalls the journey into exile in Swaziland after her father's arrest in South Africa: "Ruth drove us, through one whole day of sizzling heat, across the border into Swaziland. I remembered how, on our arrival, I had rushed into the shower in a desperate attempt to cool down. All that I remembered, and all that was real" (196).

This is a central problem of the book and of healing narratives in general: How can we ever know the truth? How can we ever evaluate a life, even the life of one as close as a parent, without applying a subjectivity so profound as to render the story meaningless or so purely personally meaningful that it loses its larger context? Cathy Caruth wrote, "It is indeed the truth of the traumatic experience that forms the center of its pathology or symptoms. It is not a pathology, that is, of falsehood or displacement of meaning, but of history itself . . . The traumatized, we might say, carry an impossible history within them, or they become themselves the symptom of a history that they cannot entirely possess" (5).

This issue must be confronted by anyone who chooses to write a trauma narrative. First, since trauma is the response, not the event, we can never fully comprehend our history. Some level of dissociation is common as a response to trauma. To fully comprehend the experience is to obliterate our natural and necessary defense systems, if that were even appropriate or possible. But just as important, our memories of our experiences may not be the same as the memories of others. Patricia Hampl described this memory conflict eloquently in her essay "Memory and Imagination." Ultimately, all we can vouch for is the emotional truth of our work, even if that truth conflicts with the needs of others. Slovo's attempt to bring her parents into focus continues to crash against the public images of those lives and the meaning of their deaths. For example, after her father's death, a woman asked Slovo for a poster of him. She offered one "which shows him, glasses in hand, staring preoccupied, into the distance." The woman who had requested the poster "stared at it, long and hard. I had expected thanks, not this puzzling hesitation . . . She was frowning as eventually she put the poster down. 'Please don't take offence,' she said. 'I know I asked you for a picture of our hero, but I don't like this one. I want to remember JS as he was at the peak of his powers, not as this distracted old man'" (236).

The woman needed Joe to be a hero, not a man and certainly not a father. More important, Slovo, too, wanted to see her father as a hero, but then she discovered the devastating fact that he had an illegitimate child, a discovery that crystallized for her the dilemma between public and private, subjective and objective, personal and cultural dichotomies. What does Slovo really tell us about Joe Slovo? That he was a father to South Africa but not to his own children? And was her mother a martyr or a fool? There are no neutral readings of this text.

Justice and Healing

An underlying problem in the book, and one that contributes in significant ways to the nature of Slovo's narrative is the lack of retribution for her mother's assassination, in spite of the fact that she ultimately confronts her mother's murderer. The purpose of the Commission on Truth and Reconciliation is to make such encounters possible, their truths known, while also absolving the perpetrators of their guilt in order to assure a future peace. But of course one wonders if such a peace is possible without justice. Indeed, Joe's compatriots in South Africa were not in agreement with him that amnesty for crimes was appropriate. Slovo questions if she is above revenge. Her father knew that the amnesty he had approved of and supported would be painful to accept because it meant he had to agree to political indemnity for his wife's killers. Slovo was not sure she could accept it: "I had blithely said that I felt no need for retribution, but as my easy words issued out, I'd caught one of my companions shaking his head in disagreement. I asked him why: He said he thought revenge was one of the earliest emotions to be "civilized" out of us and that, perhaps, if I searched deeper within myself, I might locate a different, more basic range of responses. Was he right? Were rage and revenge the murderous impulses lurking beneath my easy rationalizations? . . . Ruth's side, Joe's side . . . had won—and yet, did that mean that the feelings from the traumas were now erased?" (253–54)

This turns out to be a key question in *Every Secret Thing,* one that is never directly answered. Only the process of writing the book, of telling the story can begin to address it.

The climax of the book occurs when Slovo goes to see Ruth's murderer, Craig Williamson. She hopes to find some sign that this man feels regret or seeks repentance but says she finds nothing like this in Ruth's killer: "He was happy to boast about his effectiveness as a spy . . . but those other qualities I'd been searching for—regret, repentance, or conscience—had been conspicuously absent" (267–68). Williamson was a soldier and Ruth the enemy. His murder of her had been "almost casual," as he put it. Yet later, when Slovo asks him whether Ruth's death weighed on him, he replied, "Yeah, I said that you'll never get rid of it. You can wish or regret as much as you like but you can't change it. What's done is done and if you try and analyze why it was done and how it was done and what the tragedy and belief behind it was . . . it is difficult to believe that it could have been done, but it was" (268).

For Slovo this is a failed dialogue. Whether Williamson is sincere or not is no longer the issue, as she had said earlier that it was. He has voiced a kind of regret, but this is not sufficient for her: "That was his whole approach—it was done, it was over. He had acted the good boy by following the rules of this new society, by coming forward and owning up: now, what he expected to do was to dump the past and move on" (268).

Slovo's response to the meeting is to suffer a predictable dissociation similar to that which often accompanies unacknowledged, disconnected trauma: "Our meeting had been an exercise in dissociation from which I'd emerged in a stupor that had sent me straight into a dreamless afternoon sleep" (266). The disconnection between Slovo's need for recognition, for some glimmer of real remorse on the part of the perpetrators, for some acknowledgment of the cost to her and to her family of the assassination and Williamson's need to avoid responsibility do not give Slovo what she needs to heal or to make peace. Instead, it re-traumatized her: "I thought about how I'd heard Archbishop Desmond Tutu talking . . . about the imminent opening of the truth commission and how the emphasis he's laid was on forgiveness. My rational mind knew he was right, that if South Africa did not find in itself the capacity to forgive, it might still go up in flames. And yet, in the face of the displaced responsibility and the empty justifications that the likes of Craig Williamson produced, forgiveness felt like just another effort . . . that the victims, not the perpetrators, would have to make" (269).

And of course, this is the crux of the book: What do we do when no restitution is possible? When no external justice exists, when the perpetrators walk the streets with the victims, traumatic memories are more likely to continue and to be expressed as anger or withdrawal. Slovo's book describes an incomplete narrative because justice eludes her; no culprits can be punished. So Gillian Slovo can assassinate her mother's murderer or she can write a book. They can both be seen as acts of retribution to free her from the past. The reader is, therefore, an essential component in this process.

Vengeance and Peace

Vengeance is a powerful emotion to attempt to stifle, especially in the face of murder and genocide. I grew up hearing the stories of the Armenian Genocide from both sides of my family—the great uncle who was shot by the Turks, the old men and women who perished on the forced marches, the piles of bones that littered the desert, the jackals that threatened the small children at night. My grandparents on both sides had been lucky: My maternal grandmother hid on a roof at the age of four to escape the Turks in the massacre of 1896 and in 1909 survived the siege of an Armenian village to escape to freedom in America in 1910. My paternal grandmother ran with her infant child to an American mission in the massacre of 1896. My father said her hair turned white overnight at the age of twenty-two. I learned at an early age both the healing and political power of narrative. My grandfather was the finance officer of a secret three-person subcommittee of the Armenian Revolutionary Federation. No one in my family knew until after his death that my grandfather had signed all the documents allocating funds to the man chosen to assassinate Talaat Pasha, the architect of the Armenian Genocide who was living the high life in post–World War I Berlin. The assassin was tried and acquitted by a German court on grounds of justifiable homicide. Talaat's order had caused the assassin's mother to be murdered.

But I always have wondered how my grandfather, this gentle soul whose most violent deed was to squeeze my arm when I misbehaved, negotiated with his soul the decision to murder a man, even one as reprehensible as Talaat Pasha. What happens to a soul when the violence against it goes unrecognized? What happens to a country when its misdeeds are unaccounted for? How can healing occur when recognition and atonement are not offered? My grandfather and his associates saw themselves as agents of justice in a world that did not permit public justice. Indeed, the independent Armenia mandated by the treaties after World War I dissolved when Russia and Turkey once again carved up Armenia, ensuring that no justice would prevail. So my grandfather and his associates became vigilantes. Is this what a lack of public justice will do? South Africa is seeking acknowledgment of its crimes but not justice for the victims. My grandfather decided that retribution was necessary for the Armenians. Does this make him an agent of justice or an assassin? Or both? We can ask the same questions of Joe Slovo's anti-apartheid activities.

More to the point for the author and for us, Gillian Slovo is asking us to participate in her experience, to bear witness to her trauma and to the traumas of those her parents fought to protect. A healing narrative for her can be seen as an act of vengeance, one designed to create retribution when there is none, to expose and punish her mother's murderers in the court of public opinion when the criminal courts will not. But if this is so, what do we, the readers, become? Are we the jury for a trial that is not to take place? Does this make us impotent witnesses or do we help carry the burdens of the victims?

Slovo closes her story in the airport while she and her daughter wait for their flight out of South Africa, attempting one more time to put it all together:

> I'd realized that memory, experience, interpretation, could never be fixed or frozen into one unchanging truth. They kept on moving, relentlessly metamorphosing into something other so that the jagged edges of each fragment would never, ever slot together.
>
> I thought of the images of my parents that I had collected, each one different from the one before. The dead stayed still but the rest of us kept going. When finally we looked back, distance distorted what we saw.
>
> His life, my life; they had crossed and they had diverged. I wasn't positive that what I had done was right but I knew I no longer felt so curious to dig out those surprises that might still be waiting out there for me. I, a child of secrets, had done something that I had needed to do. I had laid to rest some of the ghosts that had stalked my life and in doing so, I'd found a kind of peace. (281)

Yet this is the odd note, the note that does not quite fit with the tone of the narrative. The book ends with her reciting an old song from her childhood:

Ag pleez daddy, won't you take us to the drive-in,
All six, seven of us eight, nine, ten.
We wanna see a flick about Tarzan and the Apeman
And when the show's over, you can bring us back again. (282)

The song exudes a normalcy unavailable to Slovo. Its presence signifies the dichotomy between the reality of her life and her yearning for a normal family existence. She has struck a peace with herself, but it appears to come more from her putting to rest her desire for an absolute truth than from a sense of reconciliation with her past. This kind of awareness is hard won but essential with a trauma that can never be resolved. What she missed as a child is not healed and perhaps never can be. But Slovo's book must not be read simply as a failed trauma narrative.

Trauma narratives such as *Every Secret Thing* ask a great deal of us. First, as Dori Laub tells us in Felman and Laub's book *Testimony,* the testimony to the trauma "thus includes its hearer, who is, so to speak, the blank screen on which the event comes to be inscribed for the first time" (57). "The listener to trauma [is] a guide and an explorer, a companion in a journey onto an uncharted land, a journey the survivor cannot traverse or return from alone" (59). We must identify with Slovo, recognize the horror that she must feel when the image of her mother's feet washes through her for the millionth time, feel her rage and frustration when she goes to see her mother's murderer and realizes that he is not going to present himself as a penitent. As Dori Laub said concerning his project taping Holocaust survivors, the process of witnessing is itself being witnessed: "This re-externalization of the event can occur and take effect only when one can articulate and transmit the story, literally transfer it to another outside oneself and then take it back again, inside" (69).

While historical evidence of the trauma may exist, Laub makes it clear that until this process occurs the trauma has not been "truly witnessed yet, not been taken cognizance of. The emergence of the narrative which is being listened to—and heard—is, therefore, the process and the place wherein the cognizance, the 'knowing' of the event is given birth to. The testimony to the trauma thus includes its hearer, who is, so to speak, the blank screen on which the event comes to be inscribed for the first time" (57).

This process becomes even more crucial when we realize that this testimony may be the only venue the survivors have for justice. Gillian Slovo—

and the reader—are caught by the awareness that South Africa needs to find peace as a country. Perhaps the Truth and Reconciliation project can allow that, but at what cost? Can peace come when murderers go free, and what is our responsibility in this process? These are complicated questions with elusive answers. They are being asked by Bosnians, Albanians, Armenians, the Irish, by people in many parts of Africa, by Cambodians and Koreans, by Native Americans, African Americans—the list goes on. What we know from history is that expediency and justice cannot be mutually exclusive. When we allow this to happen, as Judith Shklar puts it, "Whatever decision we do make will . . . be unjust unless we take the victim's view into full account and give her voice its full weight. Anything less is not only unfair, it is also politically dangerous" (126).

Unacknowledged crimes, whether they be against one, many, or a whole people, can come back to haunt us. This makes the relationship between writer and reader even more significant since this dyad provides acknowledgement. In a speech at Ithaca College, Adrienne Rich quoted Muriel Rukeyser, who said, "Poetry is work done on the self first of all." Rich went on to add this: "But we also need the reader, the witness to the poem." For some survivors the reader's response is the most that can be hoped for. The relationship to a reader/listener can allow the survivor to feel safe again within a community, can help to soften anger, and can even allow for the possibility of forgiveness. While forgiveness can be freeing, even when the perpetrators do not ask for it, it is difficult to forgive those whose crimes are unknown. Therefore, the reader can help the survivor to lay the past to rest, even when no justice is possible. Acknowledgement is more important even than retribution, which is why listening can be so effective. I want to return here to an excerpt from Sharon's journal in the Trauma and the Twentieth Century class:

> How do we honor survivors? Maybe we should just listen to them, and close our mouth for a moment. Maybe we should just keep our ears ready for that moment when another image is translated into words and needs listening to. Maybe we should just be supportive, and let the survivors know we are there for them, that they have a support system in the waiting day or night. Having that emotional outlet is very important for the survivor of a trauma, especially when they are ready to begin to tell their story. Without the listener, the story gets reabsorbed and is lost. So I think that may be a start—I know I feel

honored when someone takes the time to listen to me and lets me bring my mind back to painful places without my having to worry about judgments or critical reactions.

This is what we can all do for each other: listen. For when that happens, we lighten the load survivors carry, and trauma narratives can become healing narratives for their authors, for us, and for the very damaged communities that exist around the globe. As quoted in chapter 2, Adam Mayblum wrote on the Internet after 9/11, "We write so we never forget." But of course we do. The Armenian Genocide was forgotten by all but the survivors and Hitler, who used it to pursue genocide in Europe; the lessons of Rwanda have been lost in the Sudan; those hard-earned in Vietnam have been abandoned in Iraq. And so survivors will write their traumas, and we who could or would do little at the time will expiate our collective guilt by reading those narratives. Our role as witness is essential to the recovery of victims: We become the jury that did not exist, the community that had earlier turned its back on the survivor; we become the soul of the world, the eye of God. But this can happen only when we realize that we are joined in our common humanity in spite of efforts to the contrary, that the world is too small for us *not* to be our brothers' and sisters' keepers. In 1854, when the United States government banished the Duwampo tribe to a reservation far from their homeland, Chief Seattle in his address to his white conquerors raised his arm and in a booming voice that witnesses said could be heard for a mile pronounced the following: "Tribe follows tribe, and nation follows nation, like the waves of the sea. It is the order of nature . . . Even the White Man whose God walked and talked with him as friend with friend, cannot be exempt from the common destiny. We may be brothers after all" (841).

We found after September 11 that individual voices were essential to our understanding of that monumental trauma and to our recovery from it. It is a shame we could not hold onto the world sympathy generated by September 11 and use it to begin to build an international community, even perhaps a sense of world justice, because trauma is the great leveler. It reminds us of our vulnerability, our humanity, our need for each other. Ironically, this may be our salvation: In our grief we come together; in our pain we see each other; in our reach for justice we join with the larger world. We can do no more and no less.

Epilogue
It's Not Academic

So while our art cannot, as we wish it could, save us from wars, privation, envy, greed, old age, or death, it can revitalize us amidst it all . . . Writing is survival.

Ray Bradbury

You must write, and read, as if your life depended on it.

Adrienne Rich

All art, like all love, is rooted in heartache.

Alfred Stieglitz

I AM IN THE PROCESS of grading a set of personal essays that exemplify the range of human experience demonstrated in this book: two papers on incest, one on a mental condition that is in remission, two on dysfunctional families, one on a terrible mistake with public repercussions, one on drug abuse, one on the cancer of a beloved relative , another on PTSD in a veteran, and another on the death of a grandmother and the remembered joy that returning to her house still brings. These topics all were chosen by the students within the context of an elective class. Many of these students are juniors and seniors who wanted an opportunity to write nonacademic prose before they leave college. Each of these papers has been rewritten at least twice on the initiative of the author. This is their testament to their lives, and they want to get it right. Although not every paper has been written by a naturally skilled writer, all the students have reached a level that fosters pride and satisfaction, and a couple have produced essays of publishable quality. But just as important, in adopting a process model for writing, they have developed more confidence in themselves as writers, and in using that model in the context of the personal essay, they have begun to develop a deeper understanding of themselves and their worlds. I quote here from a few of the students' journals:

> Before I wrote this essay I had too many secrets inside. Now that I have written it, I feel freer and have been able to share my story with others.

> I write this journal entry twelve days into the semester, which means for twenty-one years of my life I have been in the dark as to why it is that I hurt sometimes. Answers started to come on February 8th. Through the use of an in-class prompt I was able to identify Ms. P. as a person who made a profound impact on my life, but why? I knew she taught me that I was good at what I did, but why didn't I think I was good enough to begin with? Then it hit me. The sexual abuse that took place within that bedroom fourteen years ago didn't end in the summer of 1989. It lives on today, slowly eating away at my confidence. And it is through the writing process that I am beginning to get it back. When I sit down to write . . . the words just flow. In the first paper I stated that I couldn't keep a journal because I didn't know how to write. Well . . . I realized the problem wasn't that I didn't know how to write, but rather that I didn't know how to write about myself. And that was because I didn't know enough about myself to write anything. Or perhaps it was because I wasn't honest with myself. I now keep a journal. I find that it helps in understanding who I am as a person. I have never enjoyed writing as much as I do now.

> Reflecting back on this journal entry and the second paper assignment has been extremely liberating for me. I was able to look past the story that I had molded in my mind and uncover how I truly felt about the situation. Writing in the course has served as a release valve for many of the emotions I have kept bottled up inside of me. I am now able to write my thoughts down in a way that makes them show me something important. My writing is much more detailed. I found that by using good detail I can really take myself back to the time of the situation, which makes me a better writer.

I want to observe, read, and discover and then write and rewrite and rediscover over and over again. Writing will be the highlight of my life.

I have much more confidence in my writing. I have also gained a big understanding about how writing can help heal traumatic situations. When I had something I had a hard time talking about, it was amazing to me to be able to get it off my chest by writing it down, then learning/gaining an understanding of what the real problem is, then being able to deal with it and discuss it appropriately.

Simultaneously taking this writing class while in therapy has set the pace for therapy. The two processes work together. Therapy makes me a better writer. Writing helps me to heal. It forces me into memories I wouldn't normally revisit on my own. It has created an outlet for my anger. Through writing, I can say exactly what I want to. I am also able to trace the patterns that exist in my emotions. I know when I get angry I can come back to my computer and type it all out. It makes me feel better. I can clear my head and come back to my computer through my thought patterns.

These are representative responses from one class of seventeen students. The young people in this class are not unusual in their responses. While they are all bright and eager learners, I have received similar topics and responses from students in most of my personal essay classes. I have concluded that students are so hungry to write about what matters the most to them that they will stay up late, put off other work, and slave over their drafts again and again until they get them "right." They do this not only to produce something they are proud of that represents an important part of their lives, but also because in the doing, they can gain a feeling of control over the past. Their art has liberated them from past assumptions about their lives that constricted them. Adrienne Rich wrote, "A poem can't free us from the struggle for existence, but it can uncover desires and appetites buried under the accumulating emergencies of our lives, the fabricated needs and wants we have had urged on us, have accepted as our own. It's not a philosophical or psychological blueprint; it's an instrument for embodied experience" (13). And that's what art can do: embody experience that has been lost, forgotten, or trapped inside: "To write as if your life depended on it: to write across the chalkboard, putting up there in public words you have dredged, sieved up from dreams, from behind screen memories, out of silence—words you have dreaded and needed in order to know you exist" (Rich 33).

On Sunday, April 24, 2005, *Dateline NBC* ran a story titled "The Fight of Her Life," about a woman whose life provided part of the inspiration for the story *Million Dollar Baby*, which was turned into an Oscar-winning film by Clint Eastwood. This woman, Katie Dallam, who had recently left the military, was looking for a challenge and thought she found it in boxing. Her incompetent trainer sent her into the ring after only six weeks of training, pitting her against a strong fighter who went on to win titles. Although Dallam took over a hundred blows to the head, she did not fall. After the fight was finally called, however, she collapsed into a coma. It took her years to recover, and she has been left with instability in her walking, slowness of speech, and other residual effects of brain damage.

Although Dallam's verbal skills were compromised, her visual ability flourished. She became a painter, putting onto the canvas the nightmarish images that crowd her mind—black and white skeletons against red and black background; red, twisted figures; haunted faces. When asked why painting was important to her, Dallam said, "It's the only time I feel free." Painting gives her a voice when, because of her brain damage, she felt she had lost hers. As she said, "I have a story to tell. I can take the same horrible experience and turn it around." Art gives Dallam a connection to her deepest self, beyond the damage, beyond the pain. The original meaning of "amateur" is instructive here: Lovers of art engage in the process—writing, painting, sculpting, singing—whatever can give form to chaos, structure to the unfathomable. The experience of creating is at least as important as the final product. In *Empathic Teaching* Jeffrey Berman argues: "It may be far riskier *not* to allow our students to write about their fears and conflicts." He offers Donald Barthelme's advice to "write about what you're most afraid of," because, as Berman states, "when I do, I survive the terrors that silence me. While writing the dark clouds rise, the monster shadows retreat." Berman then quotes from Graham Greene: "Writing is a form of therapy; sometimes I wonder how all those who do not write, compose or paint can manage to escape the madness, the melancholia the panic fear which is inherent in the human situation" (375).

In *What Is Found There* Adrienne Rich offers a quotation from Leon Trotsky that speaks to this function of art: "The struggle for revolutionary ideas in art must begin once again with the struggle for artistic truth, not in terms of any single school, but in terms of the immutable faith of the artist in his [*sic*] own inner self. Without this there is no art. 'You shall not lie!'—that is the formula of salvation" (44–45). Rich herself goes on to ask, when a poet is "responsive, responsible—what can that mean? . . . To me it means that she or he is free to become artistically most complex, serious, and integrated when most aware of the great questions of her, of his, own time. When the mind of the maker is stretched to its fullest by the demands of the time—not fads, vogues, cliques, chic, propaganda, but the deep messages of crisis, hope, despair, vision" (51–52).

It is those deep messages of freedom and hope that enable art to forge connections in the midst of chaos and pain. And this can happen on a collective as well as a personal level. We see the intersection of the personal and the collective function of art most clearly in Maya Lin's Vietnam War Memorial, with its black granite wall inscribed with the names of thousands of war dead. We also see it in the AIDS quilt that travels the country, allowing each of us to participate in a national awareness of pain and loss, and in the Clothesline Project, where survivors of sexual assault write their messages of anger, loss, and hope on shirts for others to witness. Thousands of veterans and family members make a pilgrimage to the Vietnam War Memorial to run their hands over the names of lost soldiers, to weep in personal and collective grief. The AIDS quilt and the Clothesline Project offer the voices of survivors demonstrating a forceful personal vision that becomes stronger for its collective power. Art can reflect the conscience of a soul and a nation. It can give voice to the voiceless, power to the powerless, hope to the hopeless. Maya Angelou's poem about her community's response to racism quoted at the end of chapter 2 suggests she understood this well: "Oh, Black and unknown poets, how often have your auctioned pains sustained us? Who will compute the lonely nights made less lonely by your songs, or the empty pots made less tragic by your tales? . . . We survive in exact relationship to the dedication of our poets (include preachers, musicians, blues singers)." Finding a voice can take many forms: the visual arts, dance, theatre, music. The human impulse to transmute suffering into something more permanent than the clay we are composed of is universal. Art heals grief.

I am sitting in the Chapel at Colgate University listening to a student music recital. I have performed here myself, so I am familiar with the hall, but no matter how many times I am here its pristine white interior always reminds me of Hendricks Chapel at Syracuse University where I was married so long ago. The recital is informal, the singers seated in the audience waiting their turn. One by one, they step up to the stage to offer their music. These are not necessarily all budding professionals, as are the voice majors at Ithaca College, but talented young people who are true amateurs, lovers of music. It astonishes me what courage it takes to walk up onto a stage, stand there alone with open mouth, and begin to sing. Nothing feels more naked, more exposed than that. It's a wonder anyone ever does it for the first time. Yet singing is the breath, the pneuma, of life. When only professionals do it, Adrienne Rich tells us, "We're severed from a physical release and pleasure, whether in solitude or community—the use of breath to produce song. But breath is also ruach, spirit, the human connection to the universe" (82).

One young man shuffles up on stage, and with his hands stiffly at his side sings "Annie Laurie" in a muffled yet sweet bass voice: "For bonnie Annie Laurie, I would lay me down and die." His voice is untutored but sincere, and I almost believe that he would lie down and die for Annie Laurie, or at least that he believes he would, which is almost as good.

After three sweet sopranos, it is my partner's daughter's turn. Rebecca is an actor—a very good one—and her father and I have attended all her plays here at Colgate, where she is a senior, but I have never before heard her sing in recital. Rebecca looks as much like her father as my daughter looks like hers—and she has his vocal talent as well. She smiles at us, then focuses upward and begins to sing a song called "Grief," written by William Grant Still, an African American composer born in 1895:

> Weeping angel with pinions trailing
> And head bowed low in your hands
> Mourning angel with heart strings wailing
> For one who in death's hall stands
> Mourning angel silence your wailing
> And raise your head from your hands
> Weeping angel on your pinions trailing
> The white dove, promise, stands.

The music clings to A natural, intoning one repeated legato note, moving up or down only in thirds until the second verse, which then moves up in fourths, then sixths, then stretches to a seventh , returning to the original A natural again for the ending—"The white dove, promise, stands." Rebecca's voice is misty yet strong, full yet just short of a wail. The effect is eerie and peaceful, a mournful, muted grief, all intense understatement pulling out from the single note—until it comes to resolution on a B natural, a new key, never heard before. Rebecca holds that B natural on the word "stands," lets it fade away . . . then bows her head to the audience, steps down from the stage and sweeps in next to me laying her head on my shoulder. I hug her and can almost see the white dove floating upward . . . the promise meant for us all.

Works Cited

Adams, Dan P. "Redemption and American Politics." *Chronicle of Higher Education,* December 3, 2004, B14.

Agnosta, Carolyn and Mary McHugh. "Sexual Assault Victims: The Trauma and the Healing." In *Post-Traumatic Stress Disorders: A Handbook for Clinicians,* ed. Tom Williams, 239–51. Cincinnati: Disabled American Veterans, 1987.

Allen, Guy. "Language, Power, and Consciousness: A Writing Experiment at the University of Toronto." In Anderson and MacCurdy, 249–90.

Allison, Dorothy. *Two or Three Things I Know for Sure.* New York: Penguin, 1996.

Anderson, Charles, Karen Holt, and Patty McGrady. "Suture, Stigma, and the Pages That Heal." In Anderson and MacCurdy, 58–82.

Anderson, Charles M., and Marian M. MacCurdy, eds. *Writing and Healing: Toward an Informed Practice.* Urbana, Ill.: National Council of Teachers of English, 2000.

Angelou, Maya. "Graduation," *Conscious Reader.* Ed. Caroline Shrodes, Harry Finestone, and Michael Shugrue. New York: Macmillan, 1988: 59–62.

———. *On the Pulse of Morning.* New York: Random House, 1993.

Arenson, Karen W. "Class Notes." *New York Times,* June 18, 1997, B8.

Arthritis Self-Management. New York: Rapaport Publishing. September/October 2002.

Bardakjian, Kevork B. *Hitler and the Armenian Genocide.* Cambridge, Mass.: Zoryan Institute, 1985.

Barth, John. "All Trees Are Oak Trees." *Poets and Writers* 32.1 (January/February 2004): 19–25.

Bartholomae, David. "A Reply to Stephen North." *Pre/Text* 11 (1990): 121–30.

———. "Writing with Teachers: A Conversation with Peter Elbow." *College Composition and Communication* 46.1 (1995): 62–71.

Bauman, M. Garrett. "Crossing the Fine Line between Teacher and Therapist." *Chronicle of Higher Education,* July 12, 2002, B20.

Berliner, Lucy, and John Briere. "Trauma, Memory, and Clinical Practice." In *Trauma and Memory,* ed. Linda Williams and Victoria Banyard, 3–18. Thousand Oaks, Calif.: Sage Publications, 1999.

Berman, Jeffrey. *Empathic Teaching: Education for Life.* Amherst: University of Massachusetts Press, 2004.

———. *Risky Writing: Self-Disclosure and Self-Transformation in the Classroom.* Amherst: University of Massachusetts Press, 2002.

Brewin, Chris R,. *Post-Traumatic Stress Disorder: Malady or Myth.* New Haven: Yale University Press, 2003.

Bishop, Wendy. "Writing Is/and Therapy? Raising Questions about Writing Classrooms and Writing Program Administration." *Journal of Advanced Composition* 13.2 (1993): 503–16.

Booth, Roger, and Keith J. Petrie. "Emotional Expression and Health Changes: Can We Identify Biological Pathways?" In Lepore and Smyth, 157–75.

Brison, Susan. *Aftermath: Violence and the Remaking of a Self.* Princeton: Princeton University Press, 2002.

Bucci, Wilma. "The Power of the Narrative: A Multiple Code Account." In *Emotion, Disclosure, and Health,* ed. James W. Pennebaker, 93–122. Washington, D.C.: American Psychological Association, 1995.

Bruner, Jerome. *Acts of Meaning.* Cambridge: Harvard University Press, 1990.

Cahill, Larry, et al. "Beta-Adrenergic activation and memory for emotional events." *Nature* 371 (October 20, 1994): 702–4.

Caruth, Cathy. *Trauma: Explorations in Memory.* Baltimore: Johns Hopkins University Press, 1995.

Charon, Rita. "Narrative Medicine: A Model for Empathy, Reflection, Profession, and Trust." *JAMA* 286 (October 17, 2001): 1897–902.

Cheit, Ross. Address at Harvard University Conference on Psychological Trauma, Copley Square Hotel, Boston, Mass. March 23–24, 1996.

Chief Seattle, "Farewell Speech." In *The Norton Reader: An Anthology of Expository Prose,* ed. Linda H. Peterson, John C. Brereton, and Joan E. Hartman. 9th ed. New York: Norton, 1996.

Clifton, Lucille. Keynote Address. Conference of the Association for Poetry Therapy, Columbia, Md., May 6, 1996.

Coles, Robert. *The Call of Stories: Teaching and the Moral Imagination.* Boston: Houghton Mifflin, 1989.

Crews, Frederick. "Down Memory Lane." *New York Review of Books,* December 22, 1994, 77.

———. "The Revenge of the Repressed." *New York Review of Books,* November 17, 1994, 54–60.

———. "The Revenge of the Repressed: Part II." *New York Review of Books,* December 1, 1994, 49–58.

Daiute, Colette, and Ellie Buteau. "Writing for Their Lives: Children's Narratives as Supports for Physical and Psychological Well-Being." In Lepore and Smyth, 53–74.

Dallaire, Romeo. Speech at Colgate University, Hamilton, N.Y., February 15, 2005.

Dickinson, Emily. *The Poems of Emily Dickinson.* Ed. R. W. Franklin. Reading Edition. Cambridge: Belknap Press of Harvard University Press, 2003.

Elbow, Peter. ""Being a Writer vs. Being an Academic: A Conflict in Goals." *College Composition and Communication* 46.1 (1995): 72–83.

———. "Response." *College Composition and Communication* 46.1 (1995): 87–92.

———. *Writing without Teachers.* New York: Oxford University Press, 1973.

Felman, Shoshana. "Education and Crisis, or the Vicissitudes of Teaching." In *Trauma: Transformations in Memory,* ed. Cathy Caruth. Baltimore: Johns Hopkins University Press, 1995.

Felman, Shoshana, and Dori Laub. *Testimony: Crises of Witnessing in Literature, Psychoanalysis, and History.* New York: Routledge, 1991.

Fishman, Stephen, and Lucille McCarthy. "Is Expressivism Dead?" *College Composition and Communication* 54.6 (1992): 647–61.

Foster, Patricia A. "The Light of Writing." *Chronicle of Higher Education,* April 15, 2005, B2.

Freyd, Jennifer. *Betrayal Trauma: The Logic of Forgetting Childhood Abuse.* Cambridge: Harvard University Press, 1996.

Goleman, Daniel. *Emotional Intelligence.* New York: Bantam, 1995.

Goodwin, Stephen. "Breaking the Silence." *Poets and Writers* 31.6 (November/December 2003): 29–32.

Gornick, Vivian. "Memoir: An Inward Journey through Experience." *Chronicle of Higher Education,* August 3, 2001, B7–B9.

Gruwell, Erin, and the Freedom Writers. *The Freedom Writers Diary: How a Teacher and 150 Teens Used Writing to Change Themselves and the World Around Them.* New York: Broadway Books, 1999.

Hampl, Patricia. "Memory and Imagination." In *Mind Readings:An Anthology for Writers,* ed. Gary Colombo, 180–90. New York: Bedford Books, 2002.

Harris, Judith. *Signifying Pain: Constructing and Healing the Self through Writing.* Albany: SUNY Press, 2003.

Hawkins, Anne Hunsaker. *Reconstructing Illness: Studies in Pathography.* West Lafayette, Ind.: Purdue University Press, 1993.

Henke, Suzette. *Shattered Subjects: Trauma and Testimony in Women's Life-Writing.* New York: St. Martin's, 2000.

Herman, Judith. *Trauma and Recovery.* New York: Basic, 1992.

Herr, Michael. *Dispatches.* New York: Avon, 1978.

Hill, Carolyn Ericksen. *Writing from the Margins.* New York: Oxford University Press, 1990.

Hoffman, Richard. *Half the House.* New York: Harcourt, 1995.

Hopkins-Powell, Sara. "Opening Ourselves to Unconditional Love in Our Relationships with Students." *Chronicle of Higher Education,* June 28, 2002, B5.

Horner, Bruce. "Students, Authorship, and the Work of Composition." *College Composition and Communication* 59.5 (1997): 505–529.

Ithaca Journal, April 16, 1998, 2B.

Ithaca Journal, September 5, 2001, 3B.

Ithaca Journal, May 23, 2002, 2A.

Ithaca Journal, March 24, 2004, 4A.

Ithaca Journal, November 20, 2004, 3A.

Janoff-Bulman, Ronnie. *Shattered Assumption: Towards a New Psychology of Trauma.* New York: Simon and Schuster, 1992

Johnston, Jill. "Fiction of the Self in the Making." *New York Times Book Review,* April 25, 1993, 29.

Jonson, Ben. "On the Death of His First Son." In *The Norton Anthology of English Literature,* ed. M. H. Abrams (gen. ed.). 6th ed. New York: Norton, 1993.

Kamler, Barbara. *Relocating the Personal: A Critical Writing Pedagogy.* Albany: State University of New York Press, 2001.

Kirsch, Gesa, and Joy Ritchie. "Beyond the Personal: Theorizing a Politics of Location in Composition Research." *College Composition and Communication* 46.1 (1995): 7–29.

Lakoff, Robin Tolmach, and James C. Coyne. *Father Knows Best.* New York: Teachers College Press, 1993.

Laub, Dori. "Bearing Witness, or the Vicissitudes of Listening." In Felman and Laub, 57–74.

———. "Truth and Testimony: The Process and the Struggle." In *Trauma: Explorations in Memory,* ed. Cathy Caruth, 61–75. Baltimore: Johns Hopkins University Press, 1995.

LeDoux, Joseph. E. "Emotion as Memory: Anatomical Systems Underlying Indelible Neural Traces." In *Handbook of Emotion and Memory,* ed. S. A. Christianson. Hillsdale, N.J.: Erlbaum, 1992.

LeGuin, Ursula. *Dancing at the Edge of the World: Thoughts on Words, Women, Places.* New York: Grove, 1989.

———. *The Language of the Night.* New York: Berkley, 1979.

Lepore, Stephen J., and Joshua M. Smyth, eds. *The Writing Cure: How Expressive Writing Promotes Health and Emotional Well-Being.* Washington, D.C.: American Psychological Association, 2002.

Loftus, Elizabeth. *The Myth of Repressed Memory.* New York: St. Martin's Press, 1994.

Loftus E., S. Polensky, and M. T. Fullilove. "Memories of Childhood Sexual Abuse: Remembering and Repressing. *Psychology of Women Quarterly* 18.0 (1994): 67–84.

Lutgendorf, Susan K., and Philip Ullrich. "Cognitive Processing, Disclosure, and Health: Psychological and Physiological Mechanisms." In Lepore and Smyth, 177–96.

MacCurdy, Marian. "From Trauma to Writing: A Theoretical Model for Practical Use." In Anderson and MacCurdy, 158–200.

Masson, Jeffrey. *The Assault on Truth.* New York: Simon and Schuster, 1998.

McNally, Richard J. *Remembering Trauma.* Cambridge: Belknap Press of Harvard University Press, 2003.

Miller, Alice. *For Your Own Good: Hidden Cruelty in Child-Rearing and the Roots of Violence.* Trans. Hildegarde and Hunter Hannum. New York: Farrar, Straus, Giroux, 1983.

Moffett, James. "Coming Out Right." In *Taking Stock: The Writing Process Movement in the '90s,* ed. Lad Tobin and Thomas Newkirk, 17–30. Portsmouth, N.H.: Boynton/ Cook, 1994.

———. "Interchanges: Spiritual Sites of Composing." *College Composition and Communication* 45 (1994): 258–61.

Morgan, Dan. "Opinion: Ethical Issues Raised by Students' Personal Writing." *College English* 60.3 (1998): 318–25.

Morrison, Toni. *Beloved.* New York: Penguin, 1988.

Orr, Gregory. "Paths and Pearls." *Poets and Writers* 30.5 (September/October 2002): 16–21.

Pennebaker, James. *Opening Up: The Healing Power of Confiding in Others.* New York: Avon, 1992, 1997.

———. "Telling Stories: The Health Benefits of Narrative." *Literature and Medicine* 19.1 (Spring 2000): 3–18.

Pennebaker, James, and J. D. Seagal. "Forming a Story: The Health Benefits of Narrative." *Journal of Clinical Psychology* 55 (1999): 1243–54.

Perillo, Lucia. "When the Classroom Becomes a Confessional." *Chronicle of Higher Education,* November 28, 1997, A56.

Phillips, Robert. "Why I Write." *Poets and Writers* 27.2 (March/April, 1999): 18–23.

Pillemer, David. *Momentous Events, Vivid Memories.* Cambridge: Harvard University Press, 1998.

Pinsky, Robert. Quoted *in Ithaca Journal,* September 26, 2001, 4B.

Power, Samantha. *The Problem from Hell.* New York: Harper, 2002.

Raab, Laurence. "Poetry and Consolation." *Writer's Chronicle* 35.3 (2002): 10–15.

Resnick, P. A. *Stress and Trauma.* Hove, U.K.: Psychology Press, 2001.

Rich, Adrienne. Address at Ithaca College, Ithaca, N.Y. October 1, 2001.

———. *What Is Found There: Notebooks on Poetry and Politics.* New York: Norton, 1993.

———. "When We Dead Awaken: Writing as Revision." In *The Norton Reader: An Anthology of Expository Prose,* ed. Linda H. Peterson (gen. ed.), John C. Brereton, and Joan E. Hartman, 1136–49. 9th ed. New York: Norton, 1996. Originally published in *On Lies, Secrets, and Silence: Selected Prose 1966–1978.* New York: Norton, 1979.

Romano, Carlin. "Is the Rise of 'Narratology' the Same Old Story?" *Chronicle of Higher Education,* June 28, 2002, B12.

Rushdie, Salman. "Rushdie Engages Students." *Connections.* College of Arts and Sciences, Syracuse University (Fall 2002): 8.

Schacter, Daniel L. *Searching for Memory.* New York: Basic Books, 1996.

Science News 164 (November 8, 2003): 293 ("Forgetting to Remember: Emotion Robs Memory While Reviving It").

Sebold, Alice. *Lucky.* Paper Edition. New York: Little, Brown/Back Bay Books, 2000.

Segal, Carolyn Foster. "The Solace of Literature." *Chronicle of Higher Education,* October 5, 2001, B5.

Shay, Jonathan. *Achilles in Vietnam: Combat Trauma and the Undoing of Character.* New York: Atheneum, 1994.

Shklar, Judith N. *The Faces of Injustice.* New Haven: Yale University Press, 1990.

Slovo, Gillian. *Every Secret Thing: My Family, My Country.* New York: Little, Brown, 1997.

Spiegelman, Art. Quoted in the *Ithaca Journal,* September 25, 2001, 4B.

Stanton, Annette L., and Sharon Danoff-Burg. "Emotional Expression, Expressive Writing, and Cancer." In Lepore and Smyth, 31–52.

Sternberg, Robert. "It's Not What You Know, but How You Use It: Teaching for Wisdom." *Chronicle of Higher Education,* June 28, 2002, B20.

Tal, Kali. *Worlds of Hurt: Reading the Literatures of Trauma.* New York: Cambridge University Press, 1996.

Talan, Jamie. *Ithaca Journal,* October 25, 2001, 8A.

Taylor, Peter. Interview in *Poets and Writers* 31.6 (November/December 2003): 30.

Tedeschi, Richard, Crystal Park, and Lawrence Calhoun, eds. *Posttraumatic Growth: Positive Changes in the Aftermath of Crisis.* Mahway, N.J.: Lawrence Erlbaum, 1998.

Terr, Lenore C. "Chowchilla Revisited: The Effects of Psychic Trauma Four Years after a School-Bus Kidnapping." *American Journal of Psychiatry* 140 (1983): 1543–50.

———. "Time Sense Following Psychic Trauma: A Clinical Study of Ten Adults and Twenty Children." *American Journal of Orthopsychiatry* 53 (1983): 244–61.

Todd, Janet. *The Sign of Angelica: Women, Writing, and Fiction, 1660–1800.* New York: Columbia University Press, 1989.

Tompkins, Jane. "Me and My Shadow." In *Feminisms: An Anthology of Literary Theory and Criticism,* ed. Robyn R. Warhol and Diane Price Herndl, 1079–92. New Brunswick, N.J.: Rutgers University Press, 1991.

van der Kolk, Bessel. Keynote Address. Harvard University Conference on Psychological Trauma, Copley Square Hotel, Boston, March 23–24, 1996.

van der Kolk, Bessel, Alexander C. McFarlane, and Lars Weisaeth. *Traumatic Stress.* New York: Guilford Press, 1996.

Villanueva, Victor. "The Politics of the Personal: Storying Our Lives Against the Grain, Symposium Collective." *College English* 64.1 (2001): 41–61.

Von Franz, Marie Louise. *Shadow and Evil in Fairy Tales.* Zurich: Spring, 1974.

Walker, Nancy. *The Disobedient Writer: Women and the Narrative Tradition.* Austin: University of Texas Press, 1995.

Wegner, D., and L. Smart. "Deep Cognitive Activation: A New Approach to the Unconscious." *Journal of Consulting and Clinical Psychology* 65 (1997): 944–995.

Wiesel, Eli. "The Loneliness of God." In *Dvar Hashavu* (Tel Aviv). Quoted in Felman, 14.

———. "Why I Write." In *The Arlington Reader: Canons and Contexts,* ed. Lynn Bloom and Louise Smith, 93–97. New York: Bedford, 2003.

Williams, Linda M. "Recovered Memories of Abuse in Women with Documented Child Sexual Abuse Victimization Histories." *Journal of Traumatic Stress* 8.4 (1995): 649–71.

Williams, Linda M., and Victoria L. Banyard, eds. *Trauma and Memory.* Thousand Oaks, Calif.: Sage Publications, 1999.

Williams, Tom. "Diagnosis and Treatment of Survivor Guilt—The Bad Penny." In *Post-Traumatic Stress Disorders: A Handbook for Clinicians,* ed. Tom Williams, 75–91. Cincinnati: Disabled American Veterans, 1987.

Zytaruk, George J., and James T. Bolton, eds. *The Letters of D. H. Lawrence.* Vol. 2. Cambridge: Cambridge University Press, 1981.

Index

Marian Mesrobian MacCurdy, a writer, teacher, and singer, is professor of writing at Ithaca College, where she teaches both creative and expository writing. She has published scholarly articles as well as personal essays and poetry in such journals as *Raft, Ararat,* and the *Journal of Poetry Therapy.* An article, "The Four Women of the Apocalypse: Polarized Feminine Images in Magazine Advertisements," is included in an anthology titled *Utopia and Gender in Advertising: A Critical Reader.* Her essay "From Image to Narrative: The Politics of the Personal," which began her exploration of the relationship between writing and healing, was published in the spring 1995 issue of the *Journal of Teaching Writing,* and her edited collection, *Writing and Healing: Toward an Informed Practice,* coedited with Charles Anderson, was published by NCTE Press in 2000. She holds a PhD in Humanities from Syracuse University.